Ꮪᴜɴᴅᴀʏ

WEEKLY LEADER GUIDE

Sundays, Feast Days & Solemnities

Year C

SUNDAY WEEKLY LEADER GUIDE

Sundays, Feast Days & Solemnities
Year C

In Canada
NOVALIS

In England
T. SHAND PUBLICATIONS, Ltd.

In the United States
T R E E H A U S

TREEHAUS COMMUNICATIONS, INC. P.O. BOX 249, LOVELAND, OHIO 45140

Acknowledgment

Sr. Paule Freeburg, D.C., and
Christopher Walker wish
to express gratitude to the
Daughters of Charity in Belgium
for their hospitality while
working on the SUNDAY project.

Second Revised Edition: February 1994

[ ] Text that appears in brackets
    may be omitted by the reader.

United States Publisher
TREEHAUS COMMUNICATIONS, INC.
P.O. Box 249
Loveland, Ohio 45140

Canadian Publisher
NOVALIS
St. Paul University/Ottawa
P.O. Box 990
Outremont, Quebec
H2V 4S7

Great Britain Publisher
T. SHAND PUBLICATIONS, LTD.
The Chapel, St. Mary's Abbey
The Ridgeway
Mill Hill, London
England NW7-4HX

The Sunday Leader Guide includes the adapted scripture texts
from *The Sunday Book of Readings/The Lectionary Adapted for Children*
which has been endorsed for liturgical use with children in Canada by
The Episcopal Commission for Liturgy,
Canadian Conference of Catholic Bishops.

Printed and bound in the United States.

ISBN 0-929496-92-2

Contents

* *For parishes with a children's catechumenate, and in keeping with the* Order for the Christian Initiation of Adults, *the readings for the 3rd, 4th, and 5th Sundays of Lent/Year A may be used in place of the readings selected for those Sundays in Year C.*

** *In keeping with the* Directory For Masses With Children *(Paragraph 43), some of the readings assigned to the day have been changed when they appear "unsuited to the capacity of children." Changes have been made in the following occasions: First Sunday of Advent, Easter Sunday, Trinity Sunday, Body and Blood of Christ, Twentieth Sunday in Ordinary Time, All Souls, Dedication of St. John Lateran.*

The Seasons of Advent
and
Christmas

FIRST SUNDAY OF ADVENT

YEAR C

PRAYER OF THE DAY:

God, you love us so much,
you send Jesus, your Son,
into our world.
Help us be ready
to make him welcome
so that he will live
with us always.
We ask you this through him,
who lives with you
and the Holy Spirit
forever and ever.

FOCUS OF THE READINGS:

Our first reading is a reassurance of the promise that God will send salvation. This salvation is not an abstraction but will come in and through a real person to be born in the family of David. The signs of salvation are justice and peace.

The Gospel exhorts us to "stay awake" and be ready for the return of the Lord. We do not know the time, but we do know that it will be a time of justice and peace as the first reading tells us. Therefore, our "being ready" involves a constant striving for what is right and just in the world.

Our God is coming! Stay awake! Be ready!

FIRST READING: *Jeremiah 33:14-16*

A reading from the prophet Jeremiah.

Our God says:

"The time is coming
when I will keep the promise I made
to the people of Israel and Judah.

"When that time comes,
a special person
will be born in David's family,
a person who will do what is right
and will treat the people with justice.

"Then the people in the land of Judah
will be saved
and the city of Jerusalem
will be peaceful.
People will call Jerusalem
the city of God, 'The City of Justice.' "

The Word of the Lord.

RESPONSE: *Psalm 80*

1st time: Leader; 2nd time: All

God of jus-tice and peace, let your face shine on us. face shine on us.

Leader:

All:

Shine on us and we shall be saved. Shine on us and we shall be saved.

GOSPEL ACCLAMATION:

Stay a-wake, be read-y. You do not know the hour when the Lord is com-ing. Stay a-wake, be read-y. The Lord is com-ing soon! Al-le - lu - ia, al - le - lu - ia! "The Lord is com-ing soon."

*After Gospel, repeat Acclamation from here.

GOSPEL: *Matthew 24:42-44*

A reading from the Gospel of Matthew.

Jesus said to his disciples:

"Stay awake! Always be ready!
You do not know on what day
your Lord is coming.

"You know for sure
that if the owners of a house
knew at what time of night
a thief was coming,
they would stay awake
and wouldn't let the thief break in.

"And in the same way,
you must always be ready
because you do not know the time
when the Lord is coming."

The Gospel of the Lord.

REFLECTING ON THE READINGS WITH CHILDREN:

The season of Advent is filled with vivid, exciting characters who announce the coming of the Savior: the prophets, John the Baptist, Mary and Elizabeth. It might be interesting for the children to see themselves in these roles and imagine how they might announce the coming of Jesus. During this season we will invite the children to do this each week. Children love to imagine and to be part of the story. It is important that they think of actual scenes and then place themselves in those scenes. On the first Sunday, it is Jesus himself who speaks. You might try something like this.

Before reading the Gospel, explain to the children that one day the disciples asked Jesus when he would come back again in glory. Jesus told the disciples that no one could know that, but that they must always be ready and watching. *Read the Gospel.*

What example did Jesus use to tell the disciples to always be ready? People today sometimes ask the same question. When will Jesus come back in glory? Jesus still says: You must always be ready. Suppose you are Jesus and people say to you: "But what do we do to be ready? What do you want us to be doing when you come back?" How would you answer them? (Encourage the children to speak in the first person—as Jesus.)

After all the children who wish have spoken, help them see that *being ready means trying to live good Christian lives.* We don't need to be doing something extraordinary. Being ready means doing the things we do (at their age) well: loving people, helping others at home and at school, being honest, studying well, being fair in games, etc.

3

SECOND SUNDAY OF ADVENT

YEAR C

PRAYER OF THE DAY:

Loving Lord,
you want the whole world
to welcome Jesus.
Give us the strength
to avoid doing what is wrong,
and instead,
through our kindness
and love for other people,
make his way easy and gentle.
We make this prayer to you
through him,
who lives with you
and the Holy Spirit
forever and ever.

FOCUS OF THE READINGS:

The focus of the first reading is the good news of salvation to the people who were in exile in Babylon. This salvation was very real for them. It meant, literally, that they were coming home to Jerusalem. Baruch tells us that it is because of God's justice and mercy that the people are saved. Their salvation is expressed by "wearing" justice, peace and the glory of God. In other words, it is these qualities that show we are saved.

In our Gospel reading, John the Baptist calls us to change our lives so our sins will be forgiven. In so doing, we prepare the way for God. God's way is the way of justice, of equality. This justice is symbolized in Isaiah's prophecy that "Every valley will be filled in and every mountain will be made small...." Both readings use beautiful, symbolic language to speak of God's justice.

God comes with love and justice!
Prepare the way!

FIRST READING: *Baruch 5:1-9*

A reading from the prophet Baruch.

People of Jerusalem,
take off your clothes of sorrow and suffering;
put on the beauty of God's glory;
put on the robe of God's justice.
Wear on your head a crown
with the name of God on it.
For God will show all the world
how beautiful you are.
Everyone will know you
because of your justice and peace,
and because of the honor you give to God.

Rise up, people of Jerusalem!
Stand on the mountain top.
Look to the east and to the west
and see the people coming home in joy.
Enemies took them away from their home,
but God will bring them back
with justice and mercy.
They are coming home in joy,
led by the light of God's glory.

The Word of the Lord.

RESPONSE: *Psalm 80*

1st time: Leader; 2nd time: All
God of hope bring us back, let your face shine on us. face shine on us.

Leader:
Shine on us and we shall be saved. Shine on us and we shall be saved.

4

GOSPEL ACCLAMATION:

Pre - pare! He's com-ing! The one who will give peace to the world is com-ing! Pre - pare! He's com-ing! The reign of God is near! Al-le - lu - ia, al-le - lu - ia! "The reign of God is near."

*After Gospel, repeat Acclamation from here.

GOSPEL: *Luke 3:1-6*

A reading from the Gospel of Luke.

There was a man named John,
who was the son of Zechariah.
While John was living in the desert,
God spoke to him
and told him to preach to the people.
So John went around
the whole area of the Jordan River
telling everyone to change their lives
and to be baptized,
so that their sins would be forgiven.

The prophet Isaiah
had already written about this
a long time ago when he said,

"In the desert
there is the voice of a herald proclaiming:

'Prepare the way for the coming of God!
Make a straight path for the coming of God!
Every valley will be filled in
and every mountain and hill
will be made small,
the crooked roads will be made straight
and the rough land will be made smooth.
And all people on earth
will see the saving power of our God.' ''

The Gospel of the Lord.

REFLECTING ON THE READINGS WITH CHILDREN:

This Sunday we might encourage the children to imagine themselves in the role of Baruch. (Cf. *Reflecting on the Readings* for last Sunday.) Because we have John the Baptist both this Sunday and next Sunday, we will take the first reading this Sunday and John the Baptist next Sunday.

For the Old Testament prophecies of redemption to be understood, we need to imagine a people in captivity with little hope of seeing their homeland again. That is not easy for children who have rarely been away from home without their parents.

Try to help the children imagine people in a similar situation. The current events of the day may be used—perhaps, "missing children" or "prisoners of war." The children have probably heard on T.V. or in school, talk of people being held hostage. Explore that with them. Ask questions similar to these:

- What does hostage mean?
- What have you heard about it?
- How do you think a hostage feels in the beginning? after awhile? after a long time?
- How do you think their family back home feels?
- What might it be like to be a hostage for a long time?
- Have you ever seen on T.V. the release of hostages? How do you think they feel when they meet their families?
- Now, if you were the person who had the joy of telling people who were hostages that they are free and are going home, what might you say to them? (Give time for this.)

After the children have had time to "speak the good news," remind them that the Hebrew people—the people of the Old Testament—were hostages in Babylon for a long, long time. They too felt discouraged and wanted to go home to Jerusalem. After setting the stage for them to imagine the Hebrew people in captivity, read the first reading again.

Simply remind the children that the Gospel speaks of John the Baptist who came to tell the people that a Savior was coming to save them. At Jesus' time, the people were not hostages in another country, but were "hostages of sin." Jesus would free them from that.

THIRD SUNDAY OF ADVENT

YEAR C

PRAYER OF THE DAY:
God,
you made us to care
for one another.
Let us never turn away from
people who are hungry and poor,
but share with them
the good things we enjoy.
We make this prayer to you
through Jesus Christ,
who lives with you
and the Holy Spirit,
forever and ever.

FOCUS OF THE READINGS:

The Third Sunday of Advent is traditionally known as Gaudete Sunday, a day of joy. In our first reading, all fear, all sorrow, gives way to a song of joy at the wonderful thing God has done: "God has sent your enemies away." Zephaniah concludes with the tender assurance that God too rejoices in our salvation!

Again this Sunday, John the Baptist calls us to change our lives and live as people who have been saved. Each one who seeks the Lord is told to live justly according to his or her way of life. Throughout Advent, justice and peace are revealed as the signs of salvation. John points to the one who will come to baptize us in the Holy Spirit. It is this Spirit that enables us to live in justice and peace.

Shout for joy! The Savior brings justice and peace!

FIRST READING: *Zephaniah 3:14-17*

A reading from the prophet Zephaniah.

Shout for joy, O people of Jerusalem!
Sing with joy, people of Israel!
Be glad and sing with all your heart.
Be glad
because God has sent your enemies away!

Do not be afraid; do not be discouraged!
The Mighty Savior is with you
and will show God's love for you again.
And because of you,
God will dance and sing for joy,
just as we sing and dance at a celebration!

The Word of the Lord.

RESPONSE: *Psalm 80*

GOSPEL ACCLAMATION:

*After Gospel, repeat Acclamation from here.

6

GOSPEL: *Luke 3:10-16*

A reading from the Gospel of Luke.

While John was baptizing in the Jordan River,
many people came and asked him
what they should do.
John said to them,

"Anyone who has two coats
should give one to someone
who hasn't got a coat.
Anyone who has food
should share with people who are hungry."

Tax collectors came to be baptized
and they asked him,

"What must we do?"

John answered them,

"Don't make people pay more taxes
than they have to."

Soldiers also asked him,

"What about us?"

He told them,

"Don't bully people. Don't lie about anyone.
And be happy with the money you are paid."

All the people were filled with excitement.
They wondered if John might be the Messiah,
the one they were waiting for.

But John said to them,

"There is one who will come later,
who is mightier than I am.
I am not even worthy
to untie his sandal straps.
I am baptizing with water,
but he will baptize you in the Holy Spirit."

The Gospel of the Lord.

REFLECTING ON THE READINGS
WITH CHILDREN:

This Sunday we will invite the
children to take the role of John the
Baptist. Please see the *Reflections*
for the first and second Sundays
of Advent.

After the Gospel, you might
suggest the following to the children:

Try to imagine that you are living
somewhere where no one has ever
heard about Jesus. No one is
baptized; no one has ever heard
about Mass or the Bible. You are the
only person who knows about Jesus.
If God asked you to tell the people
about Jesus, what would you tell
them about him? (Allow time for
this.) If these people said they
wanted to be disciples or followers of
Jesus, how would you tell them to
live? Would you have anything
special to say to people like those
listed below?

- store owners
- students in school
- children
- doctors
- rich people
- poor people
- (other groups)

These are merely examples to
help the children begin. You may
wish to suggest others.

7

FOURTH SUNDAY OF ADVENT

YEAR C

PRAYER OF THE DAY:

Lord God,
just as Mary believed
that she would become
the mother of Jesus,
so, by your great power,
may we believe
that he will come among us
and live as our friend,
forever and ever.

FOCUS OF THE READINGS:

God chose to bring about our redemption through the small and the humble. Micah tells us that in the little town of Bethlehem—so small it goes unnoticed—the ruler of Israel will be born. The Savior comes as a baby, born of an ordinary woman, because she believed. Her faith and joy are shared by her cousin of "the hill country." But this encounter between Mary and Elizabeth reveals more than the tender affection between cousins and the desire to share their joy of conception. Women, being of little or no account, could hardly be expected to be the bearers of salvation for humankind. Yet, in this encounter, both precursor and Savior are revealed. These two women, simple and humble, are the first to receive the Holy Spirit, the power of God for salvation, and the first to proclaim that God's promise is fulfilled. Our reading reminds us that the Incarnation will bring justice to all. Here Luke emphasizes the importance and equality of women in the economy of salvation. Mary rejoices in this truth in her hymn of praise, the Magnificat.

God's power is shown in the small and humble.

FIRST READING: *Micah 5:2, 4, 5a*

A reading from the prophet Micah.

City of Bethlehem,
you are so small that you are hardly noticed
in the land of Judah.
But even though you are so small,
the person who is going to become the ruler
of all of Israel
will be born in your city.
God will make him strong.
He will be a shepherd and will feed his people.
He will be peace,
and all the world will know how great he is.

The Word of the Lord.

RESPONSE: *Psalm 80*

God our Shep-herd and Lord, let your face shine on us. face shine on us.

Shine on us and we shall be saved. Shine on us and we shall be saved.

GOSPEL ACCLAMATION:

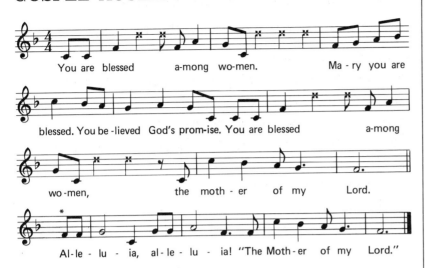

You are blessed a-mong wo-men. Ma-ry you are blessed. You be-lieved God's prom-ise. You are blessed a-mong wo-men, the moth-er of my Lord. Al-le-lu-ia, al-le-lu-ia! "The Moth-er of my Lord."

*After Gospel, repeat Acclamation from here.

GOSPEL: *Luke 1:39-45*

A reading from the Gospel of Luke.

When the angel Gabriel told Mary
that her cousin Elizabeth
was going to have a baby,
Mary went as quickly as she could
to the town where Zechariah and Elizabeth lived,
up in the hill country of Judah.
When Mary arrived,
she greeted her cousin Elizabeth.
As soon as Elizabeth heard Mary's voice,
the baby in her womb began to move.

Elizabeth was filled with the Holy Spirit,
and she said to Mary,

"Of all the women on earth,
you are most blessed.
And the baby in your womb is also blessed.
I am so honored
because you, the mother of my Lord,
have come to visit me!
You are blessed, Mary,
because you believed in the promise
that God made to you."

The Gospel of the Lord.

REFLECTING ON THE READINGS WITH CHILDREN:

During this season of Advent, we have been inviting the children to enter into the reading and take the role of the speaker. (Please see the *Reflections* for the past three Sundays.) The Gospel for today tells us of Mary's visit to her cousin Elizabeth in the hill country of Judah. It's a story that easily lends itself to imagination.

Help the children to imagine a clay house (small) in the hills. What does the area look like? There are no cars, no stores (as we know them), no telephone poles. Perhaps there is a well nearby. Perhaps there are animals. Ask the children questions similar to these:

- What do you think Elizabeth was doing before Mary came?
- Do you think Elizabeth and Zechariah had visitors often?
- How do you think Elizabeth and Mary first greeted each other?
- Why were they so happy to see each other?
- Now, suppose you are Elizabeth, the first person Mary comes to with the Good News. What would you say to her? If you, like Elizabeth, wanted to tell Mary how special she is and why, what would you say?

Help the children see that it is Mary's *faith* and *trust* in God that makes her special. She is the mother of Jesus because she said yes to God.

Next week is Christmas. Jesus wants to come into our hearts. We too, like Mary, can say yes. We can bring Jesus into the world by saying yes.

Jesus wants us to tell our family and friends and others the Good News. We too, like Mary, can tell others what God has done.

CHRISTMAS DAY

YEAR C

PRAYER OF THE DAY:

Father in heaven,
we are happy
because your Son, Jesus,
was born a baby at Bethlehem.
We thank you and praise you
for this great gift.
Be with us
as we tell others the Good News.
We pray to you
through Christ our Lord,
who lives with you
and the Holy Spirit,
forever and ever.

FOCUS OF THE READINGS:

The Gospel for Christmas Day is taken from the prologue of John's Gospel (1:1-18). This magnificent hymn of the Incarnation is perhaps one of the most beautiful passages in all of Scripture. But its language, at once poetic and highly theological, is scarcely understood by children. We have, therefore, chosen to use the nativity story of Luke which is proclaimed at the Mass of Midnight and Dawn. While it too is highly theological (please see "Introduction to the Infancy Narratives" in Leader's Handbook), it is written in a language which children can relate to, and delight in. They may miss many of the theological references, but they will surely understand the joy and excitement which accompanies our salvation. They will understand the great love God has for us expressed in this event. And this, we suggest, is the focus of our readings: God's great love for the world; God's great gift to the world. To a world of darkness and sin, a child is born, bringing light and peace.

FIRST READING: *Isaiah 9:2a-3a, 6-7*

A reading from the prophet Isaiah.

The people who were in darkness
have seen a great light.
You have filled them with great joy.

For a child is born to us, a son is given to us.
He is called:

> Wonderful Counselor, the Mighty God,
> the One Who Lives Forever,
> the Prince of Peace.

His kingdom will be great.
He will rule with justice and peace
now and forever.
The love of our God will make this happen!

The Word of the Lord.

RESPONSE: *Psalm 96*

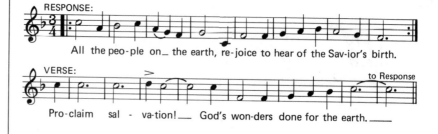

GOSPEL ACCLAMATION:

GOSPEL: *Luke 2:1-20*

A reading from the Gospel of Luke.

When Caesar Augustus, the ruler of Rome,
passed a law that everyone in the world should be enrolled,
all the people went to be registered
in the towns where they were born.

Joseph and Mary went from the town of Nazareth
to the City of David, which is called Bethlehem,
because Joseph was born in the family of David.
While they were there, the time came for Mary's child
to be born, and she gave birth to her first-born son.
She wrapped him in swaddling clothes
and laid him in a manger,
because there was no room for them in the inn.

At that time, there were shepherds in the fields
watching over their sheep during the night.
An angel of God appeared to them,
and the glory of God surrounded them with a great light.
And they were frightened.
The angel said to them,

  "Do not be afraid. I have come to bring you good news,
   news of great joy, to be shared by all the people.
   Today, in the City of Bethlehem,
   a Savior has been born for you,
   Christ the Lord!
   And this will be a sign for you:
   You will find a child wrapped in swaddling clothes
   and lying in a manger."

Suddenly, all the angels of heaven
were praising God and singing,

  "Glory to God in heaven, and peace to all people on earth."

The shepherds said to one another,

  "Let us go over to Bethlehem
   and see this wonderful thing God has told us about."

They hurried to Bethlehem
and found Mary and Joseph
and saw the baby lying in the manger.
When they saw the child, they repeated
what the angel had said about him.

Everyone was amazed
at what the shepherds told them.
And Mary thought about all these things
and kept them in her heart.

The shepherds returned to their fields,
thanking and praising God for all they had heard and seen.

The Gospel of the Lord.

REFLECTING ON THE READINGS WITH CHILDREN:

We offer two possibilities for the children's reflections.

If there has been an opportunity to prepare, the children may enjoy participating in a dramatization of the Christmas story. One example is provided on the following pages. If this is not possible, we suggest reflecting with the children as follows.

Welcome the children in the joy of this Holy Season. Usually we stand for the Gospel. Today, because this is a story and the children are likely to be excitable, we may want them to sit and listen to the story. It should be read in great story form so the children *hear* every detail.

After the Gospel, ask the children to recall the details of the story.

- What did the ruler of Rome want everyone to do?
- Where did Mary and Joseph go?
- What is the story of the inn and the manger?
- What did the angels tell the shepherds?
- What was the song the angels sang?
- What can you recall about the coming of the shepherds to the manger?
- What do you remember about Mary in the Christmas story?
- What is your favorite part of the Christmas story?

Jesus was born a long time ago in Bethlehem. But we still read the story of his birth.

- Why do we do this?
- What does Jesus want us to learn from this Christmas story today?
- How is Jesus born again today—on Christmas?
- How can we be like the angels?
- How can we be like the shepherds?
- How can we be like Mary?
- How can we be like Jesus?

CREED (If there is time)
- Do you believe God made you and loves you?
- Do you believe God sent Jesus to show us how to live and how to love each other?
- Do you believe that Jesus was born of the Virgin Mary and came to earth as a little baby so that everyone could be saved?
- Do you believe that Jesus wants everyone to know his love and live together in peace?
- Do you believe that the Holy Spirit lives in our hearts to help us live the way Jesus wants us to?

This is the faith of our Church. "Amen."

Gospel Drama for Christmas Season

Gospel: *Luke 2:1-20*

Children always enjoy acting the Christmas story. It should be prepared before Christmas. Children will be needed for the roles of:

> Mary
> Joseph
> Angel
> Shepherds
> Youngest child to bring child Jesus
> Narrator (older child)

For props, a crib or manger. A candle for each child. A doll.

This Gospel drama could replace the reflection on the reading.

Narrator: In those days, Caesar Augustus, the ruler of Rome, passed a law that everyone in the world should be counted. And so, all the people went to the town where they were born to give their names. Joseph and Mary went from Nazareth to the City of David, which is called Bethlehem, because Joseph was born in the family of David.

Action: Mary and Joseph travel to Bethlehem. Mary hides under her cloak a doll wrapped in "swaddling clothes."
or: The youngest child holds the doll, standing "off-stage."

Narrator: While they were there, the time came for Mary's child to be born. She gave birth to her first-born son and wrapped him in swaddling clothes and laid him in a manger, because there was no room for them in the inn.

Action: Mary carries the doll under her cloak and places it in the manger.
or: the youngest child brings the doll and gives it to Mary and remains at her side.

Narrator: At that time, shepherds who lived in the fields were watching over their sheep at night. An angel of God appeared to them, and the glory of the Lord surrounded them like a light. And they were very much afraid.

Action: An angel approaches the shepherds.

Angel: "Do not be afraid; I come to bring you good news—news of great joy to be shared by all people. Today, in the City of Bethlehem, a Savior has been born for you. This Savior is Christ the Lord. And here is a sign for you: you will find a child wrapped in swaddling clothes and lying in a manger."

Narrator: Suddenly, all the angels of heaven were praising God and singing:

Angels: "Glory to God in heaven, and peace to all people on earth."
(A few children join in the singing of the gloria.)

Narrator: Let us join our voices to the voices of the angels and sing:
"Glory to God in heaven, and peace to all people on earth."

All: Sing a gloria taken from the Christmas carols repertoire.

Narrator: The shepherds said to one another,

One Shepherd: "Let us go over to Bethlehem and see this wonderful thing God has told us about."

Narrator: They went quickly and found Mary and Joseph and saw the baby lying in the manger. When they saw Jesus, they understood all that they had been told about him, and they knelt down and adored Jesus, their Lord and Savior.

Action: Three shepherds kneel and sing a song.

All: Continue singing Glory to God.

Action: The shepherds slowly leave.

Narrator: The shepherds returned to their fields, thanking and praising God because of all that they had heard and seen. They told the good news to many. Those who heard what they saw were amazed at what the shepherds told them. And Mary treasured all these things in her heart.

Today we are happy to hear again "the good news" which the shepherds have told to so many. Let us take our lighted candles and bring them to the crib. Today, we come to see and worship this child, our Lord and Savior, who was born of Mary in Bethlehem, many years ago.

Action: Lighted lamps or candles are given to everyone. The children form a procession and bring the lights to the crib where they are carefully placed in sandboxes. The leader may invite the children to kneel before the child Jesus. A Christmas song or a Gloria Acclamation may be sung. After some time, all return to their places, and the celebration continues with the Profession of Faith.

HOLY FAMILY

YEAR C

PRAYER OF THE DAY:

God our Father,
you especially wanted
Jesus to live and grow
in a family with
Mary and Joseph.
Help our own families
always to be
full of happiness and peace.
We ask you this
through Christ our Lord.

FOCUS OF THE READINGS:

Our readings focus on the importance and holiness of family life. By "holiness" we mean that the family truly reflects and participates in the creative activity of God.

In the first reading, Paul gives us the Christian principles that both animate and characterize the family life of baptized Christians. We are to live in mutuality, each respecting and loving the other. We are to help each other grow by being kind, forgiving, gentle, honest, peace-making, and most of all by our love for each other. Christian families live this way because they are chosen and loved by God.

The Gospel tells us that Jesus returned to Nazareth, obeyed Mary and Joseph, and continued to grow in body and wisdom. The point of the Incarnation is that Jesus was truly, fully human. His human development is dependent, as it is for all of us, on the nurturing of a family. That Mary and Joseph provided a nurturing environment is seen in their religious devotion to their faith and their obvious concern for the well

FIRST READING: *Colossians 3:12-21*

A reading from a letter written by Paul to the Colossians.

Brothers and sisters,

You are God's chosen people, holy and well loved.
Therefore, be kind and patient with one another.

Be honest and gentle with one another.
Forgive each other as God has forgiven you.
And most of all, love one another.

Let the peace of Christ be in your hearts.
And always be thankful. Let the word of Christ, which is so wonderful, live in you.

Help each other to grow and to become better.
Everything you say or do,
do it in the name of the Lord Jesus.
And always give thanks to God through Jesus.

Wives and husbands, love one another
and take care of each other,
because this is what God asks of you.
Children, obey your parents,
because this is what God asks of you.
Parents, be patient and gentle with your children,
so that they will be encouraged.

The Word of the Lord.

RESPONSE: *Psalm 96*

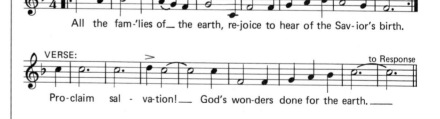

RESPONSE: All the fam-'lies of_ the earth, re-joice to hear of the Sav-ior's birth.

VERSE: Pro-claim sal - va-tion!_ God's won-ders done for the earth._ (to Response)

14

GOSPEL ACCLAMATION:

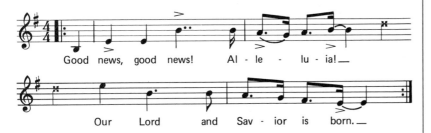

Good news, good news! Al - le - lu - ia!

Our Lord and Sav - ior is born. —

GOSPEL: *Luke 2:41-52*

A reading from the Gospel of Luke.

The parents of Jesus used to go to Jerusalem every year
for the feast of Passover.
When Jesus was twelve years old,
they went for the celebration as usual.
When the feast was over, they left to go back to Nazareth,
but Jesus stayed in Jerusalem.

Now, Jesus' parents
did not know that he had stayed behind.
They thought he was traveling with relatives and friends
who were with them.
But when they didn't find Jesus in the group,
they went back to Jerusalem to look for him.

Three days later, they found him in the temple.
He was with the teachers,
listening to them and asking them questions.
Everyone who heard him was amazed
at how intelligent he was
and at the answers he was giving.

His mother said to him,

"Son, why did you do this to us?
Your father and I have been worried about you.
We've been looking everywhere for you."

Jesus said to them,

"Why were you looking for me?
Didn't you know that I had to be in my Father's house?"

Hisparents did not understand what he meant.

Jesus went back to Nazareth with Mary and Joeseph
and obeyed them.
His mother, Mary, kept all these things in her heart.
And Jesus continued to grow in body and wisdom,
and was loved by God and all the people.

The Gospel of the Lord.

being of their son. The reading shows
us the authenticity of this family,
concerned with the practices of their
time. It is important to notice that
the boy Jesus was pleasing to God
and also pleasing to the people.

Rejoice, all families of the earth!
Our Savior is born, and lives among us.

REFLECTING ON THE READINGS
WITH CHILDREN:

Help the children to see that it is
mutuality that makes for peaceful
and loving family life. In this
environment each one can grow, as
Jesus did, physically, mentally and
spiritually. One example might be
the growth of a plant. It needs sun,
rain, good soil, etc. But rain alone
will not produce growth. Sun alone
will not produce growth, etc. Each
one is needed for good growth. Help
the children see that we live this way
because God loves us and because we
are baptized Christians.

MARY, MOTHER OF GOD

YEAR C

PRAYER OF THE DAY:

Loving God,
through the power
of your Spirit,
you have made
Mary the mother
of your only Son, Jesus.
In the name of Mary,
we proclaim your glory.
In the name
of Jesus, our Savior,
we rejoice in the gift
of your Spirit,
and we bless your name
forever and ever.

FOCUS OF THE READINGS:

The focus of both of our readings is the significance of "the name." In the first reading from the book of Numbers, we have the well known blessing of the Jewish people. But the meaning of the blessing comes from the last line: "When they bless . . . . *in my name*, I will bless them." In other words, when we bless in God's name, it is actually God who is blessing. The name stood for the whole person. To say, "in God's name," is to say in or with all that God is and all that God does. To bless in God's name is to make God totally present.

The Gospel reading for today recounts the circumcision and naming of Jesus. It is interesting that in the past this feast has been called both the Feast of the Circumcision, and the Feast of the Holy Name. At the presentation, Jesus was given the name foretold by the angel at the Anunciation—Jesus, the name which means "Savior." Because the whole

FIRST READING: *Numbers 6:22-27*

A reading from the book of Numbers.

God said to Moses,

"Tell Aaron and all the priests of Israel
  that when they bless the people,
  they must say,

   'May God bless you and keep you.
   May God's face shine on you.
   May God be kind to you and give you peace.'

"When they bless the people like this,
  in my name,
  I will bless them."

The Word of the Lord.

RESPONSE: *Numbers 6:24-26*

RESPONSE:
May God bless and keep you, may God's face shine on you:
May God be kind to you and give you peace.

16

GOSPEL ACCLAMATION:

The an-gel said to Ma-ry: "You shall call him Je - sus."
Al - le - lu - ia! "Ma - ry, you shall call him Je - sus."

GOSPEL: *Luke 2:16-21*

A reading from the Gospel of Luke.

When the shepherds went to Bethlehem,
where Jesus was born,
they found Joseph and Mary,
and they saw the baby lying in the manger.
When they saw the child,
they repeated what the angel had said about him.

Everyone who heard it
was amazed at what the shepherds told them.
And Mary thought about all these things
and kept them in her heart.
The shepherds went back to their fields,
thanking and praising God
for all they had heard and seen.

When the baby was eight days old,
he was circumcised,
and Mary and Joseph gave him the name Jesus,
which was the name
the angel Gabriel told Mary to call him.

The Gospel of the Lord.

person is represented by the name, Scripture tells us that "at the name of Jesus, every knee should bend" and "those who call upon the name of the Lord will be saved." When Mary proclaims in the Magnificat, "Holy is God's name!" she proclaims that all that God is and all that God does is holy! Today's feast celebrates the naming of Jesus. This feast proclaims that Jesus is the Savior!

He is God's blessing and peace! You shall call him Jesus!

REFLECTING ON THE READINGS WITH CHILDREN:

You might ask the children if they know why they received their name or if they know what their name means. It would be interesting to share with them the meaning of some common names. There are several little books available that give brief meanings.

Explain to the children that in the past, people's names often stood for who they were and what they did. For example, people who made bread often had the name "Baker." The name Smith comes from families who were blacksmiths, etc. In the Old Testament, people often had names that indicated their mission in life or some significant event in their life. The name "Moses" means "I drew you out of the water." Moses was saved from drowning when he was a baby and later became the leader of his people.

This introduction to the significance of names will lead naturally to a discussion of today's Gospel which recounts the naming of Jesus. Jesus was given this name because it means "Savior."

EPIPHANY

YEAR C

PRAYER OF THE DAY:

Lord God,
you want the whole world
to know
that you have sent
Jesus your Son
to save us from our sins.
Give us a share of your power,
so that we will be
like bright stars
leading others to discover him,
who lives with you
and the Holy Spirit,
one God, forever and ever.

FOCUS OF THE READINGS:

The birth of Christ is the manifestation (epiphany) of God in the world. In Christ, salvation has come for everyone, Jew and Gentile alike.

Our first reading tells us that the light has come, a light for all to walk in. In this light, the glory of God shines forth. This light is the epiphany of God. The Gospel tells us that this light shone in the east and brought visitors from afar to see this manifestation of God's love. Christ is the One to whom all people will come, bringing gifts fit for a king. He is the "newborn King of the Jews" and, indeed of all the earth. He reveals the limitlessness of God's love for all.

God's love is made known to all the world! Let all the nations rejoice!

FIRST READING: *Isaiah 60:1-4, 6*

A reading from the prophet Isaiah.

People of Jerusalem, arise! Stand up!
Your light has come!
The glory of God shines on you!
And the rulers of nations
will come to your shining light.

Look all around you and see;
people are gathering and coming to you.
They will come from far away,
bringing gifts of gold and frankincense,
and singing the praises of God.

The Word of the Lord.

RESPONSE: *Psalm 96*

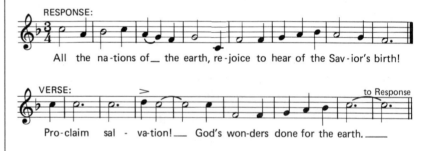

RESPONSE:
All the nations of the earth, re-joice to hear of the Sav-ior's birth!

VERSE:
Pro-claim sal-va-tion! God's won-ders done for the earth.

GOSPEL ACCLAMATION:

Good news, good news! Al-le-lu-ia!

The world will know of his love!

18

GOSPEL: *Matthew 2:1-12*

A reading from the Gospel of Matthew.

When Jesus was born in Bethlehem of Judea,
while Herod was king,
some magi came from the east.
When they arrived in Jerusalem, they asked the people,

"Where is the newborn King of the Jews?
We have seen his star in the east,
and we have come to worship him."

When they heard this,
King Herod and all the people of Jerusalem
became very disturbed.
Herod gathered the leaders of the Jewish people
and asked them
where the Messiah was supposed to be born.
They told him,

"In Bethlehem of Judea."

Then Herod asked the magi
to tell him the exact time
they had seen the star in the east.
When they told him, Herod said,

"Go to Bethlehem and find out all you can about this child.
When you have found him, come back and tell me,
so that I, too, may go and worship him."

And so they left for Bethlehem.
The star, which they had seen in the east,
went ahead of them,
and it stopped over the place where Jesus was.

When they went in,
they found the child with Mary, his mother.
And they were filled with joy.
They knelt down and worshipped Jesus.
And they gave him gifts of gold, frankincense and myrrh.

That night, God told the magi in a dream
not to go back to Herod.
So they went back to their own country by another way.

The Gospel of the Lord.

REFLECTING ON THE READINGS
WITH CHILDREN:

Children will not grasp the
profound theological signs in these
readings. But they will experience
the joy and wonder at such an event.
Again we suggest that, rather than a
discussion as such, the children
participate in a dramatization,
allowing them to experience the
"signs" Matthew presents.

Mention should be made by way of
summary, of God's love for all people,
of every race, nationality and belief.

Gospel Drama for Epiphany

Gospel: *Matthew 2:1-12*

The Story of the Wise Men

Children will be required for the roles of:

      Narrator   Mary
      Herod   Joseph
      Three Wise Men   (Jesus)
      Child hold a star

Props required: Star
                 Gifts
                 (Jesus/doll)

Narrator: This is the good news from the Gospel of Matthew.

    Action: Mary, Joseph and the child Jesus take their place on one side. A child holding a star leads the magi to Herod, who is seated on the other side.

Narrator: After Jesus was born in Bethlehem of Judea, while Herod was king, wise men from the east came one day to Jerusalem. They asked:

The Magi: Where is the newborn King of the Jews? We saw his star in the east, and we have come to worship him.

    Action: Herod's friends at the back of the stage murmur to one another: Where is the Messiah? Where was he born?

Narrator: When they said this, King Herod and all the people of Jerusalem became very disturbed. Herod gathered the leaders of the Jewish people and asked them where the Messiah was to be born. They said:

All: In Bethlehem of Judea.

Narrator: Herod asked the wise men to tell him the exact time they had seen the star. Then he sent the wise men to Bethlehem, and he told them:

Herod: Go and find out all you can about the child. When you have found him, come back and tell me so that I may go too and worship him.

Narrator: And so they set out for Bethlehem. The star, which they had seen in the east, went ahead of them, and it stopped over the place where the child was.

Action: The wise men kneel before the child and give their gifts. All kneel before the child and sing an epiphany song which is familiar to the children.

BAPTISM OF THE LORD

YEAR C

PRAYER OF THE DAY:

God of heaven and earth,
when Jesus was baptized
in the River Jordan,
you sent the Holy Spirit
upon him to show the world
that he was your Son.
Send us the Holy Spirit also,
that we may be the messengers
of your Good News.
We ask you this
through Christ our Lord.

FOCUS OF THE READINGS:

The first reading describes the mission of the servant who is chosen by God to bring justice and truth to the world and to make God known to the people. At his baptism Jesus is revealed as the Son of God and is anointed with the Spirit. Coupled with our first reading, the Baptism of the Lord also reveals Jesus as the servant described in Isaiah. He is anointed for mission. His mission is to bring justice, to be a light to the nations, to be a healer and a liberator. In this liturgy, the Church holds before us the power and the challenge of our own baptism: we are children of God, anointed with the Spirit, and the mission of Jesus is our mission.

FIRST READING: *Isaiah 42:1, 6-7*

A reading from the prophet Isaiah.

Our God says,

"This is my servant, my chosen one.
I give him my strength and my spirit
to bring justice to all the people.
And I say to him,

'I, your God, have called you.
I have taken you by your hand.
I have sent you
as my covenant to the people,
as a light for the world.
I have sent you
to open the eyes of the blind,
to free those in prison,
and to give light to those who live in darkness.'"

The Word of the Lord.

RESPONSE: *Psalm 146*

RESPONSE: I praise you, O God, for your faith-ful love. I praise you, O God, for all that you do.

VERSES: [repeat by singing or clapping rhythm]   to Response
1. You free the op-pressed and save the poor.
2. The hun-gry are fed, the blind can see.
3. Hap-py are all who hope in you.

22

GOSPEL ACCLAMATION:

A voice from heav-en said,___ "This is my be-lov-ed Son."___ Al-le-lu-ia. Al-le-lu-ia.___ Al-le-lu-ia. Al-le-lu-ia.___ Al-le-lu-ia. Al-le-lu-ia. Al-le-lu-ia.

GOSPEL: *Luke 3:15-16, 21-22*

A reading from the Gospel of Luke.

When John the Baptist
was baptizing at the Jordan River,
all the people were filled with excitement,
and they wondered if he might be the Messiah.

But John said to them,

"I am baptizing you in water,
    but someone is coming later
    who is mightier than I am.
I am not even worthy to untie his sandal straps.
He will baptize you in the Holy Spirit."

Then, after all the people were baptized,
Jesus also was baptized.
While he was praying,
the Holy Spirit came to him in the form of a dove,
and a voice from heaven said,

"You are my beloved Son
    with whom I am very pleased."

The Gospel of the Lord.

REFLECTING ON THE READINGS WITH CHILDREN:

In reflecting on the Baptism of the Lord with children, we encounter a particular difficulty. The Baptism of Jesus, and indeed the norm in the early church, was an adult experience. While the essential truth of gratuitous grace was certainly recognized, baptism was intimately linked with conversion and a life of service. The Baptism of Jesus is the inauguration of his public life, a life of service. Our baptism, like that of Jesus, calls us to the service described in our reading from Isaiah. This connection is more difficult to see and reflect on in light of infant baptism, which is the case of most of the children with whom we are ministering. And so, we hope in this reflection to plant a seed of this truth which the children will gradually come to understand and live more fully.

After the Gospel, ask the children to recall what they heard. Help them to recall especially "water," "Spirit," "You are my Son." Ask them if they have been present for a baptism or if their parents have told them about their own baptism. Help them to recall what happens at a Christian baptism. Draw from them comments about the following:

1) Water, 2) Spirit ("I baptize you in the name of the Father, and the Son and the Holy Spirit."), 3) We receive the Holy Spirit at our baptism, as Jesus did, 4) We are sons and daughters of God.

Ask the children if they remember what the first reading was about. You may want to read it again. Ask them if they can find things that are alike in this reading and the Baptism of Jesus: Spirit, with whom I am well pleased.

What did God ask the "servant" to do? (bring justice, heal people, free people.)

Did Jesus do these things after his baptism? Can you recall any stories about that?

God said to the servant:
"I have sent you as a light to the people."

Remind the children that we receive a lighted candle when we are baptized. Because we are baptized and receive the Holy Spirit, we are like Jesus. We can be a light for other people. We are like Jesus, we can serve other people.

How can we be a light for people? How can we help people as Jesus did? (As always, it is important that this reflect their age.)

You might conclude by asking the children to ask their parents to share with them pictures and memories of their baptism.

The Season of Lent

FIRST SUNDAY OF LENT

YEAR C

PRAYER OF THE DAY:

God our protector,
you wanted Jesus
to be one with us.
We are sometimes tempted
to be greedy,
to control other people's lives,
and to forget
that all good things
come from you.
Hold us in your care
and never let us forsake you.
We ask you this
through Christ our Lord.

FOCUS OF THE READINGS:

Both of our readings focus on our total commitment to the one true God. The reading from Deuteronomy is the summary of the great saving act of God in the Exodus. Here the people recount that saving act, from their entry into Egypt to their entry into the promised land. It is because of their salvation by their faithful and loving God that they give thanks and bow down in worship.

In the Gospel for today, Jesus is tempted in the desert by Satan, but Jesus resists the temptation and three times proclaims that God and God alone is the Savior. Only God gives real life, real power, real security.

To you alone will I bow in worship. By your word alone will I live.

FIRST READING: *Deuteronomy 26:4-10*

A reading from the book of Deuteronomy.

Moses said to the people,

"When you come to the place
which God is giving to you,
you shall take some
of the first things grown on the land
and put them in a basket.
You shall take the basket
to the place that God has chosen
and there you shall say to God:

'My family lived in the country of Aram.
They traveled down to Egypt
and stayed there as refugees.
The people of Egypt were cruel to us
and made us work very hard.
Then he cried out to you,
the God of our people, and you heard us.
You saw how much we were suffering
and how we were being oppressed.
So you took us out of Egypt
and brought us here
and gave us this wonderful land,
a place filled with milk and honey.
And so now, I am bringing to you
some of the first things
we have grown on this land,
which you, our God, have given us.' "

And then Moses said,

"You shall put the basket in front of the altar
and there you shall bow down
and worship your God."

The Word of the Lord.

RESPONSE: *Psalm 138*

RESPONSE:
I will bow down in your ho - ly tem - ple.

VERSE:
I will give thanks to your name, for your
to Response
love and your faith - ful - ness. ____

26

GOSPEL ACCLAMATION:

(sing and clap)

If you live by my Word, the Good News of God is for you.

[sing and clap]

GOSPEL: *Luke 4:1-13*

A reading from the Gospel of Luke.

After Jesus was baptized in the Jordan River,
the Spirit led him into the desert for forty days,
and the devil tried to tempt him.
For all those days, Jesus did not eat any food,
and he was hungry.
So the devil said to Jesus:

"If you are the Son of God, tell this stone to become bread."

But Jesus said to the devil:

"It is written in the books of Moses,

'People do not live just by eating food.' "

Then the devil took Jesus up and showed him
all the kingdoms of the world, and said:

"I will give you all the power and glory of these kingdoms
if you will worship me."

But Jesus said,

"It is written in the books of Moses,

'You must worship God, and only God!' "

Then the devil took Jesus to the very top of the temple
in Jerusalem, and said to him:

"If you are the Son of God, jump down from here,
because it is written in the book of Psalms,

'God will tell the angels to take care of you,
and they will catch you
so that you will not hurt your foot on a rock.' "

But Jesus said,

"It is also written,

'You shall not test your God.' "

After these temptations, the devil left Jesus
and waited for another time to come again.

The Gospel of the Lord.

REFLECTING ON THE READINGS
WITH CHILDREN:

The security found in God may
seem abstract to the children,
especially in comparison with the
things the world offers for security.
It is clear to them that money and
power do buy the things we need to
live. Our emphasis should not be that
these things are unimportant. The
Jews thanked God for providing the
food they needed. And Jesus said we
do not live by bread *alone*. We should
never pit God against the necessities
of this world as though the things of
this world are evil. Rather, help the
children to see two things:

- *All these things ultimately come
  from God*. For example, one can
  work and acquire a home, food,
  clothes, etc., because of good
  health, etc.
- *It is the exaggeration* and
  dependence on personal money
  and power *that Jesus warns
  against*.

27

SECOND SUNDAY OF LENT

YEAR C

PRAYER OF THE DAY:

God of heaven and earth,
we do not really understand
why Jesus, your Son,
suffered and died
on the cross for us.
Help us listen
to everything he teaches
and to follow him
to his home with you
where you live forever and ever.

FOCUS OF THE READINGS:

Our readings focus on God's promise of salvation. This salvation is seen in the first reading as the promised land. In the Transfiguration, Jesus shows us the glory to which we are ultimately called. Peter, James and John saw a glimpse of the Resurrected Jesus, and of our future glory. We will live in light and splendor. This revelation is accompanied by its requirement—Listen to him.

Jesus is the One promised by God. Listen to him.

FIRST READING: *Genesis 15:5-10a, 18*

A reading from the book of Genesis.

God said to Abraham,

"Look up at the sky. Can you count all those stars?
That's how many people will be in your family."

Abraham believed God,
and God was pleased with Abraham's faith,
and said to him:

"I am your God,
who brought you away from your home
in Ur of the Chaldeans.
I brought you here
so that I could give you this land."

But Abraham asked,

"How can I know that this land will truly be mine?"

God said,

"Bring me a young cow, a young goat,
a young ram, a turtledove and a pigeon."

Abraham brought all of these
and offered a sacrifice to God.
On that day, God made a covenant
with Abraham, saying,

"I will give all this land to your family;
all this land from the river of Egypt
to the great river Euphrates."

The Word of the Lord.

RESPONSE: *Psalm 89*

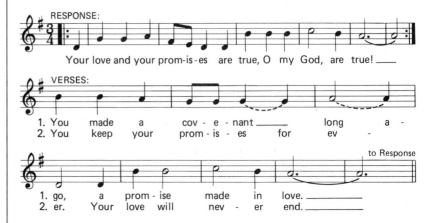

RESPONSE:
Your love and your prom-is-es are true, O my God, are true! ___

VERSES:
1. You made a cov-e-nant ___ long a-
2. You keep your prom-is-es for ev-

to Response
1. go, a prom-ise made in love. ___
2. er. Your love will nev-er end. ___

28

GOSPEL ACCLAMATION:

"This is Je - sus my Son, lis - ten, his words are for you."

GOSPEL: *Luke 9:28-36*

A reading from the Gospel of Luke.

One day Jesus took Peter, James and John
and went up on a mountain to pray.
While Jesus was praying,
his face changed
and his clothes became shining white.
Then Moses and Elijah were there with Jesus,
and they too were shining in glory.
They were talking with Jesus
about how he was going to die in Jerusalem.

Peter, James and John had fallen asleep.
When they woke up,
they saw Jesus shining in glory,
and they saw the two men with him.
As Moses and Elijah were leaving,
Peter said to Jesus,

"Master, it's good for us to be here!
Let us make three tents:
one for you, one for Moses and one for Elijah."

Peter was so confused by what was happening
that he didn't know what he was saying.
As he was speaking,
the shadow of a cloud came over them,
and when it was all around them,
they became frightened.

Then a voice came from the cloud, saying,

"This is my son, my chosen one. Listen to him."

After the voice had spoken,
they saw only Jesus standing there.

The Gospel of the Lord.

REFLECTING ON THE READINGS WITH CHILDREN:

After the Gospel, ask the children to recall what they heard. If they have difficulty recalling, you may wish to help them with questions such as:

- Who did Jesus take with him to the mountain?
- What happened while they were there?
- Who did Peter, James and John see with Jesus?
- What did Peter say?
- What did Peter, James and John hear God say?

Ask the children if they have ever seen previews of coming attractions on television or in a theatre. Help them understand that previews tell us what the coming attraction is going to be like and help us look forward to it.

Help them see that at the Transfiguration, Jesus was giving a preview of what he will be like after the resurrection. He was also showing us that we will be like him. We will live with him in glory. As Jesus was showing this to Peter, James and John, God told them what we must do to live with Jesus in glory forever.

Do you remember what God said to Peter, James and John? God tells us too,

"This is my beloved son; listen to him."

- How do we listen to Jesus today in the Bible?
- in our parents and others who teach us?
- in the good thoughts we have that encourage us to do the right thing?

THIRD SUNDAY OF LENT

YEAR C

PRAYER OF THE DAY:

Forgiving God,
you know how we try
to please you,
and how often we fail.
Be with us
in this season of Lent,
that we may fight
against our faults
and love you more sincerely.
We ask you to do this
through Christ our Lord.

FOCUS OF THE READINGS:

The first reading presents the ultimate paradox of God: always "other," yet ever "near." God is revealed in the burning bush as a God of holiness and power. It is the image of the totally other, transcendent God. Yet this is a God who speaks to and works through humanity, a God who acts in human history.

Our Gospel focuses on our need for conversion. In strong language, Jesus warns that if we do not change our ways, we will not be saved. Yet this very warning is filled with hope. We are always given the time and the help we need for conversion. The image of the fig tree so simply illustrates this.

Our God is holy and is here with us. Change your lives and believe.

FIRST READING: *Exodus 3:1-8a, 10, 13-15*

A reading from the book of Exodus.

One day, while Moses was taking care of the sheep
that belonged to his father-in-law, Jethro,
he led the sheep to the mountain of Horeb,
God's holy mountain.

While Moses was there, he saw a bush burning,
but it wasn't being burned up. So Moses said to himself,
  "I'm going to go closer so I can see this better.
    How can it be that this bush is burning,
    but isn't being burned up?"
God called from the bush,
  "Moses, Moses!"
Moses said,
  "Here I am!"
Then God said,
  "Don't come any closer. And take off your shoes,
    for the place where you are standing is holy ground.
    I am the God of your people,
    the God of Abraham, the God of Isaac,
    and the God of Jacob."
Moses put his hands over his eyes
because he was afraid to look at God.
Then God said,
  "I have seen how much my people are suffering in Egypt.
    I have heard them cry for help,
    and I have come to free them
    and to bring them away from Egypt
    to a wonderful place,
    a land that is filled with milk and honey.
    Go now, I am sending you
    to bring my people away from Egypt."
Then Moses asked God,
  "When I tell the people that you sent me,
    they will ask me what your name is.
    What shall I tell them?"
God said to Moses,
  " 'I am who I am!'
    Tell them that my name is 'I Am'—and
    that I sent you to them.
    This is my name
    and this is how I want to be remembered forever."

The Word of the Lord.

RESPONSE: *Psalm 34*

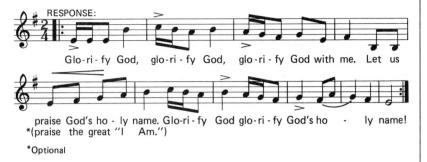

Glo-ri-fy God, glo-ri-fy God, glo-ri-fy God with me. Let us
praise God's ho-ly name. Glo-ri-fy God glo-ri-fy God's ho - ly name!
*(praise the great "I Am.")

*Optional

GOSPEL ACCLAMATION:

Change your lives and be-lieve! The Good News_ of God is for you! _

GOSPEL: *Luke 13:3, 5-9*

A reading from the Gospel of Luke.

One day as Jesus was teaching,
he said to the people,

"Unless you change your lives
and give up your sinful ways,
you will not have eternal life."

Then he told them this parable:

"There was a man who had a fig tree in his garden.
When he went to pick some figs,
there weren't any on the tree.
So he said to the gardener,

'I have been waiting for three years
for figs to grow on this tree,
and I never find any. Cut it down.
Why should it take up space in my garden?'

"But the gardener said,

'Master, leave it here for one more year.
I will dig up the dirt around it
and put manure in the ground to help it grow.
Let's wait and see if figs grow on it next year.
If they do, that's good!
But if not, then we'll cut it down.' "

The Gospel of the Lord.

REFLECTING ON THE READINGS WITH CHILDREN:

If you choose to reflect on the first reading, you might begin by asking the children how they would feel if the President or the Queen or a very important sports star (heroes will vary!) came to their home and said, "Hello, my name is . . . and I just wanted to be with you because I care about you." Let them explore those thoughts for awhile. Then help them come to a sense of appreciation and awe of the majesty of God. Help them see the reverence implied in "take off your shoes." God is not one among many wonderful people. God is absolutely unique, different, beyond. God's name is holy and demands reverence. Then, help the children to appreciate that it is this same God who chooses to be so close to us, to love us, to save us. God came to us and said, "My name is 'I Am Who I Am,' and I am here to save you because I love you."

If you choose to reflect on the Gospel, you might ask the children what they would do with a tree that didn't produce fruit. Help them see that it is perfectly natural to want to remove it. And that's just the point of the parable. God doesn't "remove" us when we don't do what is right. Instead, God always gives us a chance to change. Lent is a special time to help us change our lives. Help the children reflect on how they think they might change to live more like Jesus. Allow them time to reflect on their own lives. Be sure that this focuses on things appropriate to their age and situation. They are not responsible for the evils of the world, and a discussion along those lines will not help them deepen their relationship with Jesus.

FOURTH SUNDAY OF LENT

YEAR C

PRAYER OF THE DAY:

Lord our God,
you are like a father,
waiting for your children
to return home.
Teach us to be sorry
for all we have done wrong,
turn back to you,
and be happy as you forgive us.
We pray to you through
Christ our Lord,
who lives with you
and the Holy Spirit,
forever and ever.

FOCUS OF THE READINGS:

Our Gospel focuses on God's loving response to our conversion. In this story, God is compared to a father who rejoices when his child returns home. The story tells us that we can never be truly happy when we turn away from God. When we realize that and want to go back, God is always there waiting to meet us with open arms.

God looks for those who are lost.

FIRST READING: *Joshua 5:9a, 10-12*
A reading from the prophet Joshua.

*When the people of Israel
crossed over the Jordan River,
they came into the promised land,
the place that God had told them about.*

God said to Joshua,
  "Today I have saved you and your people
    from the sufferings you had in Egypt."
And while they were staying
in a place called Gilgal,
they ate the Passover meal.
On the day after the Passover,
the people began to grow their own food
in the promised land.
They grew brown grain
and they ate unleavened bread.
From that time on
they didn't eat manna anymore,
because now they ate the food
that they grew on the land in Canaan.

The Word of the Lord.

RESPONSE: *Psalm 104*

You are the one who feeds us, giv-ing us food from your hand.
You are the one who feeds us, giv-ing us all we need.

GOSPEL ACCLAMATION:

"The lost has been found!" The Good News of God is for you!

GOSPEL: *Luke 15:11-32*
A reading from the Gospel of Luke.

One day Jesus told this story.
There was a man who had two sons.
The younger son said to his father,
  "Give me my half of all the family property—
    all that would be mine after you die."
So the father divided everything he owned
between his two sons.
A few days later the younger son packed up all his things
and left home to live in a far away country.
But he wasted all of his money living a wild life.
After he had spent everything,

there was a bad famine in that country
and he became very hungry but could not buy any food.

He went to work for a farmer
who sent him out to feed the pigs.
The young man was so hungry
that he could have eaten the food the pigs ate,
but no one offered him even that.

At last, he came to his senses and said to himself,

"The people who work for my father
have more than enough food to eat,
and here I am starving to death.
I will go back to my father and I will say to him,
'Father, I have sinned against God and against you;
I am no longer good enough to be called your son.
Treat me like one of your workers.' "

So the young man started home.
But while he was still a long way off,
his father saw him coming and ran out to meet him.
He took his son in his arms and kissed him.

The young man said,

"Father, I have sinned against God and against you.
I am no longer good enough to be called your son."

But his father said to the servants,

"Quick! Bring out the best clothes and put them on him.
Put a ring on his finger and shoes on his feet.
Get our best calf and prepare a feast.
Let's eat and celebrate because my son was dead
and he has come back to life.
He was lost and has been found!"

[Now the older son was out in the field working.
But when he came close to the house, he heard music and dancing.
So he asked one of the servants what was going on.
The servant said,

"Your brother has come home
and your father has killed the best calf.
We are having a big party
because your brother is home safe and sound."

The older brother was very angry and would not go into the house.
His father went out and begged him to come in.
But the older son said to his father,

"I have worked for you all these years
and I have never once disobeyed you.
But you never gave me anything
so that I could have a party with my friends.
Now this son of yours comes back
after wasting all your money on wild living,
and you kill the best calf for him."

The father said to his older son,

"Son, you are always here with me.
Everything I have is yours too.
But we must be happy and celebrate now
because your brother was dead and now he is alive.
He was lost and now he has been found."]

The Gospel of the Lord.

[ ] *Reader may omit text that appears in brackets.*

REFLECTING ON THE READINGS
WITH CHILDREN:

Ask the children if any of them
has ever been lost or separated from
their parents in a big store or
elsewhere. What did that feel like?
Give them time to talk about that.
How did they feel when they saw
their parents again?

Ask them to retell the story in the
Gospel. Help them to visualize the
story. They should know that the
younger son was not a child. His
father freely gave him what he asked
for. His problem was that he didn't
use it wisely. He tried to be totally
independent.

We want to focus, not so much on
what the boy did while he was away,
but on his return. Why did he decide
to go home? What was his father
doing? It should be noted that
"While he (the son) was still a long
way off, his father saw him coming."
*This implies that he was waiting and
watching for his son.* What did he do
when he saw his son? How do you
think the father felt? How do you
think the son felt? What did the
father do then? Help the children see
that Jesus is telling a story about
God and us. We sometimes go our
own way. But *when we turn back to
God, God rejoices and welcomes us
with open arms.*

If you read the second half, ask the
children why they think the older
brother felt as he did. Do we
sometimes feel that way? What did
the father say to his older son? Do
you think the older son ever
changed?

33

FIFTH SUNDAY OF LENT

YEAR C

PRAYER OF THE DAY:

God of mercy,
you always forgive those
who are truly sorry
for what they have done wrong.
Today we stand
in need of your help.
Show us how to avoid
all wrong-doing
and please you in everything.
We ask you this
through Christ our Lord,
who lives with you
and the Holy Spirit
forever and ever.

FOCUS OF THE READINGS:

Our readings focus on God's forgiveness. In the first reading, we are told that the people have, more or less, forgotten about God, have become "bored" with God. They have forgotten that it was God who brought them out of Egypt (the past). But God is going to work even new wonders for them, to bring them back from exile (something completely new, a path in the wilderness). And besides all this, God is even ready to forgive their sin of rejection, and even to forget about it!

The Gospel, of course, puts this into a concrete situation. It should be noted that Jesus does not ignore the woman's sin of adultery, but rather forgives it. And the manner in which Jesus deals with this situation teaches us that in the community, there is no room for self righteousness that condemns others.

I am the one who forgives your sins. Go, now, and do not sin again.

FIRST READING: *Isaiah 43: 18-19, 21, 24-25*

A reading from the prophet Isaiah.

Our God says,

"Forget about the things of the past.
 Don't think about them anymore.
 Look, I am doing something completely new.
 Really, it is already here, don't you see it?
 I am making a path in the wilderness
 and rivers in the desert so my people can drink.

"My people, I have created you for myself
 so that you would give me praise.
 But you did not call upon me
 because you got tired of me.
 You went on sinning and doing evil things.

"But I am your God,
 and so I forgive all you do wrong
 and forget about your sins."

The Word of the Lord.

RESPONSE: *Psalm 51*

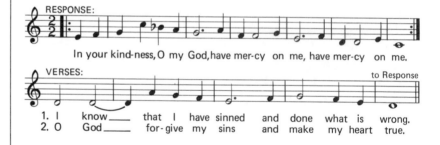

In your kind-ness, O my God, have mer-cy on me, have mer-cy on me.

1. I know_____ that I have sinned and done what is wrong.
2. O God_____ for-give my sins and make my heart true.

GOSPEL ACCLAMATION:

"Go now, do not sin." The Good News__ of God is for you! ____

34

GOSPEL: *John 8:1-5, 6b-11*

A reading from the Gospel of John.

One day while Jesus was at the Temple,
some of the teachers of the law
and some of the Pharisees came,
bringing a woman with them.
They made her stand in front of everyone,
and they said to Jesus,

"Teacher,
   this woman was caught committing the sin of adultery.
   The law of Moses tells us to kill her
   by throwing stones at her until she is dead.
   What do you say we should do?"

But Jesus didn't say anything.
He knelt down
and started writing on the ground with his finger.
They kept on asking him
what they should do with the woman.
So Jesus stood up and said to them,

"Anyone here who has never sinned
   can throw the first stone at her."

Then Jesus knelt down and wrote on the ground again.
The people started leaving, one by one.
First the older ones, and then the others.
When everyone was gone,
Jesus was there alone
with the woman standing in front of him.

Jesus looked up at her and said,

"Where are all those people who were here?
   Didn't any of them stay to punish you?"

She said,

"No, Lord, no one did."

And Jesus said,

"I don't punish you either.
   Go now—and don't sin anymore."

The Gospel of the Lord.

REFLECTING ON THE READINGS
WITH CHILDREN:
   You will need to explain the
meaning of adultery and the
seriousness with which it was
considered. That will not be easy,
because of their age, but also because
today it is considered the norm as
evidenced on television and in films.
But only in its proper context can the
woman's fearful situation and the
gratuitous forgiveness of Jesus be
appreciated. Try to have the children
enter into the mood and feelings of
this Gospel.
   ● Read the story slowly to: *"they
     made her stand in front of
     everyone."*
        —Help the children to visualize
          the woman standing in front
          of an angry crowd, eager to
          stone her. Help them to
          visualize the crowd.
   ● Read slowly to: *"What do you
     say we should do?"*
        —Ask the children how the
          crowd felt.
        —How did the woman feel?
        —What did she do? Did she
          look at Jesus? At the crowd?
   ● Read slowly to: *"Then Jesus
     knelt down and wrote on the
     ground again"* (the second
     time).
        —Ask the children how the
          crowd felt.
        —How did the woman feel?
          What did she do?
   ● Read slowly to: *"Jesus was
     there alone with the woman
     standing in front of him."*
        —How did the woman feel?
   ● Read slowly to: *"I don't punish
     you either. Go now and don't sin
     anymore."*
        —How did the woman feel at
          this moment?
        —How would you feel?
        —Do you think her life
          changed? How? Why?
This story, while seemingly very
adult, can be well used to help
children feel the loving, freeing
forgiveness of Jesus.

35

PASSION SUNDAY
YEAR C

PRAYER OF THE DAY:

God of all things,
through the death of Jesus
you forgive us all our sins.
Let us never forget the cross
because it is the sign
of how much you love us.
We make this prayer to you
through Christ our Lord.

FOCUS OF THE READINGS:

Jesus, eternal God, humbled
himself to be identified with
humankind. Those who sought their
own importance humiliated Jesus
and denied his identity: Messiah,
King of the Jews, builder of the
Temple. They put him to death,
but God raised him up and
proclaimed his true identity:
Jesus Christ is Lord!

Jesus suffers and dies.

THE PROCESSION WITH PALMS:

Sing ho-san-na, sing ho-san-na, to the King, sing ho-san-na!

GOSPEL: *Luke 19:28-40*

A reading from the Gospel of Luke.

Jesus and his disciples
were on their way to Jerusalem.
And when they were close to Bethany,
a town near the Mount of Olives,
Jesus said to two of his disciples,

"Go into the next town
and you will see a young donkey tied there.
Untie it and bring it to me.
If anyone asks you why you are doing that,
just say, 'The Lord needs it.' "

When the two disciples went into the town,
they found the donkey,
just as Jesus had said they would.
While they were untying it, the owners asked,

"Why are you untying that donkey?"

The disciples said,

"The Lord needs it."

Then they took it to Jesus.
They put their coats on the back of the donkey
and then helped Jesus up on it.
People came and spread their coats
on the road in front of him.
When he came close to Jerusalem,
at the bottom of the Mount of Olives,
a large crowd of his followers
began to rejoice and praise God
for all the wonderful and powerful
things they had seen. They shouted,

"Blessed is the King
who comes in the name of the Lord.
Peace in heaven, and glory to God."

[Some of the Pharisees who were there said to Jesus,

"Teacher, tell your disciples to stop shouting."

But Jesus answered,

"I tell you that, if they stop,
these stones will start shouting it out."]

The Gospel of the Lord.

36

REFRAIN:

"Bless-ings on the King who comes in the name of the Lord!" They came run-ning down the streets so ex-cit-ed were the chil-dren as he came, sing-ing:

FIRST READING: *Philippians 2:5-11*

A reading from Paul's letter to the Philippians.

Brothers and sisters,

You must think and live like Christ.
Even though he was always God,
Jesus did not try to hold onto that.
Instead, he became a human being just like us.
As a human being, he lived a humble life.
Jesus obeyed God in everything,
even though it meant he would die on a cross.
Because he obeyed God in everything,
God raised Jesus up and gave him the name
which is above every other name,
so that at the name of Jesus
everyone should kneel and worship.
Everyone in heaven, on earth and everywhere
should give glory to God by proclaiming,

   "Jesus Christ is Lord!"

The Word of the Lord.

RESPONSE: *Psalm 34*

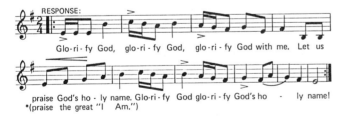

RESPONSE:
Glo-ri-fy God, glo-ri-fy God, glo-ri-fy God with me. Let us
praise God's ho-ly name. Glo-ri-fy God glo-ri-fy God's ho-ly name!
*(praise the great "I Am.")

GOSPEL ACCLAMATION:

Leader:
Je-sus has giv-en his life for
All:
us.
Je-sus has giv-en his life for us.

REFLECTING ON THE READINGS WITH CHILDREN:

We suggest that the Passion be read in parts as has become customary in many parish communities.

The experience of Holy Week is more of a meditation than a theological study. These reflections should allow the children to enter into the drama of the Passion in a way that touches them personally.

After the Passion, ask the children to recall the scene.

- Who was there? (Jesus, chief priests and other leaders, Pilate, a crowd of people, soldiers, Simon, the two criminals crucified with him.)
- Why did the people take Jesus to Pilate?
- Why did they want him crucified?
- How do you think Jesus felt when they made fun of him as a king?
- Who was the man Pilate wanted to let out of prison?
- How do you think Jesus felt when his own people kept shouting, "Crucify him, crucify him"?
- Why were the people making fun of him on the cross?
- What did they say? How do you think Jesus felt when they said these things?
- What did the two criminals say to Jesus? How do you think the criminal felt when Jesus said, "Today you will be with me in Paradise."
- After Jesus died, what did one of the soldiers say? How do you think that soldier felt?

If some of the older children have done the reading, you might ask those who read:

- How did you feel being Jesus?
- How did you feel being Pilate?
- How did you feel being the chief priests and leaders?
- How did you feel when you were shouting, "Crucify him"?
- How did you feel being the first criminal?
- How did you feel being the second criminal?
- How did you feel being the soldier at the end?

Gospel Drama for Passion Sunday

Gospel: *Luke 23:1-7, 9-11, 13-26, 32-34, 36-47*

Narrator: The story of the suffering and death of Jesus, taken from the Gospel of Luke. The chief priests and the scribes took Jesus to Pilate and accused Jesus of doing wrong. They said to Pilate,

Priests: "This man has been trying to confuse our people and change the way they think and live. And he told us not to pay taxes to Caesar. He also says that he is the Christ, a king."

Narrator: So Pilate asked Jesus,

Pilate: "Are you the king of the Jews?"

Narrator: Jesus answered,

Jesus: "You have said so."

Narrator: Then Pilate said to the leaders and to all the people who were there,

Pilate: "I do not find this man guilty of doing anything wrong."

Narrator: But the people said over and over again,

Crowd: "He has been teaching and making trouble all over Judea. He started in Galilee and now he is doing the same thing here in Jerusalem!"

Narrator: When Pilate heard that Jesus was from Galilee, he sent him to Herod because Herod was the ruler of Galilee. Herod asked Jesus many questions, but Jesus did not answer any of them. Then Herod and his soldiers started making fun of Jesus. They put a beautiful robe on him, like a king would wear. Then they sent him back to Pilate. Pilate called all the people and their leaders together and said to them,

Pilate: "I don't find Jesus guilty of any of the things you have said. And Herod didn't find him guilty either. He has not done anything wrong and does not deserve to be put to death. I will have him whipped and let him go."

Narrator: But the people shouted,

Crowd: "Kill him. Let Barabbas go free."

Narrator: Now, Barabbas was a man who was in prison because he had started a riot in the city, and he was also a murderer. Pilate told the people again that he wanted to let Jesus go. But they shouted,

Crowd: "Crucify him! Crucify him!"

Narrator: For the third time, Pilate said to the people,

Pilate: "Why? What has he done wrong? I haven't found him guilty of anything. He does not deserve to die."

Narrator: But the people kept on shouting that Jesus should be killed. They wouldn't stop shouting, so Pilate finally gave in to them. He let Barabbas, a murderer, go free, and he let them have their way with Jesus. As they were taking Jesus away, they saw a man named Simon of Cyrene coming into the city. They made him carry the cross on his shoulder and walk behind Jesus. Two men who were criminals were also led away with Jesus to be killed. And when they came to the place which is called "the Skull," they crucified Jesus. And Jesus said,

Jesus: "Father, forgive them! For they do not know what they are doing!"

Narrator: The soldier made fun of him, and said,

Soldiers: "If you are the King of the Jews, save yourself."

Narrator: There was a sign at the top of his cross which said, "This is the King of the Jews." And they crucified the two criminals beside him, one on his left and one on his right. One of the criminals yelled at Jesus,

Thief 1: "Aren't you the Christ? Then save yourself and save us too!"

Narrator: But the other criminal scolded him, and then said to Jesus,

Thief 2: "Jesus, when you come into your kingdom, remember me."

Narrator: Jesus said to him,

Jesus: "I promise you, today you will be with me in Paradise."

Narrator: It was now about noon, and the sun stopped shining, and it was dark until about three o'clock in the afternoon. Then Jesus cried out loud,

Jesus: "Father, I put myself in your hands; I give you my spirit."

Narrator: Then he died.
One of the soldiers in the Roman army who saw all of this began to praise God, and he said,

Soldier: "Surely, this man was good and he was innocent."

Narrator: This is the Passion of our Lord, Jesus Christ.

PASSION (PALM) SUNDAY

PASSION: *Luke 23:1-47*

REFRAIN:

Leader: Jesus has given his life for us.
All: Jesus has given his life for us.

The story of the suffering and death of Jesus,
from the Gospel of Luke.

After Jesus had been on trial before the leaders of his people,
the chief priests and the scribes took him to Pilate.
They accused Jesus of doing wrong and they said to Pilate,

"This man has been trying to confuse our people
and change the way they think.
And he told us not to pay taxes to Caesar.
He also says that he is the Christ, a king."

So Pilate asked Jesus,

"Are you the King of the Jews?"

Jesus answered,

"You have said so."

Then Pilate said to the leaders and to all the people who were there,

"I do not find this man guilty of doing anything wrong."

But the people said over and over again,

"He has been teaching and making trouble all over Judea.
He started in Galilee
and now he is even teaching here in Jerusalem!"

When Pilate heard that Jesus was from Galilee,
he sent him to Herod because Herod was the ruler of Galilee.
Herod asked Jesus many questions,
but Jesus did not answer any of them.
The soldiers put a beautiful robe on him like a king would wear,
and made fun of him
because they thought he was pretending to be a king.

Then Herod sent him back to Pilate. Pilate called all the people
and their leaders together and said to them,
"You brought this man to me
and told me that he has been making trouble among the people.
He has not done anything wrong
and does not deserve to be put to death.
I will have him whipped and then I will let him go."

But the people shouted,
"Kill him. Let Barabbas go free."

Now, Barabbas was a man who was in prison
because he had started a riot in the city and he was also a murderer.

Pilate told the people again that he wanted to let Jesus go.

But they shouted,
"Crucify him! Crucify him!"

For the third time, Pilate said to the people,
"Why? What has he done wrong?
I haven't found him guilty of anything.
He does not deserve to die."

But the people kept on shouting that Jesus should be killed.
They wouldn't stop shouting, so Pilate finally gave in to them.
He let Barabbas, a murderer, go free.
And he let them have their way with Jesus.

REFRAIN:

Leader: Jesus has given his life for us.
All: Jesus has given his life for us.

As they were taking Jesus away to crucify him,
they saw a man from Cyrene, named Simon, coming into the city.
They made him carry the cross on his shoulder and walk behind Jesus.
Many people were following Jesus and there were some women
in the crowd who were crying. Jesus turned around and said to them,

"Women of Jerusalem, don't cry for me.
Cry for yourselves and for your children."

Two criminals were also led away with Jesus to be killed.
And when they came to the place which is called "the Skull,"
they crucified Jesus.

And Jesus said,

"Father, forgive them! They do not know what they are doing!"

REFRAIN:

Leader: Jesus has given his life for us.
All: Jesus has given his life for us.

And they crucified the two criminals beside him,
one on his left and one on his right.

The people who were there watching made fun of Jesus, saying,

"He saved other people. If he is truly the Christ,
God's chosen one, let him save himself."

The soldiers also made fun of him, and said,

"If you are the King of the Jews, save yourself."

At the top of his cross, there was a sign which said,

"This is the King of the Jews."

One of the criminals yelled at him,

"Aren't you the Christ? Then save yourself and save us too!"

But the other criminal scolded him and then said to Jesus,

"Jesus, when you come into your kingdom, remember me."

Jesus said to him,

"I promise you, today you will be with me in Paradise."

It was now about noon, and the sun stopped shining and it was dark
until about three o'clock in the afternoon. Then Jesus cried out loud,

"Father, take my life. I give you my spirit."

And he died.

REFRAIN:

Leader: Jesus has given his life for us.
All: Jesus has given his life for us.

One of the soldiers in the Roman army who saw all of this
began to praise God, and he said,

"Surely, this was a great and good man!"

The Passion of our Lord, Jesus Christ.

Easter Sunday
and
The Season of Easter

EASTER SUNDAY
YEAR C

PRAYER OF THE DAY:

God of everything that lives,
we are happy today
because Jesus was dead
and now he is alive,
and through our baptism
you give us a share in his life.
By what we do and say,
make us true sisters
and brothers of Jesus
and of each other,
and so live together
forever and ever.

FOCUS OF THE READINGS:

The first reading is a proclamation of the Good News that Jesus is risen from the dead! Peter gives witness to those who killed Jesus, and his witness is based on experience: "We have seen him." It is based on the command of Jesus: "to preach to the people." And what they are to preach is that Jesus has overcome death and his resurrection brings forgiveness and salvation to all who believe.

In the Gospel, the women, the first disciples to return to the tomb, find not the body of Jesus but an empty tomb. They are filled with confusion. But even in their fear and confusion, they are greeted with the "Good News." He is alive! If you are looking for Jesus, the One who was crucified, he is not here—in a tomb. He is risen! And they hastened to tell the apostles and the others. And so our readings focus on the central message of our faith:

Christ has died, Christ has risen, Christ lives among us.

FIRST READING: *Acts 10:34a, 37-43*

A reading from the Acts of the Apostles.

Peter said to the people:

"I am sure that you know what has been told
all over Judea about Jesus of Nazareth:
that it all began in Galilee
when John was preaching about baptism,
and God anointed Jesus
with the Holy Spirit and power;
that Jesus went from place to place
doing good works and healing people from evil,
for God was with him.

"We ourselves saw all that he did
in the land of the Jews and in Jerusalem.

"They killed him by hanging him on a cross.
But God raised him up on the third day.

"And we have seen him.
We ate and drank with him
after he rose from the dead.
He told us to preach to the people,
and to tell them that he is the one
chosen by God to be the judge of all people,
both living and dead.

"All the prophets tell us that everyone
who believes in Jesus
will have their sins forgiven in his name."

The Word of the Lord.

RESPONSE: *Psalm 118*

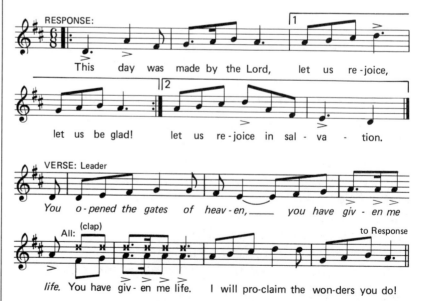

44

GOSPEL ACCLAMATION:

"Christ is ris - en from the dead," Al - le - lu - ia!

"He is ris - en as he said," Al - le - lu - ia!

GOSPEL: *Luke 24:1-12*

A reading from the Gospel of Luke.

On the first day of the week, very early in the morning,
Mary Magdalene, Joanna, Mary the mother of James,
and some other women went to the place
where Jesus had been buried.
They took the sweet-smelling spices
which they had prepared to put on his body.
When they got to the tomb,
they saw that the stone in front of it had been rolled away.
They went inside, but Jesus' body was not there.
They didn't know what to think.

Then two men, wearing bright clothes,
were standing beside them.
The women were afraid
and knelt down and covered their faces.
The men said to them,

"Why are you looking here, in this cemetery,
for someone who is alive?
Jesus is not here. He is not dead. He has risen!
Remember, he told you
that he would be handed over to people
who would crucify him,
but on the third day he would rise from the dead."

Then the women remembered that Jesus had said this.
They went back and told the eleven apostles
and all the others what had happened.
The men thought the women were talking nonsense
and didn't believe them.
But Peter got up and ran to the tomb.
He looked in and saw the cloths
that the body of Jesus had been wrapped in.
Peter went home, wondering what all of this meant.

The Gospel of the Lord.

REFLECTING ON THE READINGS WITH CHILDREN:

We are a symbolic people! And often it is in the rich symbols that God's self-revelation is available to us. We are accustomed to certain symbols that surround Easter, and they are not without meaning, for they generally have to do with "newness." You might explore these symbols with the children.

Why do we wear new Easter clothes? Why do we see bunnies and chicks on cards? Why do we have Easter eggs?

All of these are signs of "newness" —new life.

We see signs of new life even in nature: new grass, flowers, buds on trees. Everything is beginning to grow—new life!

Perhaps some will visit relatives or friends today—perhaps a grandparent, an elderly person, someone who is alone. How can we bring new life to those we visit?

Help the children to see that all of these signs remind us that Jesus rose from the dead to New Life. *We celebrate today that Jesus is alive and that he is with us.* He will live forever, and because of him, we too will live forever! Today is a joyous celebration of New Life!

45

SECOND SUNDAY OF EASTER

YEAR C

PRAYER OF THE DAY:

God of peace,
we believe that Jesus died
and rose again from the dead.
Send your Holy Spirit
into our hearts
that we may believe more firmly
what we cannot see.
We ask you this
through our Lord, Jesus Christ,
who lives with you
and the Holy Spirit,
forever and ever.

FOCUS OF THE READINGS:

Both of our readings focus on the presence of the Risen Lord. In the first reading, this presence is witnessed in the actions of the disciples; their life in "peace and unity," their miracles and their belief in the Resurrection. This witness led more and more men and women to believe.

Jesus' first words to his disciples are of peace and forgiveness. "Peace be with you . . . if you forgive the sins of anyone, they are forgiven." Thomas represents those of us who find it hard to believe that Christ is truly present among us and that living in peace and unity is possible. To him, Jesus says, "Don't be unbelieving, but believe." The evangelist tells us that he has written this for us, so that we will recognize the signs of the Risen Lord and believe.

FIRST READING: *Acts 5:12-16*

A reading from the Acts of the Apostles.

All the disciples lived in peace and unity,
and the people respected them very much.
The apostles did many miracles
and wonderful things.
People who were sick
were carried out into the streets on mats
so that Peter's shadow
would touch them as he walked by.
People came from all the towns around Jerusalem,
bringing those who were sick
or who had evil spirits in them,
and they were all healed.
Every day more men and women
came to believe in the Lord.

The Word of the Lord.

RESPONSE: *Psalm 118*

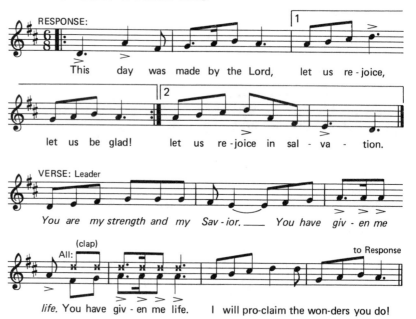

RESPONSE: This day was made by the Lord, let us re-joice, let us be glad! let us re-joice in sal-va-tion.

VERSE: Leader
You are my strength and my Sav-ior. ___ You have giv-en me

(clap) All:
life. You have giv-en me life. I will pro-claim the won-ders you do!

GOSPEL ACCLAMATION:

"We have seen the ris-en Lord!" Al-le-lu-ia!

"I be-lieve my Lord and my God!" Al-le-lu-ia!

46

GOSPEL: *John 20:19-29*

A reading from the Gospel of John.

On Sunday evening
(the same day the women had been to the tomb of Jesus),
the disciples were gathered in a room upstairs.
They had locked the doors
because they were afraid of the people
who had crucified Jesus.
Then Jesus came and stood in the room and said,

   "Peace be with you!'

Then he showed them his hands and his side.
The disciples were filled with joy when they saw the Lord.
Jesus said again,

   "Peace be with you.
      As God has sent me to you,
      now I am sending you to others."

Then he breathed on the disciples and said to them,

   "Receive the Holy Spirit.
      If you forgive the sins of anyone, they are forgiven.
      If you do not forgive them, they are not forgiven."

Now one of the apostles, Thomas, was not there
when Jesus came. So, later, the disciples told him,

   "We have seen the Lord!"

But Thomas said,

   "I'll never believe it
      until I see the marks made by the nails in his hands
      and touch the wound in his side."

One week later, the disciples were in the same room again.
This time, Thomas was with them.
Even though the doors were locked,
Jesus came in and stood among them. He said,

   "Peace be with you."

Then he said to Thomas,

   "Here, touch the marks on my hands
      and feel the wound in my side.
      Stop doubting and believe."

Thomas said to Jesus,

   "My Lord and my God!"

Then Jesus said to Thomas,

   "You believe now because you see me.
      How blessed are people who have not seen me
      and still believe!"

The Gospel of the Lord.

REFLECTING ON THE READINGS
WITH CHILDREN:

   Like the Passion, the theology of
the resurrection is difficult to discuss
with children. Let the text speak
for itself.

   After the first reading, ask the
children to recall how the first
Christians lived and what they did.
Ask them why the Christians lived
that way. How did it show they
believed in Jesus?

   After the Gospel, ask the children
to recall the story:
   • Where were the apostles? Why?
   • Wasn't it normal that they
      should be there?
   • What did Jesus say when he
      came in? Why?
   • Which disciple was not there?
   • What did he say when the
      others told him about Jesus?
   • Wasn't that a normal way to
      react?
   • What happened one week later?
   • What did Jesus say again to the
      disciples?
   • What did he say to Thomas?
   • What did Thomas call Jesus?

Help the children to understand
that when Jesus said, "those who
have not seen," he meant, "seen my
body." Help them understand, also,
that it is truly difficult to believe in
things we haven't seen. Often we
come to believe because someone we
trust tells us. For example, we
believe certain foods are good for us
because our parents told us so.

   St. John tells us that he wrote
this story and others to help us
believe.

THIRD SUNDAY OF EASTER

YEAR C

PRAYER OF THE DAY:
Lord God,
through your Son, Jesus,
you call upon us to love
and care for all people.
Make us able to see those
who need us most
and give us the courage
to overcome all difficulties.
We ask you this
through Christ our Lord.

FOCUS OF THE READINGS:

The focus of the readings is the mission of the Church. In the first reading, the apostles are persecuted for preaching about Jesus and they respond by preaching even to their persecutors.

The Gospel tells us that at the word of Jesus the disciples caught so many fish they could hardly bring them in. All of this is in the context of the Church (the boat). We see in this reading references to the Eucharist: the bread which they shared and the mission to Peter to "feed my sheep."

FIRST READING: *Acts 5:27b-32, 40b-41*
A reading from the Acts of the Apostles.

*The high priest and the other leaders had a meeting
to decide what to do with the apostles,
because they were teaching the people about Jesus.*

The soldiers brought the apostles in
and made them stand in front of the leaders.
The high priest said to the apostles,

  "We told you not to teach anyone about Jesus.
    But you have told everyone in Jerusalem about him.
    And now you are trying to say
    that we are the ones who killed him
    and that we are guilty."

Peter and the apostles answered,

  "We must obey God, not you.
    You killed Jesus by hanging him on a cross,
    but our God raised him from the dead
    and made him our Savior and Leader.
    Jesus is the one who forgives all those
    who change their hearts and lives.
    We have seen these things, and we know they are true."

The high priest and the leaders
were very angry when they heard this.
They beat the apostles and sent them away telling
them again that they must stop teaching about Jesus.
The apostles left and were happy
because they had to suffer for being faithful to Jesus.

The Word of the Lord.

RESPONSE: *Psalm 30*

GOSPEL ACCLAMATION:

48

GOSPEL: *John 21:3-19*

A reading from the Gospel of John.

One day, Peter said to the other disciples,
  "I'm going fishing."

They said, "We'll come with you."

So they went. They got into their boat
and they fished all night long, but they didn't catch anything.

Early the next morning, as the sun was rising,
Jesus was standing on the beach,
but the disciples didn't know that it was Jesus. He called to them,
  "Did you catch any fish?"

"No," they answered.

Then Jesus said,
  "Put your net down into the water on the right side of the boat
    and you will catch some."

So they did what he said, and they caught so many fish
they could not pull the net back into the boat.
One of the disciples said to the others,
  "It's the Lord!"

They were not too far from shore, only about a hundred yards.
When they got to the beach, they saw a charcoal fire
with some fish on it and some bread.

Jesus said to them,
  "Bring some of the fish you've just caught."

So Peter went back to the boat to bring the fish.
Then Jesus said to them,
  "Come and have breakfast."

None of them asked Jesus, "Who are you?"
because now they knew he was the Lord.
Jesus took the bread and gave it to them.
He also gave them the fish to eat.
When they had finished eating, Jesus said to Peter,
  "Peter, do you love me more than the others do?"

He answered, "Yes, Lord, you know that I love you."

Jesus said, "Feed my lambs."

Jesus asked Peter again, "Peter, do you love me?"

He said, "Yes, Lord, you know that I love you."

Jesus said, "Feed my sheep."

A third time Jesus asked Peter, "Peter, do you love me?"

Peter was sad that Jesus asked him this question a third
time. He said,
  "Lord, you know everything! You know that I love you."

Jesus said, "Feed my sheep."

Then Jesus said to Peter, "Follow me."

The Gospel of the Lord.

REFLECTING ON THE READINGS
WITH CHILDREN:

Ask the children to recall the Gospel story. Remind them that most of the apostles were fishermen and that they were doing their work. Help them recall the story with questions such as:
- Who was there?
- How long did they fish?
- Did they catch anything?
- Who called to them?
- What did he say to them?
- Then what happened?
- What did they find on the beach?
- What did Jesus ask Peter?
- What did he tell Peter to do?

Help the children reflect on the meaning of those words "feed my sheep." Help them see that it is the ministry of the Church (us) to bring people in and to "feed" them. We do this especially in the Eucharist and the Word.

You may wish to end by inviting the children to sing the Gospel Acclamation as a response to short prayers such as:

Jesus, you are our Good Shepherd.
  (Gospel Acclamation)

Jesus, you are always there to
  protect us.
  (Gospel Acclamation)

Jesus, you bring us to live with
  you forever.
  (Gospel Acclamation)

FOURTH SUNDAY OF EASTER

YEAR C

PRAYER OF THE DAY:

Loving Lord,
you have put us
in the care of Jesus
who watches over us.
With your help,
may we stay faithful to him
as he gives himself to us,
and now lives with you
and the Holy Spirit,
forever and ever.

FOCUS OF THE READINGS:

The focus of the readings is the spread of the Gospel to the Gentile world. In the first reading, Luke presents the preaching of the apostles with the usual results: some converts, some violent opposition, and the apostles turning to the Gentiles.

The Gospel is our assurance that when we belong to Christ, we will live forever. Nothing can take us from the loving protection of our Shepherd (as we witnessed with the apostles in the first reading). This little section of John is a return to his theme of the Good Shepherd a few verses earlier. In the previous section (reading for this Sunday in Cycle B), Jesus says, "I have other sheep who aren't in this flock yet. I must lead them too, and they will listen to my voice. Then there will be only one flock with one shepherd."

FIRST READING: *Acts 13:14-16, 43-48, 52*

A reading from the Acts of the Apostles.

Paul and Barnabas went together to Antioch.
And on the Sabbath day they went to the synagogue
to listen to the readings from the law of Moses
and the writings of the prophets.
Then the leaders of the synagogue
said to Paul and Barnabas,

"Brothers, if you have something to say
to the people gathered here,
you may speak now."

So Paul stood up and spoke to the people.
Many of the Jews believed
what Paul and Barnabas taught
and became followers.
The two apostles told them to keep trusting in God.

The next Sabbath day,
almost everyone in the city came to the synagogue.
When the Jews saw how many people
came to hear Paul preach,
they were jealous.
They told the people that Paul was wrong
and not to listen to him.
But Paul and Barnabas went on speaking boldly:

"God sent us to preach to you first of all.
But you have refused to listen to God.
So now we are going to preach
to the people of other nations.
For God has told us,

'I have made you a light to the nations.
I am sending you
to tell people all over the world
about salvation.' "

When the Gentiles heard about this,
they were filled with joy,
and they gave praise to God.
And the disciples were filled with joy
and with the Holy Spirit.

The Word of the Lord.

RESPONSE: *Psalm 100*

(Leader) We sing to you _____ with songs of joy _____
(All) We sing to you, _____ with
songs of joy. _____ We bless your Ho - ly name! We
come to you _____ with thank - ful hearts _____
We come to you _____ with
thank - ful hearts. _____ We en - ter your house with praise!

VERSE: to Response

1. You are God, you made us.   We are your sheep _ we be - long to you.
2. You are al - ways faith - ful.   Your love will last _ till the end of time.

GOSPEL ACCLAMATION:

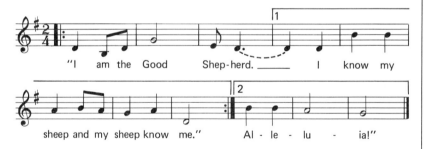

"I am the Good Shep - herd. _____ I know my
sheep and my sheep know me."   Al - le - lu - ia!"

GOSPEL: *John 10:27-30*

A reading from the Gospel of John.

Jesus said,

"My sheep listen to my voice.
I know my sheep and they follow me.
My sheep will live forever
because I give them eternal life.
No one can take them out of my hand
for the Father, who is greater than anyone,
gave them to me.
And the Father and I are one."

The Gospel of the Lord.

REFLECTING ON THE READINGS WITH CHILDREN:

Before the Gospel, ask the children what they know about sheep and shepherds. Have they ever seen sheep with a shepherd? For many children, especially those living in cities or suburbs, the image of sheep and shepherd will not be a familiar one. It is a powerful and frequently used image in both the Old and New Testaments. It will be well worth the time to familiarize the children with both the shepherding of Jesus' time and of today. Perhaps you will find pictures or even a short film on shepherding today.

The image rests on the reality of the intimacy that exists between sheep and their shepherd, for it is this intimacy and care that Jesus speaks of here.

After the Gospel, ask the children how they feel when Jesus says this. Children have experience with "protection." Allow them time to share experiences of being protected by parents, perhaps scout leaders, etc. Help them see that Jesus promises that protection forever to all his sheep, those who follow him.

Ask the children how we listen to Jesus' voice today. What are the signs that we are following Jesus?

FIFTH SUNDAY OF EASTER

YEAR C

PRAYER OF THE DAY:

God of all people,
you made us
to live and love together
in peace,
and Jesus shows us the way.
Help us to be
more and more like him
that the whole world may see us
and believe in him
who lives with you
and the Holy Spirit
forever and ever.

FOCUS OF THE READINGS:

Again our readings focus on God's universal love. In the first reading, we again see the apostles preaching everywhere, proclaiming that "people of all nations can have faith and be saved."

The Gospel gives us the heart of the Christian message: Love. This is not an option for Christians, but a commandment. It is the proof of our discipleship. Others will come to believe because we love one another.

FIRST READING: *Acts 14:21-27*

A reading from the Acts of the Apostles.

Paul and Barnabas went back to all the cities
where they had taught the people about Jesus.
They encouraged the people
to stay strong in their faith in Jesus.
They chose leaders in each church,
and prayed that the Lord would take care of them.

Then Paul and Barnabas
went to preach in many other cities,
and finally they sailed back to Antioch.
This is the city where the disciples
had prayed especially for Paul and Barnabas
and had sent them off to preach the Word of God.
So when they got to Antioch,
they gathered all the believers together
and told them all that had happened.
They told them how God had shown them
that people of all nations can have faith
and be saved.

The Word of the Lord.

RESPONSE: *Psalm 96*

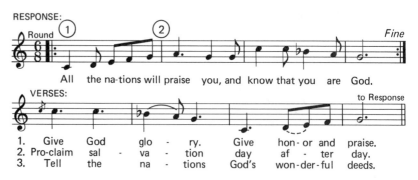

RESPONSE:
All the nations will praise you, and know that you are God.

VERSES:
1. Give God glo - ry. Give hon- or and praise.
2. Pro-claim sal - va - tion day af - ter day.
3. Tell the na - tions God's won-der-ful deeds.

52

GOSPEL ACCLAMATION:

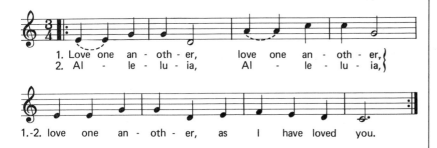

1. Love one an-oth-er, love one an-oth-er,
2. Al - le - lu - ia, Al - le - lu - ia,

1.-2. love one an-oth-er, as I have loved you.

GOSPEL: *John 13:31-33a, 34-35*

A reading from the Gospel of John.

After Judas left the room
where the disciples were gathered,
Jesus said,

"Now my glory begins.
And when I receive glory, God receives glory.
My friends,
I am going to be with you
for only a little while longer.
But I am giving you a new commandment:
love one another.
You must love one another
just as I have loved you.
Everyone will know that you are my disciples
if you love one another."

The Gospel of the Lord.

REFLECTING ON THE READINGS WITH CHILDREN:

Jesus tells us how he wants us to love others. What did he say? What do you think Jesus meant when he said, "Love one another as I have loved you."

Note: This is a crucial point in our Christian faith. Christian love is a commitment. But children can easily misunderstand this. Jesus loves with "divine love." God *is* love. We are not commanded to love "as much as"— that is, with divine love. We are commanded to love "in the way" Jesus loved. This commandment is first given in an earlier part of this "last discourse of Jesus," just after he has washed the feet of his disciples in an attitude of service. Thus we are commanded to love (serve) one another. The greatest love is shown by giving our lives for others—in service. Loving everyone equally is difficult to achieve, even for adults. Such love is unconditional and attained by few. Jesus teaches us to show loving service to anyone and everyone. He tells us that when we live this way, we show that we are his disciples. How can children live out this commandment today? Children can begin to learn to love, as Jesus did, by being helpful to others. Help them to see ways of doing this (things possible for children),

- including all children in games;
- talking to a child who feels alone;
- helping someone with a task;
- taking time, perhaps from play, to help someone;
- accepting people just as they are.

Jesus asks us to love this way because he loves us so much. Jesus loves everyone and wants us to love everyone too. That's what a Christian is—someone who believes Jesus is living and who lives like him.

SIXTH SUNDAY OF EASTER

YEAR C

PRAYER OF THE DAY:

God, lover of us all,
Jesus came among us
to bring us peace.
Take away all worry and fear,
and make us ready
for the coming of your Spirit.
We ask this
through Christ our Lord.

FOCUS OF THE READINGS:

The first reading, from Acts,
continues Luke's presentation of the
mission of the Church to spread the
Gospel to the "ends of the earth." In
today's section, we read the letter
written by the apostles and elders
in Jerusalem. Seemingly, the
decisions taken at the meeting
were to determine the status of
the Gentile believers. Even after
the Resurrection, there were those
who believed that salvation was only
for the Jews. This passage rejects
that notion.

The Gospel is part of John's
discourse on the Holy Spirit. Jesus,
before his death, assures his
followers that he will return and will
take the faithful to be with him
forever. There is no need to fear;
God's own Spirit will be with us and
will teach us and remind us of all
that Jesus said. The Spirit brings the
peace of Jesus. True believers live,
not in fear, but in peace.

FIRST READING: *Acts 15:1-2, 22-29*

A reading from the Acts of the Apostles.

Some people went
from Jerusalem to the city of Antioch
and said to the new Gentile believers there,

 "If you don't follow the law of Moses,
  you cannot be saved."

Paul and Barnabas did not agree with this,
so they went to Jerusalem
to ask the leaders of the Church
what they should do.
After they talked about it,
the leaders decided to send Judas and Silas back
with Paul and Barnabas,
and they sent this letter to the Gentiles:

 "Greetings from the apostles and elders,
  to the Gentile believers in Antioch.

 "Dear friends,
  We have heard that some people from here
  have come to you and have confused you
  by what they said.
So we are sending Judas and Silas
  along with Paul and Barnabas
  to tell you what we have decided is best.
This is what the Holy Spirit has taught us:
  don't eat food that has been offered to false gods,
  and keep yourselves pure.
  If you do this, you will be doing what is right.
We send you our greetings. Farewell."

The Word of the Lord.

RESPONSE: *Psalm 71*

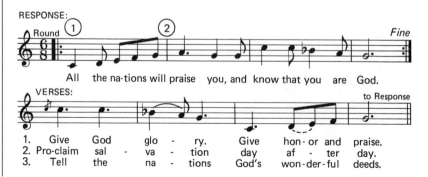

RESPONSE:
All the na-tions will praise you, and know that you are God.

VERSES:
to Response

1. Give God glo - ry. Give hon- or and praise.
2. Pro-claim sal - va - tion day af - ter day.
3. Tell the na - tions God's won-der-ful deeds.

54

GOSPEL ACCLAMATION:

"My peace I give you. Do not be a-fraid!

My peace I give you." Al - le - lu - ia!

GOSPEL: *John 14:23-29*

A reading from the Gospel of John.

Jesus said to his disciples,

"I am going to prepare a place for you,
and I will come back and take you with me.
If you love me, you will obey my words
and do as I have said.
For everything I have said to you
came from the Father who sent me to you.

"I have told you this while I am here with you.
But the Father is going to send the Holy Spirit,
who will teach you everything
and remind you of all that I have said.

"I leave you my peace.
The peace I give you
is not like the peace that the world gives,
so don't be afraid.
Let your hearts be at peace.

"I told you that I am leaving,
but I will come back to you.
I am telling you this so that when it happens,
you will believe it."

The Gospel of the Lord.

REFLECTING ON THE READINGS WITH CHILDREN:

Ask the children if they have ever experienced an inner desire to do something good for someone. Perhaps some examples would help. Sometimes children decide with excitement that they are going to "surprise Mom or Dad" by cleaning the house while they're out. Some children like to sneak in and put flowers on a teacher's desk. Sometimes they see an elderly person or a smaller child having difficulty, and they instinctively want to help. Allow them time to share their own experiences.

Tell them that it is the Holy Spirit that inspires us to do good things. We don't see the Holy Spirit, but the Holy Spirit—the Spirit of Jesus—is in us and helps us. Remind the children that they received the Holy Spirit when they were baptized. Jesus promised that the Holy Spirit would always be with us.

What else did Jesus promise in today's readings? Jesus tells us that he is giving us his peace. Jesus really wants us to have peace and not be afraid. He is always with us.

"Peace" in this context seems to mean a "sense of well-being." Ask the children if they experience that when they follow their feelings to do good things. Help them see that following the Holy Spirit—living like Jesus—brings peace.

55

ASCENSION OF THE LORD

YEAR C

PRAYER OF THE DAY:

Lord,
just as the disciples were happy
that Jesus returned to you,
make us happy
to know about him
and keep us always
praising you.
We ask this
through Christ our Lord.

FOCUS OF THE READINGS:

The mission of the Church is to evangelize.

Our Gospel tells us that before Jesus left his disciples physically, he called them to be his witnesses. And to what are they to witness? All that they have seen and heard. They are to tell everyone to turn from their sins and receive God's forgiveness. But Jesus does not leave them alone in this mission. He promises them the Holy Spirit and then gives them his blessing.

In the passage from Acts, the disciples are baptized in the Holy Spirit and receive power to preach in the name of Jesus.

Like love, evangelization is not an option for the Church. We are commanded in today's readings: "Go . . . you are to be my witnesses . . . ."

FIRST READING: *Acts 1:3-5, 8-11*

A reading from the Acts of the Apostles

After Jesus died and rose,
he appeared to his apostles many times
to show them that he was really alive.
They saw him,
and he talked to them about the reign of God.

He told them not to leave Jerusalem
but to wait for the gift of the Holy Spirit.
Jesus said,

> "I have told you about the promise.
> John baptized with water, but in a few days,
> you will be baptized with the Holy Spirit.
> The Holy Spirit will give you power
> to be my witnesses in Jerusalem, Judea,
> Samaria, and all over the world."

After he said this, Jesus was taken up to heaven.
Even though they couldn't see him anymore,
the disciples stayed there staring into the sky.
Two men, dressed in white robes,
appeared to them and said,

> "Jesus has been taken up to heaven,
> but he will come back to you!"

The Word of the Lord.

RESPONSE/GOSPEL ACCLAMATION: *Psalm 47*

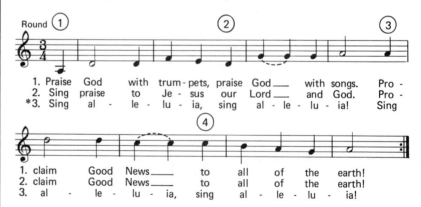

1. Praise God with trum-pets, praise God___ with songs. Pro-
2. Sing praise to Je-sus our Lord___ and God. Pro-
*3. Sing al-le-lu-ia, sing al-le-lu-ia! Sing

1. claim Good News___ to all of the earth!
2. claim Good News___ to all of the earth!
3. al-le-lu-ia, sing al-le-lu-ia!

56

GOSPEL: *Luke 24:44-53*

A reading from the Gospel of Luke.

Jesus said to his disciples,

"While I was with you, I told you
about all that was going to happen to me."

Then he helped them understand
all that was written about him
in the books of Moses,
the prophets and the Psalms.
Jesus said,

"It was written in those books
that Christ would have to suffer and die,
but that he would rise from the dead
on the third day.
It was also written that everyone in Jerusalem
and in every part of the world
should be told to turn away from their sins,
and God will forgive them.
And you are witnesses of this
because you have seen all of this happen.
Now you must stay in Jerusalem
until I send you the power from heaven
that God has promised."

Then Jesus led the disciples to Bethany.
When they were there,
Jesus raised his hands and blessed them.
As he blessed them, he was taken up to heaven.
The disciples went back to Jerusalem
filled with joy
and went every day to the temple to praise God.

The Gospel of the Lord.

REFLECTING ON THE READINGS
WITH CHILDREN:

After the Gospel, ask the children to retell what they heard. Ask them to listen to the Gospel again, this time listening for the words they think are very important. Hopefully they will give a variety of words such as:

- Jesus rose,
- appeared,
- gift of the Holy Spirit,
- promise,
- baptized,
- water,
- power,
- witnesses.

You may wish to write on newsprint the words the children say.

Help the children reconstruct Jesus' directions that everyone should be told to turn away from sin and accept God's forgiveness.

Ask the children how the disciples were able to do this. Remind them of the first reading that tells us that the disciples were baptized in the Holy Spirit. With that power they were able to do many things, especially to be witnesses for Jesus. Be sure the children understand the meaning of "witness."

We also received the Holy Spirit when we were baptized:
"In the name of the Father, and of the Son, and of the Holy Spirit."

And so, we too have the power of the Holy Spirit to be witnesses for Jesus. How can we do this?

Jesus said he wants everyone to hear the Good News that he is alive and wants everyone to live with him forever. Jesus said, "Go . . . tell everyone the Good News." How can we help do that?

(As always, it is important to keep the children focused on ideas truly possible for them at their age.)

SEVENTH SUNDAY OF EASTER

YEAR C

PRAYER OF THE DAY:

God in heaven,
as you and Jesus are one,
so share his life with us,
we pray,
that we may all live as friends.
Take away
our selfishness and pride;
let nothing come between us,
so that the world may know
that Jesus came from you
and now lives with you
forever and ever.

FOCUS OF THE READINGS:

As we near the conclusion of the Easter season, our readings focus on our future life with Christ. It is a life with the risen Lord which begins here on earth and culminates in our being with him forever.

In the first reading, Stephen, the first martyr, is given a vision of the risen Lord, "standing at the right hand of God." Stephen has fulfilled his mission; he has witnessed to Christ and now he goes willingly to be with him forever.

Chapter 17 of John's Gospel contains the priestly prayer of Jesus for the Church. This Sunday's Gospel gives us a small portion of that prayer. The first half is a plea that the Church will be united for mission, to give witness to Christ so that the world will believe that God sent Jesus into the world. The second half assures us that we will be with him always and will know fully God's love for us.

FIRST READING: *Acts 7:55-60*

A reading from the Acts of the Apostles.

When Stephen told the leaders of his people that they were guilty of killing Jesus, they became very angry.

But Stephen was filled with the Holy Spirit.
He looked up to heaven and said,

> "I can see Jesus standing
> at the right hand of God."

The leaders of the people were so angry
that they screamed at him
and covered their ears so they couldn't hear him.
Then they all ran at him,
and threw him out of the city, and stoned him.

As they were throwing stones at him,
Stephen prayed,

> "Lord Jesus, take my life; I give you my spirit."

Then he knelt down and prayed,

> "Lord, do not blame them for this sin."

After Stephen said these words, he died.

The Word of the Lord.

RESPONSE: *Psalm 15*

RESPONSE:
They will live with you, O God, they will live for - ev - er.

VERSES 1 & 3:   to Response
1. Those who speak the___ truth:
3. Those who do what is right:

VERSE 2:   to Response
2. Those who show great kind - ness:

GOSPEL ACCLAMATION:

Al-le-lu-ia, al-le-lu-ia, "May they all be one in

Fine

love." Al-le-lu-ia, al-le-lu-ia, "May they all be one in love."

GOSPEL: *John 17:20-26*

A reading from the Gospel of John.

While Jesus was teaching his disciples, he looked up to heaven and prayed,

"Father, I pray for my disciples.
I pray also for all those people
who will believe in me
because of what my disciples teach.
I pray that they will be united
as you and I are united.
You are in me and I am in you.
I pray that my disciples will be united with us,
so that everyone will believe that you sent me.
I have shown them what you are like,
so that they will love each other
just as you love me.

"Holy Father, I want my disciples
to be with me always,
and to know that you love them
just as you love me."

The Gospel of the Lord.

REFLECTING ON THE READINGS WITH CHILDREN:

After the first reading, ask the children to recall the story.

- Why were the leaders angry with Stephen?
- How did Stephen act like Jesus?
- What did he say? Explain to the children what a martyr is. Stephen was the first martyr to give his life for Jesus. Ask the children how we can give witness to our faith in Jesus today.
- How can we show others that we believe in Jesus?
- Is that sometimes difficult to do?
- Why do people sometimes get angry with us when we speak the truth or stand up for Jesus and what he teaches?

After the Gospel, explain to the children that it is easier to stand up for Jesus when we are united with other Christians. Jesus prayed that we would be united so that others would see how we live and would believe in him.

- What did Jesus say in his prayer? Jesus also prayed that we would love one another very much, just as he is loved by God. He promises that those who are his disciples will be with him forever.
- How can we show that we are united with Jesus and that we are his disciples?

PENTECOST

YEAR C

PRAYER OF THE DAY:

God of all the nations,
we praise you for your gift to us
of the Holy Spirit.
Through the power
of that same Spirit,
enable us to tell
the whole world about Jesus,
and to forgive those
who have harmed us,
as we ourselves pray
to be forgiven.

FOCUS OF THE READINGS:

The mission of the Church is to do the work of the Holy Spirit.

Jesus breathed into his disciples his own life, the Holy Spirit. By the power of that Spirit, the Church is born. They are now to do what his death and resurrection was all about—forgive. Peace is the greeting of the Risen Lord, and peace is his continued presence in the Church.

This Spirit comes upon the disciples with power. In the name of Jesus, in every language, they are empowered to preach about "the great things God has done."

REFLECTING ON THE READINGS WITH CHILDREN:

Before the first reading, remind the children of the first reading for Ascension. Reread to them the center part of the reading:

"One day when Jesus was with the disciples, he told them not to leave Jerusalem but to wait for the gift of the Holy Spirit. Jesus said,

'I have told you about this promise. John baptized with water, but in a few days you will be baptized with the Holy Spirit. The Holy Spirit will give you

FIRST READING: *Acts 2:1-8, 11b*

A reading from the Acts of the Apostles.

On the day of Pentecost,
the believers were gathered together in one room.
All of a sudden they heard a sound
like a strong wind
that seemed to fill the whole house.
Then they saw what looked like tongues of fire
coming and resting on each one of them.
They were all filled with the Holy Spirit,
and immediately they started to speak
in other languages.

At that time, there were visitors in Jerusalem
who had come from all over the world.
They were amazed
because they heard the believers
speaking in so many languages.
They said,

"How are they able to speak like this?
Aren't all of these people from around Galilee?
Yet we can all hear them
telling in our own languages
about the great things God has done."

The Word of the Lord.

RESPONSE: *Psalm 104*

RESPONSE: Send us your Spir-it, O Lord, and re-new the face of the earth!

VERSE: May your glo-ry last for-ev-er. May you re-joice in all we do!

60

GOSPEL ACCLAMATION:

"Peace_ be with you!
Al - le - lu - ia!

Re - ceive the Ho - ly Spir - it."

GOSPEL: *John 20:19-23*

A reading from the Gospel of John.

On Sunday evening (the same day
the women had been to the tomb of Jesus),
the disciples were gathered in a room upstairs.
They had locked the doors
because they were afraid of the people
who had crucified Jesus.
Jesus came and stood in the room and said,

"Peace be with you!"

Then he showed them his hands and his side.
The disciples were filled with joy
when they saw the Lord.
Jesus said again,

"Peace be with you!
As God has sent me to you,
now I am sending you to others."

Then he breathed on the disciples
and said to them,

"Receive the Holy Spirit.
If you forgive the sins of anyone,
they are forgiven.
If you do not forgive them,
they are not forgiven."

The Gospel of the Lord.

power to be my witnesses in Jerusalem, Judea, and Samaria, and all over the world.' "

Now invite the children to listen to today's first reading.

After the first reading, ask the children how Jesus kept the promise that he had made. Ask them what it must have been like for the disciples when they received the Holy Spirit. It is important to help them understand that the Holy Spirit is not "strong wind" and "tongues of fire." These are images used to describe an event which really cannot be put into words. We often do this. We say things like: "She is like a cute little kitten." Or we say, "She is as strong as a rock." We are using similes to help us express a feeling or a quality rather than a physical presence. The disciples were able to preach with clarity and so, later, when writing this account, described the event as receiving "tongues of fire." We don't know what the event was like. They (and we) knew they had received the Holy Spirit by the power they had to do Christ's work, especially of preaching and healing.

Ask the children (as we have before) what words are said at a Christian baptism.

"I baptize you in the name of the Father, and of the Son, and of the Holy Spirit."

Help them to understand that we too have received the Holy Spirit. Ask them what the disciples did when they received the Holy Spirit. The stress here should not be on "speaking other languages" but on "telling . . . about the great things God has done."

Ask the children how we can do this today, because we, too, have the Holy Spirit. Ask them to give some examples of how they can "tell about the great things God has done." What great things (*now*)? Whom can we tell?

After the Gospel, ask them what other thing (besides "telling the great things God has done") Jesus gave us the power to do. Explore ways in which they can "forgive others." Help them see that if we forgive someone, that person truly feels forgiven. If we refuse this, that person feels unforgiven. We have the power of the Holy Spirit to free people by being forgiving. Help them see that when we live this way, "the face of the earth will be like new." (The Psalm refrain.)

Feasts of the Lord
and
Sundays in Ordinary Time

TRINITY SUNDAY
YEAR C

PRAYER OF THE DAY:
God of all creation,
you embrace us
with the love
of a mother and father.
You send your own son,
Jesus, to save us.
Through the power
of your Holy Spirit,
you raise us
to life everlasting.
Your life is a mystery
that we will celebrate
and proclaim
forever and ever.

Note: Consistent with other specific feasts, we have chosen to keep the same readings for all three cycles. Of the readings available for this feast, these two seem to be the most easily understood by children.

FOCUS OF THE READINGS:
The focus of our readings is the experience of God acting in our lives in various ways. We have no adequate language for God, because God is beyond any single image we may have. We experience God in Jesus Christ who shares with us his experience of God, as creator, as redeemer, and as a person of intimate relationship. Our experience of this relationship is the Spirit of God living in us.

In the first reading, Paul tells us that because we live in the Holy Spirit, and because we are brothers and sisters of Christ, we are children of God. We too can enjoy the intimate relationship that Jesus called "Abba."

In the Gospel, Jesus tells his disciples to preach, baptize and teach in the name of God—the God who is intimate like a parent (Father), who comes as Savior (Son), and who lives within us (Holy Spirit).

FIRST READING: *Romans 8:14-17*

A reading from the letter of Paul to the Romans.

Brothers and sisters,

Everyone who is guided by the Holy Spirit
is a child of God.
We have been adopted by God,
and when we pray, "Abba, Father,"
it is the Holy Spirit and our own spirit
telling us that we truly are God's children.
And if we are God's children,
we will have eternal life like Jesus
who is God's Son.

The Word of the Lord.

RESPONSE: *Psalm 104*

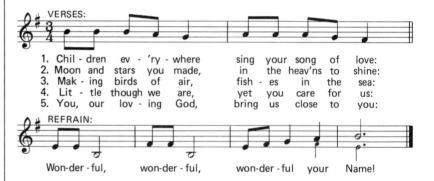

VERSES:
1. Chil - dren ev - 'ry - where   sing your song of love:
2. Moon and stars you made,   in the heav'ns to shine:
3. Mak - ing birds of air,   fish - es in the sea:
4. Lit - tle though we are,   yet you care for us:
5. You, our lov - ing God,   bring us close to you:

REFRAIN:
Won-der - ful,   won-der - ful,   won-der -ful your Name!

GOSPEL ACCLAMATION:

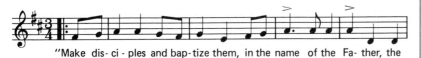

"Make dis-ci-ples and bap-tize them, in the name of the Fa-ther, the name of the Son, the name of the Spir-it." Al - le - lu - ia!

GOSPEL: *Matthew 28:16-20*

A reading from the Gospel of Matthew.

The eleven disciples
went to the mountain in Galilee,
just as Jesus had said.
When Jesus met them there, he said,

  "God has given me all the power
    and authority of heaven and earth.
  Now I am sending you out
    to preach to all the nations.
  I want you to make disciples
    and baptize them
    in the name of the Father,
    and of the Son,
    and of the Holy Spirit.
  Teach them to keep my commandments
    and do all that I have taught you.
  And I promise you
    that I am with you always—
    yes, to the very end of the world."

The Gospel of the Lord.

REFLECTING ON THE READINGS WITH CHILDREN:

As noted previously, Trinitarian language poses difficulties for children (as well as adults!), and even well-intentioned analogies serve only to confuse them more. We suggest that with the children we not concern ourselves with doctrinal language for Trinity, but rather with the experience of God in our lives.

After the Gospel, ask the children what Jesus asked the disciples to do (preach, baptize and teach). Are the disciples of Jesus still doing those things today?

Jesus said, "preach to all nations." This might be a good time to tell the children a little about missionary work. Besides preaching in our own parishes, some people are called to go to other parts of the world.

Jesus said, "teach them to keep my commandments." Help the children discuss the many ways the church teaches (religious education classes for children and adults, special classes on the Bible, informal teaching by parents, teachers, friends, and so forth). Draw attention especially to teaching activities in your own parish.

Jesus said, "baptize them in the name of the Father and of the Son and of the Holy Spirit." Ask the children if they remember being at a baptism. What words does the priest or deacon say? Remind them that we proclaim that we are baptized Christians every time we make the sign of the cross and say those words.

If time permits, you may wish to reflect on the first reading as well. Remind the children that Jesus often used the name "Father" or even "Abba" which is like our word "Daddy." What is important here is not the masculine image of God, but rather the intimate relationship that Jesus experienced with God. St. Paul tells us that because Jesus chose us to be his brothers and sisters and gave us his Holy Spirit, we too are children of God and can call God "Abba!" The children should leave today's liturgy of the Word knowing that God loves them and wants to be close to them.

BODY AND BLOOD OF CHRIST

YEAR C

PRAYER OF THE DAY:

God of life, help us to know
that when we share our food,
as you do,
with all who are in need,
we satisfy our hunger;
when we share our drink,
as you do,
with all who are in need,
we satisfy our thirst.
We offer this prayer
as we gather
to eat the bread
and drink the wine
of your son, Jesus,
who lives with us
now and forever.

Note: Consistent with other specific feasts, we have chosen to keep the same readings for all three cycles. Of the readings available for this feast, these two seem to be the most easily understood by children.

FOCUS OF THE READINGS:

Our readings for today focus on the presence of Christ in the Eucharist. In the first reading, Paul presents what he was taught concerning the actions and words of Jesus at the Last Supper. While the words may vary in the four accounts (Matthew, Mark, Luke and 1 Corinthians), we have here a straightforward account of Jesus' institution of the Eucharist. In the sharing of bread and wine, Christ is present.

The Gospel proclaims that Christ himself is our life. It is he who satisfies our hunger and thirst. He chose to make this reality concrete in language, bread and wine. Jesus invites us to share his body and blood, which in Hebrew are symbols of person and life. In these symbols we encounter the living Lord, ever present to us. To share in his life, to be one with him, is to live forever.

FIRST READING: *1 Corinthians 11:23-26*

A reading from the first letter of Paul to the Corinthians.

Brothers and sisters,

This is what the Lord taught me
and I am now telling you.
At supper, on the night before he died,
Jesus took bread,
and after he gave thanks,
he broke the bread and said,

"This is my body,
which I am giving for you.
When you eat this bread,
remember me."

After supper,
he took a cup of wine and said,

"This cup is the new covenant in my blood.
When you drink from this cup,
remember me."

For when you eat this bread
and drink from this cup,
you are proclaiming the death of the Lord
until he comes again.

The Word of the Lord.

RESPONSE: *Psalm 104*

You are the one who feeds us, giv-ing us food from your hand.

You are the one who feeds us, giv-ing us all we need.

GOSPEL ACCLAMATION:

1. "I am the Bread of Life," says the Lord.
2. Al - le - lu - ia, al - le - lu - ia!

1.-2. "All who eat this Bread will live for ev - er."

GOSPEL: *John 6:35, 51, 53, 55-56, 54*

A reading from the Gospel of John.

Jesus said to the people,

"I am the bread of life.
Anyone who comes to me
will never be hungry,
and anyone who believes in me
will never be thirsty.
I am the living bread
that came down from heaven.
Anyone who eats this bread,
which is my life, will live forever.
This bread gives life to the world.
Unless you eat this bread
and drink from this cup,
you do not have real life in you.
For I am real food and real drink for you.
Everyone who eats this bread
and drinks from this cup
lives in me,
and I live in each of them.
Those who eat this bread
and drink from this cup
have eternal life
and I will raise them up on the last day."

The Gospel of the Lord.

REFLECTING ON THE READINGS WITH CHILDREN:

Discuss with the children the many times we celebrate our unity by sharing in a special meal: Christmas, Easter, Thanksgiving, birthdays, and so forth. Are there other times? Ask the children what their family eats on these special occasions. Help them see that certain foods have become symbols of what we are celebrating. When we see and eat certain food, it makes the event real and even brings to our memory past celebrations. For example, many families have turkey for dinner every year on Christmas. It has become symbolic for the celebration of an important event. And sharing in that special dinner brings members of the family closer together.

Jesus celebrated a special meal with his disciples the night before he died. They shared bread and wine. Jesus told them that from now on, whenever his disciples share that bread and wine and remember him, he is there in a special way. When we come together for Mass, we remember what Jesus said and did. We too share that bread and wine which is the very life of Jesus, and it brings us all closer together. When we eat this bread and drink from this cup, we say that we believe in Jesus, and we believe that he gives us life and that he will give us life forever.

SECOND SUNDAY IN ORDINARY TIME

YEAR C

PRAYER OF THE DAY:

Lord God,
when Jesus changed water
into wine at a wedding,
he showed for the first time
the power he had from you.
With Mary, our mother,
praying for us,
change our lives
that we may love you
with all our heart.
We ask this of you
through Christ our Lord.

FOCUS OF THE READINGS:

The first reading focuses on the restoration of Jerusalem after many years of exile. The people have returned and now await the rebuilding of their city. This day of joy, when all will see her glory, is described in beautiful imagery of a marriage.

In the first of his miracles, Jesus reveals that *the glory of God has indeed come.* This glory is imaged also in a marriage scene. What is revealed, in concrete terms, is that the glory of God, in Jesus, makes all things new. Water is changed into wine. Jesus can and does change things. *That revelation is realized because Mary, a symbol of the faithful, asked in faith. Jesus makes all things new.*

FIRST READING: *Isaiah 62:1-5*

A reading from the prophet Isaiah.

The prophet Isaiah said,

"Because I love you Jerusalem,
I will not be silent.
I will not rest
until you shine like a burning torch
and everyone sees your salvation.
All nations will know
that you have been saved,
and all the kings of the world
will see your glory.
God will give you a new name, a special name
and will hold you like a precious crown.
Just as a bridegroom is happy
and rejoices with his bride,
so God will be happy and rejoice because of you."

The Word of the Lord.

RESPONSE: *Psalm 96*

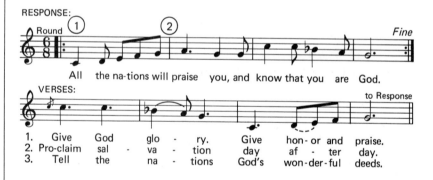

All the nations will praise you, and know that you are God.

1. Give God glory. Give honor and praise.
2. Proclaim salvation day after day.
3. Tell the nations God's wonderful deeds.

GOSPEL ACCLAMATION:

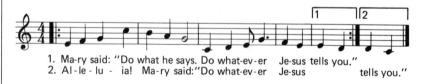

1. Ma-ry said: "Do what he says. Do what-ev-er Je-sus tells you."
2. Al-le-lu-ia! Ma-ry said: "Do what-ev-er Je-sus tells you."

GOSPEL: *John 2:1-11*

A reading from the Gospel of John.

One day there was a wedding at Cana in Galilee,
and Mary the mother of Jesus was there.
Jesus and his disciples
were also invited to the wedding.
Now when Jesus' mother
saw that there wasn't any wine left,
she said to him,

"They don't have any more wine."

Jesus said,

"Why are you telling me about this?
It is not time for people to know who I am."

Then Jesus' mother said
to those who were serving at the celebration,

"Do whatever Jesus tells you."

Now there were six large water jugs there,
and each of them held about twenty or thirty
gallons. Jesus said to the servers,

"Fill those jugs with water."

After the servers filled the jugs, Jesus said,

"Now take some of it to the waiter
in charge of the celebration."

The waiter did not see what happened,
so when he tasted the water
which Jesus had turned into wine,
he called the bridegroom over and said to him,

"People usually serve the very best wine first.
Then after the guests
have been drinking for a long time,
they serve the cheaper wine.
But you have saved the best wine until now!"

And so, the first miracle that Jesus did
was at Cana in Galilee.
With this sign, Jesus revealed his glory,
and his disciples believed in him.

The Gospel of the Lord.

REFLECTING ON THE READINGS
WITH CHILDREN:

Ask the children to retell the
story and help them visualize the
scene. Perhaps some of them have
attended a wedding and can share
their remembrance of the ceremony
and the reception. It is important
that the children see Jesus, his
mother, the newly married couple
and the guests as real people at a real
event. Ask the children how they
think the couple might have felt
when they didn't have enough wine
for their guests. Help the children
see that Mary believed that Jesus
could do something about this
problem. How do we see that Mary
believed in Jesus? Because she asked
in faith, Jesus acted, and in doing so,
revealed God's glory and power. *It is
important that the children see in this
event, not the power of Mary, but the
faith of Mary, and the power and
glory of God in Jesus.* Jesus wants to
make all things new and does when
we ask in faith.

THIRD SUNDAY
IN ORDINARY TIME

YEAR C

PRAYER OF THE DAY:

God, always faithful and true,
you promised to send
the Good News
to all those who love you.
We know
that Jesus is that Good News.
May we show
how much we love you
by opening our hearts
to his words
and obeying his commandments.
We make this prayer to you
through Christ our Lord.

FOCUS OF THE READINGS:

Our first reading focuses on the
law of Moses and worship of God.
When Ezra stood on the platform,
read the law and explained it to all
the people, they accepted it by
saying, "Amen, amen." "Then they
bowed their heads and worshipped
God." The reading tells us that
true happiness is found in following
God's ways.

In our Gospel, Jesus, too, stands
before the people and reads from the
Word of God. He, too, explains it to
those gathered there. This passage in
Luke is, as it were, Jesus' own "job
description." He declares that he is
the one sent and anointed by God to
fulfill the prophecy which he has
read from Isaiah. Here Jesus reveals
the meaning of the Scriptures and
his own mission. Throughout
Ordinary Time, we will see this
mission to the poor, the oppressed
and the downtrodden unfold in the
teachings and actions of Jesus.

Jesus brings Good News to the poor.

FIRST READING:
Nehemiah 8:1-2, 4a, 5-6, 3, 8-10

A reading from the prophet Nehemiah.

When all the people were gathered
outside the Temple,
Ezra, the priest,
brought the book of the law of Moses
to read it to them.
He stood on a wooden platform
which the people had made for him,
and he held the book up high
so that everyone could see it.
When he opened the book of the law,
all the people stood up.
Ezra praised God,
and all the people raised their hands high and said,

"Amen, amen!"

And he read to them
from early morning until noon.
All the people,
the men, women, and the children
who were old enough to understand,
listened carefully to what Ezra read.
Then he explained the law of Moses to them
so that they could understand it.

[Then Nehemiah, who was the leader,
said to the people,

"Today is a special day for God, a holy day.
Eat and drink whatever you like.
And be sure to give something to those
who don't have anything to eat or drink,
because this is a holy day for God. Be happy.
You will be strong
when you find your joy in God."]

The Word of the Lord.

[ ] *Reader may omit text that appears in brackets.*

RESPONSE: *Psalm 19*

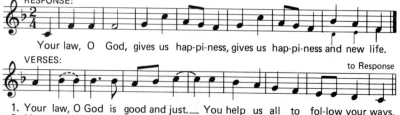

RESPONSE:
Your law, O God, gives us hap-pi-ness, gives us hap-pi-ness and new life.

VERSES:
to Response

1. Your law, O God is good and just.__ You help us all to fol-low your ways.
2. Your words_teach us what is right.__ Your word, O God gives joy to my life.

GOSPEL ACCLAMATION:

"The Spir-it__ of God is on me. I bring Good News to the poor." Al - le - lu - ia,____ al - le - lu - ia,____ "Good News to the poor."

GOSPEL: *Luke 4:14-21*

A reading from the Gospel of Luke.

Jesus had been in the desert for forty days.

Jesus then came back to Galilee
filled with the power of the Holy Spirit.
He taught in the synagogues,
and people all around heard about him
and said wonderful things about him.

When he went to the town of Nazareth
where he had grown up,
he went to the synagogue
on the Sabbath day as he always did.
He stood up to read,
and the book of the prophet Isaiah
was handed to him.
Jesus opened the book
and found the place where it says,

   "The Spirit of God is upon me.
     God has anointed me
     and sent me to bring Good News to the poor,
     to proclaim freedom
     to those who are oppressed by others,
     to give sight to the blind,
     and to announce a special time of blessing from God."

Then Jesus closed the book,
gave it back to the server and sat down.
Everyone in the synagogue was looking at him.

Jesus said to them,

   "What I have just read to you has come true
    right here and now, while you are listening."

The Gospel of the Lord.

REFLECTING ON THE READINGS WITH CHILDREN:

Since it would be difficult to reflect on both of these readings, we have chosen to concentrate on the Gospel.

Even with children, it is important to proclaim clearly that Jesus' mission was to help those in need. He consistently speaks of helping the poor, the blind, the lame, the deaf, the oppressed—in short, those who are most in need.

The reflections on the Gospel should center on two things:

1) Jesus tells us that he was anointed by the Spirit for his mission. *How do we see Jesus carrying out his mission in the Gospels?* Help the children recall examples of this from the life of Jesus, stories he told (the Good Samaritan), his own actions (healing the blind, etc.)

2) *Since we too are anointed by the Spirit in our Baptism, we have the same mission.* How can we carry it out?

Help the children discover in themselves a real concern for the poor and those in need. Help them realize tangible ways they can help. Be sure that this discussion stays within the capabilities of their age. While there are genuine ways they can live this, we are, for the most part, planting seeds for the future. What is important is that they see that *service is the Christian way.*

FOURTH SUNDAY IN ORDINARY TIME

YEAR C

PRAYER OF THE DAY:

Saving God,
to live as Jesus taught us
is hard, and we often fail.
Fill us with confidence
in your strength
because you love us
and you are always by our side.
We make this prayer to you
through Christ our Lord.

FOCUS OF THE READINGS:

In both of our readings, the one called to announce God's revelation is rejected by his own people. Jeremiah is called at an early age and set apart to proclaim God's message. He sees already that it will not be easy. "I don't know what to say, for I am too young." But God is the source and strength of every vocation. Jesus, too, is rejected, not because of his youth, but because he is "too local." The people find it hard to accept a prophet who comes from their own town. Both readings focus on God's call to vocation, and the stubbornness of those to whom the called are sent. Both Jeremiah and Jesus suffer at the hands of those to whom they offered God's message.

God is the source and strength of all vocations.

FIRST READING: *Jeremiah 1:3-7, 17-19*

A reading from the prophet Jeremiah.

During the time when Josiah
was the king of Judah,
God said to me,

"Even before
I created you in your mother's womb,
I knew you.
Even before you were born,
I chose you to be a prophet
to all the nations of the world."

Then I said,

"But God, I can't do this.
I won't know what to say, for I am too young."

God said,

"Do not say you are too young. I am with you.
Go now and tell the people
everything I tell you to say.
Don't be discouraged by them
and don't give up.
I will make you as strong as iron and bronze.
The people and their leaders
will fight against you,
but they will not win,
for I am with you to save you."

The Word of the Lord.

RESPONSE: *Psalm 71*

RESPONSE:

I have been yours since the day of my birth, and you have been my God. ___ been my God. ___

GOSPEL ACCLAMATION:

Leader:

All: (sing and clap)

1. Your Word brings us heal - ing. Al - le - lu - ia, al - le - lu - ia!
2. Your Word Lord is all we need. Al - le - lu - ia, al - le - lu - ia!

GOSPEL: *Luke 4:15, 22-30*

A reading from the Gospel of Luke.

When Jesus taught on the Sabbath day
in the synagogue in his home town of Nazareth,
all the people said wonderful things about him.
But, in fact, they wondered
how he could be so wise, and they said,

"Isn't he the son of Joseph?"

Jesus said to them,

"I am sure you are thinking,

'Doctor, why don't you heal yourself?
Why don't you do the miracles here
that you did in Capernaum?'

"But I tell you, people never believe
or accept a prophet
who comes from their own town.

["For example, when Elisha was a prophet,
there were many people
living right here in Israel who had leprosy.
But the only leper who was healed by Elisha
was Naaman, a man who lived in Syria."]

When Jesus said this,
the people in the synagogue became very angry.
They forced him out of the town
and took him to the top of a hill
so that they could throw him over the cliff.
But Jesus escaped through the crowd
and walked away.

The Gospel of the Lord.

[ ] *Reader may omit text that appears in brackets.*

REFLECTING ON THE READINGS
WITH CHILDREN:

Help the children appreciate
these points.

1) God's call is not limited.
Jeremiah was called as a youth.
Children, too, can proclaim God's
Word. How?

2) Prophets are often not accepted
because they speak the truth. Many
people don't want to hear the truth.
Sometimes we don't either. Why?

3) Jesus can do all things if we
believe. Sometimes our lack of faith
keeps Jesus from doing all he would
like to do for us.

FIFTH SUNDAY IN ORDINARY TIME

YEAR C

PRAYER OF THE DAY:

God of the peoples,
it is your desire
that the whole world
should hear
the message of Jesus.
Put your power into our lives
and send us out to do your work.
We make this prayer to you
through Christ our Lord.

FOCUS OF THE READINGS:

Both of our readings focus on call and response. Both Isaiah and Simon (Peter) acknowledge unworthiness even to be in the presence of God. After admitting their sinfulness, each receives the call to act in God's name.

Isaiah's confession finds immediate forgiveness, and he hears God's call: "Whom shall I send? Who will go for me?" Filled with God's grace, Isaiah responds, "Here I am! Send me."

Simon (Peter) too, having witnessed the power of Jesus, confesses his sin and receives immediate forgiveness followed by the call, "Do not be afraid" and "From now on you will be gathering people (for me), not fish." As in the case with Isaiah, Simon (Peter), filled with grace, can respond by leaving everything to follow Jesus.

Who will go for me? Here I am! Send me. And they left everything to follow Jesus.

FIRST READING: *Isaiah 6:1-2a, 3-8*

A reading from the prophet Isaiah.

One day, when I was in the temple, (I had a vision.)
I saw God sitting on a high throne,
and there were angels standing all around it.
One angel called to another,

"Holy, holy, holy is the Lord!
The whole earth is full of God's glory!"

When the angel spoke,
the doors of the temple shook.
And the temple filled with smoke.

Then I said,

"I am a sinner, and my people are sinful people,
and yet I have seen God. Now I am doomed."

Then one of the angels came to me
holding a piece of burning coal.
The angel touched my mouth
with the hot coal and said,

"Now that this has touched your mouth,
your sin is forgiven."

Then I heard the voice of God say,

"Who will go and speak for me?
Who will I send?"

And I answered,

"I am here! Send me."

The Word of the Lord.

RESPONSE: *Psalm 40*

RESPONSE:
Here I am, O my God, I come to do your will.

VERSES:
to Response
1. You have put a new song in my mouth, a song of praise to you.
2. I pro-claim your kind-ness. I will sing, your love is won-der-ful.

74

GOSPEL ACCLAMATION:

1. Je - sus said: "From now on you will be
2. Al - le - lu - ia! "You will be

1.-2. gath - er - ing peo - ple in."

[1] peo - ple in."

GOSPEL: *Luke 5:1-11*

A reading from the Gospel of Luke.

One day when Jesus was standing on the shore
beside Lake Gennesaret,
he saw two boats by the lake.
The fishermen were busy washing their nets.
Jesus got into the boat that belonged to Simon,
and he said to him,

"Row the boat out where the water is deep.
Put your nets into the water,
and you will catch some fish."

Simon said,

"Master, we fished all night long
and didn't catch anything!
But if you say so, we will try again now."

So they put their nets into the deep water.
Soon they caught so many fish
that their nets began to tear.
They called to their partners in the other boat
to come and help them.
James and John came,
and both boats were so full of fish
that they almost sank.
James and John were amazed at what happened.
When Simon saw how many fish they caught,
he fell down in front of Jesus and said,

"Lord, go away from me! I am a sinner!"

But Jesus said to Simon,

"Don't be afraid!
From now on you will be gathering people, not fish!"

They brought their boats onto the shore
and left everything to follow Jesus.

The Gospel of the Lord.

REFLECTING ON THE READINGS
WITH CHILDREN:

Last week we saw that God's call
is not limited to age or location. In
today's readings we hear that God
calls even those who feel unworthy
because of their sinfulness.

Help the children recall the story
of Isaiah. Help them see that Isaiah
confessed his sin because he saw how
holy God is. But God is always ready
to forgive and fill us with grace. Then
we *can* respond to God's call. This
should be brief so we can concentrate
on the Gospel story.

Help the children visualize the
scene by Lake Gennesaret:
- the crowd, the boats, fishermen
  busy washing their nets
  (perhaps a picture would be
  helpful);
- Jesus teaching the crowd, the
  dialogue between Jesus and
  Simon (Peter), and the
  wonderful catch of fish.

Help the children see that Simon
(Peter) confessed his sin because he
saw how holy Jesus is. Again, stress
the readiness of Jesus to forgive and
give us grace to do what he wants.
- Ask the children what Jesus
  meant when he said, "From now
  on, you will be gathering people,
  not fish."
- How does the Church do that
  today?
- *How can we follow Jesus and do
  that too?*

75

SIXTH SUNDAY IN ORDINARY TIME

YEAR C

PRAYER OF THE DAY:

God, heavenly teacher,
show us how we ought to live.
Although following Jesus
may at times be difficult
and even unpopular,
give us the confidence
always to be faithful to him.
We make this prayer to you
through Christ our Lord.

FOCUS OF THE READINGS:

Both of our readings focus on trust in God. In the reading from Jeremiah, this is imaged by living plants. Those who trust in this world are like plants deprived of water, the source of life. Those who trust in God produce fruit because they receive water from the source of life. We must put our trust in God, who alone gives real life.

In our Gospel, Luke also contrasts those who live by the ways of the world and those who live the ways of God. The Beatitudes present the ultimate paradox of Christian life and can only be lived (or even seen as worthwhile) by the believer whose source of grace is Christ. It takes complete trust to live the Beatitudes.

Live by my Word, and you will be blessed.

FIRST READING: *Jeremiah 17:5-8*

A reading from the prophet Jeremiah.

Our God says,

"People who don't trust in God
and who don't love God
do not have real joy.
They are like plants in the desert,
plants that don't have water.
But people who trust in God and love God
are blessed.
They are like trees
that are planted beside running water.
Their leaves stay green,
and they always bear fruit."

The Word of the Lord.

RESPONSE: *Psalm 18*

RESPONSE:
I love you God, for you are my strength. You are my God. I give you my praise. praise. You are my God.

GOSPEL ACCLAMATION:

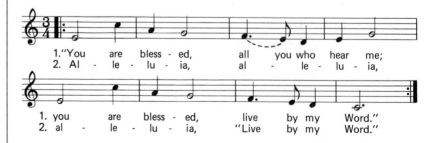

1. "You are bless-ed, all you who hear me; you are bless-ed, live by my Word."
2. Al-le-lu-ia, al-le-lu-ia, al-le-lu-ia, "Live by my Word."

GOSPEL: *Luke 6:17, 20-26*

A reading from the Gospel of Luke.

When Jesus and his disciples
came down from the mountain,
a great crowd of people
came from all over to hear him teach
and be healed of their diseases.
Jesus looked at his disciples and said,

"Blessed are you if you are poor now,
because God's kingdom belongs to you.

"Blessed are you if you are hungry now,
because later you will have all the food you need.

"Blessed are you if you are sad now,
because later you will laugh.

"Blessed are you if people hate you
and say bad things about you
just because you believe in me.
Be happy about that,
because you will have a great reward in heaven.
People have always treated the prophets
in just the same way.

["But pay attention you who are rich now.
It will be sad for you later,
because you have already had
what you wanted.

"It will be sad for you later
if you have more food than you need,
because one day you will be hungry.
It will be sad for you later
if you can laugh now,
because one day you will cry.

"It will be sad for you later
if everyone says only good things
about you now,
because people have always treated
the false prophets in the same way."]

This is the Good News of the Lord.

[ ] *Reader may omit text that appears in brackets.*

REFLECTING ON THE READINGS
WITH CHILDREN:

Reflecting on the Beatitudes will
not be easy with children, for they
present the opposite of all that seems
reasonable. Poverty, sorrow, hunger,
and mistreatment will hardly seem
like blessings. But two things may be
hoped for with the children.

1) To provide familiarity with the
Beatitudes, the heart of the
Christian way of life. Here again, we
are planting seeds that, with life's
experience and God's constant grace,
will grow to maturity. It is enriching
for children to hear and be familiar
with the truths of our faith even if
they are not completely understood.

2) To help the children
understand that, *whatever our
condition in life, God asks for our
trust.* If we are poor or hungry, or sad
or mistreated, God can and will make
things right. This may, of course,
only be known in heaven. Likewise, if
we have more than we need, we must
trust that when we share what we
have, *God will continue to take care
of us and bless us.* Sorrow comes
when we don't trust God and,
therefore, live selfishly rather than
for others.

77

SEVENTH SUNDAY IN ORDINARY TIME

YEAR C

PRAYER OF THE DAY:

God,
you have shown us your love
most of all by sending Jesus
who died for us.
With your aid,
may we love everybody we meet,
those who are good to us
and those who do us harm.
We make this prayer to you
through Christ our Lord.

FOCUS OF THE READINGS:

Both of our readings focus on a willingness to forgive others, even when they mistrust us. And in both readings, we are presented with the only motive for this: God.

In our reading from Samuel, David, who has been hunted and hounded by Saul, finally finds the opportunity to kill his persecutor. But he does not do it because "God has chosen Saul." For David, to act in an unforgiving way would be to act against the ways of God.

The Gospel for today echoes this attitude in the golden rule: "Treat everyone the way you would like them to treat you." We are presented with several examples of this: forgiving slander, forgiving physical abuse, forgiving greed and selfishness—in short, all actions of our enemies, those who hate us. And we are commanded not only to forgive, but to act positively in these situations:

Love your enemies, pray for them, lend to them. And why? Because that is the way God treats us!

Treat everyone the way you would want them to treat you.

FIRST READING:
1 Samuel 26:2, 7-9, 12-13, 22-23

A reading from the first book of Samuel.

Saul and his army were looking for David
who was in the wilderness in a place called Ziph.
That night, while Saul
and all the men in his army were asleep,
David and Abishai got into the camp
and crept into Saul's tent.
Saul was asleep, and his spear
was stuck in the ground beside his head.
Abishai said to David,

"Here is your enemy asleep and at your mercy.
Let me kill him with his own spear."

But David said,

"No, do not kill him.
For God has chosen him and anointed him.
It would be wrong for us
to kill the one God has chosen."

So David took Saul's spear and left the camp.
No one saw or heard him, and no one woke up.
Then David went to the top of the mountain
and called out,

"O King Saul, here is your spear.
Send one of your soldiers over to get it.
This will show you that I could have killed you,
but I didn't because God has chosen you.
God will reward everyone
who is good and faithful."

The Word of the Lord.

RESPONSE: *Psalm 103*

RESPONSE:
My God, my God, have mer-cy on me, for all my hope is in you, my God, all my hope is in you.

VERSES: to Response
1. I give you thanks, O God,___ and bless your Ho-ly Name.__
2. You take a-way our sins___ and bring us to new life.__
3. As par-ents love their chil-dren, you love your faith-ful peo-ple.

78

GOSPEL ACCLAMATION:

"Treat peo-ple as you would like them to treat you." Al-le - lu - ia!

GOSPEL: *Luke 6:27-36*

A reading from the Gospel of Luke.

Jesus said to his disciples,

"Love your enemies,
  and be good to people who hate you.
  Pray for people who are unkind to you
  and who say bad things about you.
  If someone hits you on the side of your face,
  let them hit the other side too.
  If someone takes your coat,
  give your shirt with it.
  When anyone asks you for something,
  give it right away and don't ask for it back.
  Treat everyone
  the way you would like them to treat you.

"If you love only those people who love you,
  why should you be rewarded?
  Even sinners love people who love them.
  And if you are good only to people
  who are good to you,
  why should you be rewarded?
  Even sinners are good to people
  who are good to them.

"But I tell you, love your enemies,
  be good to everyone,
  lend people things freely,
  and God will reward you.
  You will be true children of God
  because God is kind to all people,
  even those who are selfish or ungrateful.
  You must be kind and loving just like God."

The Gospel of the Lord.

REFLECTING ON THE READINGS
WITH CHILDREN:

Our reflections should be centered on the golden rule. Taken apart from that, commandments like "love your enemies," "pray for those who hate you," "turn the other cheek," "lend to those who are greedy or selfish," etc., will not seem fair to children. And indeed they aren't! The point of the Gospel is that God does not treat us fairly. We are not always what we should be. We do not always behave well. But God is kind to all people, even those who are selfish and ungrateful. And we, as Christians, are to be like God. Help the children to appreciate two things:

1) We often act in an unchristian way toward others. *Just as we want them to forgive and start over with us, we must do the same with others.* The children can easily share examples of this.

2) We are called to be like God. *When we treat others as we want to be treated, we are acting like God.*

79

EIGHTH SUNDAY IN ORDINARY TIME

YEAR C

PRAYER OF THE DAY:

God of truth,
Jesus matched his words
with his actions.
Help us to be like him,
so that we will always
say and do
what you want of us.
We make this prayer to you
through Christ our Lord.

FOCUS OF THE READINGS:

The focus of both readings is simply that our actions reveal our inner selves. We are known to be honest and just if we act honestly and justly. People know who we really are by the way we act. Both of our readings use the image of a fruit tree to illustrate this truth. Quite simply, a rotten tree does not give good fruit, and if we harbor evil on the inside, our actions will reveal that. Further, figs grow only on fig trees and grapes grow only on vines and not vice versa. Both readings point to interior integrity.

Plant your word in our hearts. Let it bear fruit in us.

FIRST READING: *Sirach 27:5-6*

A reading from the book of Sirach.

We know that pottery is well made
if it does not break
when it is put into the fire to harden.
And we know that a tree has been well cared for
if it gives good fruit.
It is just the same with human beings.
We know the kind of people they are
from the things they say.

The Word of the Lord.

RESPONSE: *Psalm 92*

RESPONSE:
1. I will sing praise to you. I will sing to you, my God.
2. I will sing praise to you. I will sing for all you do.

VERSE:
We pro-claim you are great. We pro-claim your faith-ful love.

GOSPEL ACCLAMATION:

Al - le - lu - ia, al - le - lu - ia. Al - le - lu - ia, al - le - lu - ia!

*VERSE:

Plant your Word in our hearts. Let it bear fruit in us!

GOSPEL: *Luke 6:43-45*

A reading from the Gospel of Luke.

Jesus said to his disciples,

"Good trees give good fruit
and bad trees give bad fruit.
You don't see figs growing on bushes with thorns.
No, they grow on fig trees.
And grapes don't grow on bramble bushes,
but only on grape vines.

"It is the same with human beings.
People who have a good and kind heart
do good things.
But people who have evil in their hearts
do evil things.
People show what is truly in their hearts
and how they truly are by what they do."

The Gospel of the Lord.

REFLECTING ON THE READINGS WITH CHILDREN:

This may be an occasion when you will want to reflect with the children *before the readings.*

Ask the children a series of questions. They may even find them humorous and fun.
- Did you ever see a rose on a grape vine?
- Did you ever see corn growing on a banana tree?
- Did you ever see oranges growing on a tulip plant?

After some time with this, ask the children why those things don't happen. In their own language, they will tell you that "things are what they are!"

Read the first reading. Help the children see that what is true of trees and plants is also true of people. *We can tell what kind of people we are by the way we act.*

Invite them to sing the Psalm Response, which is our prayer to live by God's ways.

Invite them to sing the Gospel Acclamation, to pray that God's Word be planted in us.

After the Gospel, simply point out to the children that Jesus has just said what they have already said. Again remind them that Jesus used the example of fruit trees to teach us something about people: Just like figs grow only on fig trees, *good actions come only from people who are good in their hearts.* A few examples of this will suffice for the children to understand the parable.

Sing again the Gospel Acclamation.

NINTH SUNDAY IN ORDINARY TIME

YEAR C

PRAYER OF THE DAY:

God, you care for us,
and we know we are precious
in your sight.
Help us to believe
and trust in you
with all our might.
We make this prayer to you
through Christ our Lord.

FOCUS OF THE READINGS:

Both of our readings focus on the revelation of God to the Gentiles.

In our first reading, Solomon prays that all people (Gentiles) will come to the Temple to pray. Since the Temple represented the "place of God" to the Israelites, Solomon's prayer is that all people will come to know God even as Israel knows God.

In today's Gospel, we have an example of the Gentiles coming to Jesus and, indeed, showing more faith than Israel. The healing of the Roman officer's servant points up two things:

1) the outreach to the Gentiles prayed about in the first reading,

2) the healing power of Jesus' Word.

Your Word brings us healing and sets us free.

FIRST READING: *1 Kings 8:41-43*

A reading from the first book of Kings.

King Solomon was praying in the temple.
This is what he prayed:

"Dear God, people everywhere
will hear how great you are
and about all the mighty things you have done.
People will come from foreign countries
to pray in this temple.
When they come to pray,
listen and answer their prayers.
Then everyone from every nation
will know your name and will worship you,
just as we, the people of Israel,
know and worship you."

The Word of the Lord.

RESPONSE: *Psalm 96*

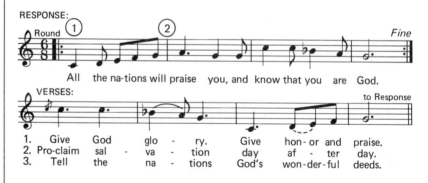

GOSPEL ACCLAMATION:

GOSPEL: *Luke 7:1-10*

A reading from the Gospel of Luke.

While Jesus was in Capernaum,
there was a Roman army officer
whose servant was very sick and was dying.
The officer liked his servant very much, and so,
when he heard about Jesus,
he sent two of his friends who were Jewish leaders
to ask Jesus to come and heal his servant.
When the two men came to Jesus, they said,

"We beg you to come.
This Roman officer deserves your help.
He loves our people,
and he even gave us the money
to build our synagogue."

Jesus went with them.
But as he was getting close to the house,
the officer sent some other people to say to Jesus,

"Lord, you don't need to come.
I am not good enough
to have you come into my house.
I sent my friends to speak to you
because I am not even good enough to talk to you.
But if you just say the word,
my servant will get well.
I know this because I am an officer in the army.
When I tell a soldier to come, he comes.
Or if I tell him to go, he goes.
And when I tell my servants to do something,
they do what I tell them."

When Jesus heard what the Roman officer said,
he was amazed at how much faith he had.
And he said to the people who were following him,

"This Roman man has more faith
than the people of Israel."

The friends of the officer went back to his house
and found that the servant was completely healed.

The Gospel of the Lord.

REFLECTING ON THE READINGS
WITH CHILDREN:

Ask the children to recall the
Gospel story.
- Who are the people?
- What do they do and say?
- Why does Jesus praise the
  Roman officer?
- Why was the servant healed?
- Did Jesus go to the officer's
  home? Why?
- How was the servant healed?

Point out to the children that we
have sung our belief in the healing
power of Jesus in our Gospel
Acclamation. Invite them to sing
it again.

Note: We suggest that you not
draw a parallel between the words of
the Roman officer and the words
used in the liturgy before
communion, "Lord, I am not
worthy," etc. Since this was not the
meaning intended by Luke, it would
be best to leave it in its Gospel
context.

TENTH SUNDAY IN ORDINARY TIME

YEAR C

PRAYER OF THE DAY:

God of the living
and of the dead,
all our life comes from you.
Look with love
on those who are sick
in mind or in body,
and raise us up like Jesus
to live with you forever.
We make this prayer to you
through Christ our Lord.

FOCUS OF THE READINGS:

Both of our readings focus on God's power over death. In the first reading, the prophet, Elijah, raises the son of the widow of Zarephath. In the Gospel, Jesus raises the son of the widow of Nain. In addition to the manifestation of God's power over death, we find in both stories the revelation of this power at work specifically in and through the words of the prophet Elijah and the words of Jesus. What is recognized is not simply the miracle, but who it is that acts. The widow's response to Elijah's miracle is, "Now I am sure that you are truly a man of God, and that God speaks through you." The response of the crowd at Nain is similar, "God has truly come to us." We have tried to highlight this two-fold focus, power over death and the power of the Word, in our psalm response and Gospel acclamation.

Young man, get up, I tell you. You have given me life. I will tell others of the wonderful things you do.

FIRST READING: *1 Kings 17:8-9, 17-24*

A reading from the first book of Kings.

God said to the prophet Elijah,

  "Go to the town of Zarephath.
  There is a widow living there
  who will feed you and take care of you."

While Elijah was staying there,
the widow's son became so ill
that he was no longer breathing.
The widow said to Elijah,

  "What do you have against me?
  Did you come to my home just to tell me
  that I am a sinner and to make my son die?"

Elijah said to her,

  "Give me your son."

And he carried the boy upstairs to his room
and laid him on his own bed.
Elijah bent over the boy three times and cried out to God,

  "O God, I beg you to make this child alive again."

God heard the prayer of Elijah
and brought the child back to life.
Elijah took the child downstairs to his mother
and said to her,

  "See, your son is alive!"

And the widow said to Elijah,

  "Now I am sure that you are truly a man of God,
  and that God speaks through you."

The Word of the Lord.

RESPONSE: *Psalm 30*

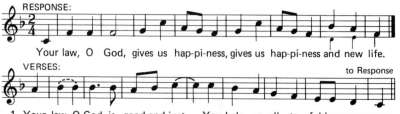

RESPONSE:
Your law, O God, gives us hap-pi-ness, gives us hap-pi-ness and new life.

VERSES:
to Response

1. Your law, O God is good and just.— You help us all to fol-low your ways.
2. Your words—teach us what is right.— Your word, O God gives joy to my life.

84

GOSPEL ACCLAMATION:

Je-sus said for all_ to hear: "Young_ man, get up, I tell you."

Al-le-lu-ia, praise_the Lord, al-le-lu-ia, praise the Lord!

GOSPEL: *Luke 7:11-17*

A reading from the Gospel of Luke.

Jesus went to a town called Nain.
His disciples and a large group of people
were with him.
As they were coming into the town,
they saw some people carrying a stretcher
with the body of a young man who had died.
This man was an only child,
and his mother was a widow.
Many people from the town
had come to be with her.
When Jesus saw the young man's mother,
he felt very sorry for her, and he said to her,

"Don't cry."

Then he went over and touched the stretcher.
The people carrying it stopped. Jesus said,

"Young man, I say to you, get up!"

And the dead man sat up and began to speak.
Jesus took the boy over to his mother.
All the people were amazed
and began to praise God, saying,

"This man is a great prophet!
God has truly come to us!"

Soon people all over Judea
and all the neighboring countries
heard about this wonderful thing that Jesus did.

The Gospel of the Lord.

REFLECTING ON THE READINGS
WITH CHILDREN:

Both of these stories will appeal
to children.

After the first reading, ask the
children to recall what they heard.
Ask them then to retell the story.
Two aspects should be highlighted:

1) The power of God acting
through Elijah.

2) Gratitude for life that leads to
the psalm refrain.

The psalm prayer is truly ours as
well because God has given us life,
continually gives us life, and
promises us life forever. *After the
Gospel*, ask the children to recall the
story. Take time to be aware of the
feelings of the boy's mother and how
Jesus treats her. What did Jesus do
and say? And again we highlight:

1) The power of God in Jesus, "I
say to you, get up."

2) Gratitude for life, "Soon people
all over . . . heard about this
wonderful thing Jesus did."

ELEVENTH SUNDAY IN ORDINARY TIME

YEAR C

PRAYER OF THE DAY:

Forgiving God,
anyone who has done wrong
can come back to you
through Jesus.
We are sorry
for going our own way,
for not loving you as we ought.
May we see the smile
of your forgiveness.
We make this prayer to you
through Christ our Lord.

FOCUS OF THE READINGS:

Both of our readings focus on God's forgiveness. In the first reading, Nathan reveals David's sin: he is responsible for the death of Uriah for clearly selfish motives. But David's confession is followed immediately by Nathan's assurance, "God has forgiven you."

In our Gospel, Jesus points out the difference between the arrogance of the self-righteous (Simon) and the love of the woman who has been forgiven. God's forgiveness is not meant to "hold us in check," as it were, but to arouse us to love. The focus is clear:

Your sins are forgiven. Go in peace.

FIRST READING: *2 Samuel 12:7-10, 13*

A reading from the second book of Samuel.

The prophet Nathan said to David,

"This is what God told me to tell you.

'I anointed you and made you king of Israel.
I saved you when Saul tried to kill you.
I made you ruler over all of Israel and Judah.
And I told you that I would give you everything.

'Why, then, have you not obeyed me?
Why have you done evil things?
You sent Uriah into the war so he would be killed!
And you killed him so that you could marry his wife.
Because of the bad example of your sin,
people in your family
will continue to kill and be killed.' "

When David heard this, he said to Nathan,

"Yes, I have sinned against God. I confess it."

Nathan said to David,

"God has forgiven you. You will be saved."

The Word of the Lord.

RESPONSE: *Psalm 51*

In your kind-ness, O my God, have mer-cy on me, have mer-cy on me.

1. I know____ that I have sinned and done what is wrong.
2. O God____ for-give my sins and make my heart true.

GOSPEL ACCLAMATION:

"Be-cause you be-lieve, your sins are for-giv-en. Go in peace." Al-le - lu - ia!

GOSPEL: *Luke 7:36-50*

A reading from the Gospel of Luke.

One day a Pharisee named Simon
invited Jesus to come and eat with him. So Jesus went.

Now there was a certain woman in that city,
and everyone knew she was a sinner.
When she heard that Jesus was having dinner at Simon's house,
she came, bringing with her a jar of perfumed ointment.
She knelt beside Jesus and began to cry.
Her tears fell on his feet, and she dried them with her hair.
She kissed his feet and put the perfumed ointment on them.
When Simon, the Pharisee, saw all of this, he said to himself,

"If Jesus were really a prophet,
he would know that this woman is a sinner,
and he wouldn't let her touch him."

Jesus said to the Pharisee,

"Simon, there is something I want to say to you."

Simon said,

"What is it, Teacher?"

Jesus said,

"There was a certain man who lent money to people,
but two of them were not able to pay him back.
One owed him 50 silver coins,
and the other one owed him 500 silver coins.
The man told both of them
that they didn't have to pay him back.
Now which of these two do you think
will love the man the most?"

Simon answered,

"I suppose it would be the one
who owed the man the most money."

Jesus said,

"You are right."

Then Jesus looked at the woman who was there,
and he said to Simon,

"Look at this woman.
When I came into your home,
you didn't give me any water to wash my feet.
But this woman has washed my feet with her tears
and dried them with her hair.
You didn't kiss me when I came in,
but she has been kissing my feet since she came.
You didn't even anoint my head with oil,
but she has put perfumed ointment on my feet!
I tell you that all of her sins have been forgiven.
And you see how much she loves!
But people who are forgiven only a little
will only love a little."

Then Jesus said to the woman,

"Yes, your sins are forgiven."

The people who were there at the dinner said to each other,

"Who is this man who forgives sins?"

Jesus said to the woman,

"Because you believed, your sins are completely forgiven.
Go in peace."

The Gospel of the Lord

REFLECTING ON THE READINGS
WITH CHILDREN:

After the Gospel, ask the children
to recall what they heard. Who was
there? What did they say and do?
Allow time for all of the details and
even a bit of visualizing this dramatic
story. Concentrate for a while on the
attitude of Simon. Is our attitude
sometimes like his: rejecting those
who do wrong? The point of the story
is that Jesus doesn't reject those who
do wrong.

This may be a good Sunday to
help the children understand that
confessing our faults (to one another
or sacramentally) should be joyful.
*We don't ever have to be afraid to say
we have done wrong because Jesus
always says, "Your sins are forgiven.
Go in peace."*

TWELFTH SUNDAY IN ORDINARY TIME

YEAR C

PRAYER OF THE DAY:

Generous God,
you will fill us with your gifts
if we give ourselves to you.
Through the example of Jesus,
show us how this can be done,
and by the power
of your Spirit
give us the courage
to carry it out.
We make this prayer to you
through Christ our Lord.

FOCUS OF THE READINGS:

Our focus today calls us to practice our faith in Christ by living like him. It is of little use to believe in Christ, but not believe in his cross. Acceptance of Christ means acceptance of his cross and also of our own cross in union with him. To take up our cross daily is to live a life of service. Christ's death on the cross is the culmination of his life for others. For us, too, they must go together.

If you want to be my disciple, accept the cross and follow me.

FIRST READING: *Zechariah 12:10*

A reading from the book of Zechariah.

Our God says:

"I am going to give a new spirit
to my people in Jerusalem.
When my spirit is in them,
their hearts will be changed.
They will look with compassion
on the one they have killed.
They will weep
as if they had killed their only child."

The Word of the Lord.

RESPONSE: *Psalm 51*

Give me a new heart, O God. Put your Spirit in me. Keep me with you, give me joy. Give me a new heart, O God.

GOSPEL ACCLAMATION:

1. "If you would be my disciples, accept the cross and follow me."
2. Alleluia, alleluia, "Accept the cross and follow me."

GOSPEL: *Luke 9:18-23*

A reading from the Gospel of Luke.

One day, while Jesus was alone praying,
his disciples came to be with him.
Jesus asked them,

  "Who do people say that I am?"

The disciples answered,

  "Some people think you are John the Baptist,
    and some people think you are Elijah.
    But there are other people
    who think you are a prophet
    who died a long time ago,
    and has come back to life."

Then Jesus asked them,

  "And who do you think I am?"

Peter answered,

  "You are the Christ, the one sent by God."

Jesus warned his disciples
not to tell anyone about this.
He said,

  "The one sent by God is going to suffer.
    The leaders of the people
    and the priests and the teachers of the law
    will all reject him, and they will even kill him.
    But after three days,
    he will rise from the dead and will be alive."

Then Jesus said,

  "If you want to be my disciple,
    you must not think only about yourself.
    You must accept the cross, every day,
    and live as I do."

The Gospel of the Lord.

REFLECTING ON THE READINGS WITH CHILDREN:

While this Gospel is important in the on-going formation of children as well as adults, we must be cautious in reflecting on it with small children. *"Accepting one's cross" must be explained in language and concrete examples appropriate to the age of the children.* We want to avoid burdening them with expectations beyond their understanding and capacity to fulfill.

After the Gospel, ask the children what Jesus said about those who want to be his disciples. (You may have to read the last paragraph again.)

- What does Jesus mean when he says his disciples must not think only about themselves?
- How does this help others?
- What does Jesus mean when he says his disciples must live as he lives?
- What does Jesus mean when he says that if we are willing to accept the cross every day, we will be his disciples?

Help the children understand *"accepting the cross" means living for others, living as Jesus wants us to, no matter what.* This can be a real "cross" when living the Gospel actually requires children to make difficult choices in their everyday lives.

THIRTEENTH SUNDAY IN ORDINARY TIME

YEAR C

PRAYER OF THE DAY:

God our leader,
at times we find it hard
to follow you
because so many other things
seem more important.
Help us to do what is right
and choose the things
which will make us happy
with you forever.
We make this prayer to you
through Christ our Lord.

FOCUS OF THE READINGS:

The focus of our readings is call and response. In the first reading, Elisha is called to follow Elijah. The Gospel presents us with the conditions for following Jesus. In both readings, those who are called request time to take care of things at home before following. Elijah grants this request to Elisha. But Jesus responds to his followers by insisting that the response be immediate. Why? What makes these calls different? Note that when Elisha is called, he is called to "replace" Elijah after Elijah dies. There does not seem to be an urgency in this call. But the disciples were not called to replace Jesus or even to follow at some later time. Jesus is the living Lord, always with us. And when he calls, everything else must be given up. True followers are ready to leave everything and follow immediately.

You call us, Lord, to follow you.
Here I am; I come to do your will.

FIRST READING: *1 Kings 19:16b, 19-21*

A reading from the first book of Kings.

God said to the prophet Elijah,

"Go and anoint Elisha.
He is the one
who will take your place as a prophet
when you die."

So Elijah went and found Elisha.
Elisha was working in the fields,
plowing the ground.
As Elijah passed by him,
he threw his cloak onto Elisha's shoulders.
Elisha stopped what he was doing
and ran after Elijah.
When he caught up with him, he said,

"I will come and follow you.
But first let me go
and kiss my father and mother goodbye."

Elijah said,

"Go; I'm not stopping you."

Elisha went and killed the oxen
and prepared a meal for the people
who lived there.
Then he followed Elijah,
and he became his helper.

The Word of the Lord.

RESPONSE: *Psalm 40*

RESPONSE:
Here I am, O my God, I come to do your will.

VERSES:
You have shown your ways to me, to pro-claim your word, and so I say:

GOSPEL ACCLAMATION:

Leader:
All: (sing and clap)

1. We stand to greet your Ho - ly Word:
2. You call us, Lord, to fol - low you:
Al - le - lu - ia, al - le - lu -ia!

GOSPEL: *Luke 9:57-62*

A reading from the Gospel of Luke.

While Jesus and his disciples
were on their way to Jerusalem,
someone came to him and said,

"I will follow you wherever you go."

Jesus answered,

"Foxes have dens to live in
and birds have their nests.
But I have no place that is really my home."

Then Jesus turned to another person and said,

"Come, follow me."

But that person answered,

"Lord, let me go to bury my father."

Jesus said,

"Let others worry about things like that.
You go and tell others
about the Kingdom of God."

Then someone else said to Jesus,

"I will follow you, Lord,
but first I want to say goodbye to my family."

Jesus said,

"Anyone who begins to plow a field,
but keeps looking back,
isn't ready to follow God."

The Gospel of the Lord.

REFLECTING ON THE READINGS WITH CHILDREN:

Jesus' response to the person who wished to wait until his father has died, may seem rather harsh, especially to children. Certainly Jesus is not implying that we should not be concerned about our parents. But since it will not be possible to explain to the children the Semitic teaching technique used here which puts this response into focus, it · would be best not to dwell on it. The reflections might bring out this point.

Jesus' response to the man who said, "I will follow you wherever you go" was "I have no place that is really my home," which does not mean he had no home. It means that he goes from place to place to preach the Good News. *And so the disciple must be ready to go and do whatever is necessary, in everyday life.*

- What does that mean to a child?
- Help them see how they can be ready and willing to follow Jesus.

As always, it is important that the discussion be governed by their age and capabilities.

91

FOURTEENTH SUNDAY IN ORDINARY TIME

YEAR C

PRAYER OF THE DAY:

Telling the whole world
about you, God,
and your Son, Jesus,
is what you are calling us to do.
May we always be unselfish
and never count the cost.
We make this prayer to you
through Christ our Lord.

FOCUS OF THE READINGS:

There does not appear to be a
strong unity between the first
reading and the Gospel this Sunday.
The first reading speaks of the great
joy the people will have when they
return to Jerusalem from their exile.
Isaiah illustrates this joy with the
tender image of God as a mother.
"Just as a mother holds her child on
her lap, so will I hold you." Just as
one sees that the child belongs to its
mother, so everyone will know that
the people of Jerusalem belong
to God.

The Gospel focuses on the
mission of the seventy-two disciples.
Jesus send them out with the
message, "The reign of God has
come." This "sending" is accompanied
by several specific instructions, the
general idea being an attitude of
availability and service.

*Like a mother, God loves us
tenderly.*

FIRST READING: *Isaiah 66:10, 12-14a*

A reading from the prophet Isaiah.

Our God says:

"Rejoice and be glad, people of Jerusalem.
  Be happy, all you who love that city.
  You have been sad, but now rejoice.

"Because, I tell you,
  I will give you peace and riches.
  And everyone will know that I am with you.
  Just as a mother holds her child on her lap,
  I will hold you and take care of you.
  Just as a mother gives comfort to her child,
  I will comfort you.
  Then you will know that I am your God,
  and your heart will be happy."

The Word of the Lord.

RESPONSE: *Psalm 131*

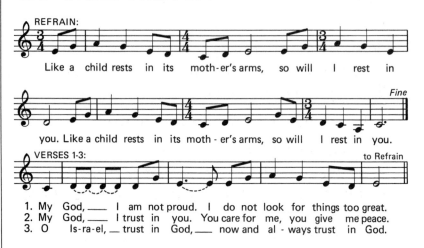

1. My God, ___ I am not proud. I do not look for things too great.
2. My God, ___ I trust in you. You care for me, you give me peace.
3. O Is-ra-el, ___ trust in God, ___ now and al-ways trust in God.

GOSPEL ACCLAMATION:

Leader: All: (sing and clap)

1. *You call us, Lord, to fol - low you:* Al - le-lu - ia, al - le - lu -ia!
2. *You send us, Lord, to speak your Word:* Al - le-lu - ia, al - le - lu -ia!

GOSPEL: *Luke 10:1-9*

A reading from the Gospel of Luke.

Jesus chose seventy-two more disciples.
He sent them, two at a time,
to all the towns and places
he was going to visit later.
Before he sent them out, he said to them,

"There is a big harvest to bring in,
but there are not enough people to do the work.
Pray that God, who is in charge of the harvest,
will send more workers to help.

"When you are traveling,
don't take any money or anything extra.
And don't stop along the way to waste time.
When you go into a house, say,

'May there be peace in this house!'

"If the people there want peace,
your peace will stay with them.
If they don't want it, it will not remain there.
Stay in only one house
instead of moving from house to house.
Eat and drink with the people there,
because if you are working with them,
you deserve to eat with them.

"While you are in a town,
heal the people who are sick and tell everyone,

'The reign of God has come!' "

The Gospel of the Lord.

REFLECTING ON THE READINGS WITH CHILDREN:

Because we have reflected on discipleship for the past two weeks, and will again on future Sundays, today it may be well to focus on the first reading.

Before the first reading, explain to the children that the people were far from their home; they were prisoners of another country. Perhaps examples of hostages, missing children, etc., may help. When they seem to understand why the people were in sorrow, read the first reading.

After the reading, ask the children how they think the people felt when they heard Isaiah's message from God. Perhaps this could be compared to a lost child finding or being found by its mother. Most children will have had the experience of being taken lovingly into their mother's arms. Most children know the joy of being held on their mother's lap.

Help them to see that God, too, is like a mother who holds us, comforts us, and gives us happiness and peace.

93

FIFTEENTH SUNDAY IN ORDINARY TIME

YEAR C

PRAYER OF THE DAY:

Loving God,
your Son, Jesus, lived and died
for all people without exception,
and so gave us an example
of how you want us to live.
See how weak we are.
Give us a share
of the strength of Jesus
so that we may help others,
especially those
who are ignored or forgotten.
We make this prayer to you
through Christ our Lord.

FOCUS OF THE READINGS:

The focus of our readings is total love of God. Both the Old and New Testament present this as a commandment, not an option or just an ideal. One cannot be an authentic believer without following this commandment; it is at the heart of our relationship with God. The reading from Deuteronomy stresses the need to express the commandment in concrete action. The Gospel gives the two-fold commandment: love of God and love of neighbor. Love is not simply a state of mind or feeling, but a way of acting. The point of the parable is not *who* my neighbor is, but am I a real neighbor. "And which of these acted like a neighbor? Now you treat others the same way." The point of the parable is to be a neighbor.

Love God with all your heart. Love your neighbor as yourself.

FIRST READING: *Deuteronomy 30:10-14*

A reading from the book of Deuteronomy.

Moses said to all the people,

"Obey God.
Keep the commandments
which are written in the book of the Law.
Turn to God with all your heart
and with all your soul.
The commandment which I am giving you today
is not too hard for you to keep.
And it isn't far away where you can't reach it.
No, God's Word is very near you.
In fact, it is in your heart.
Therefore, you can know it and live it."

The Word of the Lord.

RESPONSE: *Psalm 119*

With all my heart I turn to you. Teach me your ways, I'll fol-low you.

Your word, O God, is good and true. Help us all to fol-low you.

GOSPEL ACCLAMATION:

1. Love ___ God with all your heart:
2. Love your neigh-bor as your-self:
Al - le-lu - ia, al - le - lu - ia!

GOSPEL: *Luke 10:25-37*

A reading from the Gospel of Luke.

One day a lawyer came to Jesus and asked him,

"Teacher, what do I have to do
so that I will live forever?"

Jesus said,

"What did you read in the Scriptures about that?
What did you learn about it?"

The lawyer said,

"The Scriptures say,

'You must love God with all your heart,
with all your soul, with all your mind,
and with all your strength.
And you must love your neighbor
just as you love yourself.' "

Jesus said,

"Yes, that's right. And if you do that, you will live forever."

Then the lawyer said,

"But who is my neighbor? What does 'neighbor' mean?"

Jesus answered him by telling this story:

"One day a man was going from Jerusalem to Jericho.
On his way, some robbers came along, and they beat him,
stole his things and left him on the ground, almost dead!
After a while a priest came along, but when he saw
the man lying on the ground, he kept going.
Then a man who worked in the Temple came along.
But he also walked away and left the man lying there.
Then a man from Samaria came down that same road.
And when he saw the poor man lying on the ground,
he felt sorry for him and went over to help him.
He cleaned his cuts and put bandages on them.
Then the Samaritan lifted the man onto his donkey
and took him to an inn.
He stayed with him all night and took care of him.
The next day, when the Samaritan was leaving,
he gave some money to the owner of the inn and said,

'Please take care of this man.
If it costs more than what I am giving you,
I will pay you the rest when I come back.' "

Then Jesus asked the lawyer,

"Now, which of these three people
do you think acted like a neighbor
to the man who was beaten and robbed?"

The lawyer said,

"The one who was kind and took care of him."

Jesus said,

"Yes, that's right.
Now go and treat others the same way."

The Gospel of the Lord.

REFLECTING ON THE READINGS
WITH CHILDREN:

Invite the children to retell the
story, bringing in as many details as
possible. Help the children to
visualize the various scenes:
- Jesus and the lawyer,
- the man on the roadside,
- the three passersby,
- the Samaritan and the man,
- the Samaritan and the owner of
  the inn,
- Jesus and the lawyer.

Rather than drawing out the
lesson which the story states so
clearly, perhaps this would be a good
occasion for some children to read or
tell the story, with other children
playing the various characters. If you
wish to prepare this ahead of time,
you may have the parts written out
for them.

SIXTEENTH SUNDAY IN ORDINARY TIME

YEAR C

PRAYER OF THE DAY:

Lord God,
you have spoken to us
through your Son, Jesus,
and we still hear his voice
in the Church.
Help us pay attention
to all he says
because it is only by listening
to his words
and putting them into practice
that we show our love for you.
We make this prayer to you
through Christ our Lord.

FOCUS OF THE READINGS:

It is possible that these two readings were combined in the liturgy because of the attitude of hospitality that is evident in both. But hospitality is not the *primary* focus of either reading.

The focus of the first reading from Genesis is the announcement of the birth of a son, Isaac, to Sarah and Abraham. This annunciation is preceded by a meal graciously prepared by the elderly couple for strangers. It is in the atmosphere of hospitality that their visitors reveal the Word of God to Abraham and Sarah. The psalm response reflects the uprightness of Abraham and Sarah.

The focus of the Gospel reading is listening to God's Word. Martha is busy about many things. Mary, on the other hand, sits at Jesus' feet to listen to his word. The point here is not that doing things for others (as Martha was doing) is not important.

FIRST READING: *Genesis 18:1-10a*

A reading from the book of Genesis.

This is how God appeared to Abraham:

One day as Abraham sat at the door of his tent
during the hottest part of the day,
he saw three men coming along the road.
He ran out to meet them,
bowed down in front of them and said,

"My Lord, if you are pleased with me,
stay for a while.
Let me get some water to wash your feet,
while you rest under this tree.
Then I will bring you some food to eat
before you continue on your journey."

The visitors said,

"Yes, we will stay for a while."

So Abraham ran back to the tent
and said to his wife, Sarah,

"Hurry, get some flour
and make bread for our guests."

Then he ran to the pasture to get a young calf,
and he prepared it for dinner.
When everything was ready,
Abraham took the dinner
he and Sarah had prepared
and gave it to his guests.
And he stayed with them while they ate.

They asked Abraham,

"Where is your wife, Sarah?"

He said,

"She's in the tent."

God said to Abraham,

"I will come again next spring.
By that time Sarah will have a son."

The Word of the Lord.

RESPONSE: *Psalm 15*

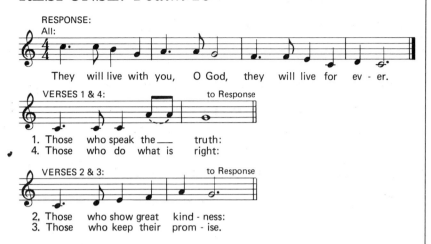

RESPONSE:
All:
They will live with you, O God, they will live for ev - er.

VERSES 1 & 4: *to Response*
1. Those who speak the___ truth:
4. Those who do what is right:

VERSES 2 & 3: *to Response*
2. Those who show great kind - ness:
3. Those who keep their prom - ise.

GOSPEL ACCLAMATION:

1. "You are bless - ed, all you who hear me;
2. Al - le - lu - ia, al - le - lu - ia,

1. you are bless - ed, lis - ten to me."
2. al - le - lu - ia. "Lis - ten to me."

GOSPEL: *Luke 10:38-42*

A reading from the Gospel of Luke.

One day Jesus went to the village of Bethany,
and a woman named Martha
invited him into her home.
Martha had a sister named Mary.
Mary was sitting on the floor
in front of Jesus listening to him,
while Martha was busy
preparing and serving the meal.
Finally, Martha came and said to Jesus,

"Lord, don't you care that my sister has left me
to do all the work by myself?
Tell her to come and help me!"

But Jesus said to her,

"Martha, Martha,
you are letting too many things bother you!
There is only one thing that is really necessary.
Mary has chosen to listen to me,
and that's more important than anything else."

The Gospel of the Lord.

That would contradict the consistent message of the Gospel and especially the Gospel of last Sunday, the Good Samaritan. Since it follows immediately after that story, its central point is one of balance: listening to the Word of God and acting on it.

Jesus says: you are blessed when you listen to me.

REFLECTING ON THE READINGS WITH CHILDREN:

Last week the children heard the story of the Good Samaritan with its concluding exhortation, "Go and treat others the same way!" This Sunday, we invite them to reflect on the source of strength for doing that. Children will be familiar with the necessity of learning the rules before playing a game well, reading or listening carefully to instructions before doing school work well, etc. Help them to see that in order to live as Jesus himself wants us to live, we must listen to him in our heart. We must hear his Word and reflect on it. *Just as we need quiet and time to hear and understand instructions for other things, so we need that in order to live like Jesus.* You might also help the children understand that Jesus is a friend, and that just spending time with him is wonderful. Just to sit quietly in his presence for a while brings us closer to him. *Jesus wants to be with us and to share his thoughts with us.*

SEVENTEENTH SUNDAY IN ORDINARY TIME

YEAR C

PRAYER OF THE DAY:

Father,
since you are always ready
to listen to our prayers,
hear us now
as we ask you to keep us safe
and in peace,
protect all the people we love,
and show special care
for those who are sick,
or who are dying.
We make this prayer to you
through Christ our Lord.

FOCUS OF THE READINGS:

The focus of both of our readings
is prayer. In the first reading we have
the sincere, yet almost amusing
pleading of Abraham for the people
of Sodom and Gomorrah. Two things
are evident here: Abraham is
comfortable in being persistent with
God and God is eager to respond.

The Gospel today presents Luke's
version of the Lord's Prayer, which,
like Abraham's prayer, is basically
one of petition. The second half of
the Gospel is a parable used to show
the effectiveness of persistent
prayer. The emphasis is not on the
seemingly unwilling neighbor, but
the persistence of the one in need.
Jesus concludes his teaching with
the reassurance that we will receive
when we ask for those things which
we truly need and will be for our good.

Ask, seek, knock: you will receive.
I thank you with all my heart, for you
have heard my prayer.

FIRST READING: *Genesis 18:20-32*

A reading from the book of Genesis.

The people who lived in the two cities
of Sodom and Gomorrah had done many evil things.
Their sins were so bad that God was going to punish
everyone who lived there by destroying the cities.

But Abraham said to God,
  "If there are 50 people there who are good,
    will you save the city for the sake of the 50 good people?
    I know you will do what is right."
And God said,
  "I will save the city for the sake of the 50 good people."
Abraham said,
  "If there are 45 good people,
    will you save the city for their sake?"
God said,
  "I will save the city if I find 45 good people."
Then Abraham said,
  "I know I am bold to speak to you this way,
    but, my God, if you find 30 good people,
    will you save the city?"
God said,
  "Yes, I will save the city if I find 30 good people."
Abraham said,
  "O God, please don't be angry with me.
    But, if you find 20 good people there,
    will you save the city for the sake of the 20 good people?"
God said,
  "For the sake of 20 good people I will save the city."
Finally Abraham said,
  "Please God, I will ask only this last time.
    If you find only 10 good people,
    will you still save the city?"
God said,
  "Even for only 10 good people, yes, I will save the city."

The Word of the Lord.

RESPONSE: *Psalm 138*

I thank you, I thank you with all my heart, I thank you.

You my God, you have heard my prayer, so I thank you, I

thank you, with all my heart, I thank you God!

98

GOSPEL ACCLAMATION:

1. "Ask and you will have. Seek and you will find.
2. Al - le - lu - ia! Al - le - lu - ia!

1.-2. Knock and the door will be o - pened to you."

GOSPEL: *Luke 11:1-13*

A reading from the Gospel of Luke.

One day when Jesus was teaching his disciples
about prayer, he said,

["When you pray, pray like this:

'Father, may your name be kept holy,
may your kingdom come.
Give us the food we need each day.
Forgive our sins,
because we forgive anyone who has hurt us.
And keep us from doing what is wrong.' "

Then Jesus said,

"Let me give you an example.]
Suppose you go to a neighbor's house at midnight
and say,

'Please lend me some bread.
A friend of mine has just arrived from a long trip,
and I don't have any food.'

"Now, your neighbor might say to you,

'Don't bother me now!
It's late, the doors are locked, and we are all in bed!'

"But if you keep on asking,
your neighbor will get up after a while
and give you what you want."

Then Jesus said,

"Ask, and you will have what you ask for.
Seek, and you will find what you are looking for.
Knock, and the door will be opened for you.
When children ask for food,
their parents don't give them a stone
or a snake that would hurt them.
No, they give them what is good for them.
In the same way,
God will give the Holy Spirit to anyone who asks."

The Gospel of the Lord.

[ ] *Reader may omit text that appears in brackets.*

REFLECTING ON THE READINGS WITH CHILDREN:

As we reflect on the efficacy of petitionary prayer, we will want to be aware of the possibility that children may see in this a sort of magic. Children tend naturally to ask for material realities—a new bicycle, a fabulous trip, to become a sports star or whatever. Believing that God is the granter of all our demands, of whatever sort, can be devastating to the child's faith.

Help them to see that in the Lord's Prayer, and in the parable, *God invites us to pray for those things which we need and which will lead us to a better life.* Nor do we want, however, to give the children the impression that their desires (a new bicycle, etc.) are unimportant. Those are things we work for and certainly may enjoy. Lead them to see that Jesus tells us to pray for the Holy Spirit. It is the Holy Spirit who will help us know what to pray for.

Nevertheless, this Gospel teaching may not be minimized. We are told, *Ask, Seek, Knock.* This is surely a Sunday to invite the children to pray. Some time should be given to this. Perhaps after each child (or several) offers a petition, all could sing the Gospel Acclamation.

EIGHTEENTH SUNDAY IN ORDINARY TIME

YEAR C

PRAYER OF THE DAY:

God of all goodness,
you know what we truly need,
and you are always ready
to help us.
Teach us to be generous
and share with others
the gifts you shower upon us.
We make this prayer to you
through Christ our Lord.

FOCUS OF THE READINGS:

The focus of both of our readings is the uselessness of life without God, and conversely, that true happiness is found in dependence on God.

The first reading presents a depressing picture of life. Life, for the author of Ecclesiastes, is something of a cruel joke. Without meaning, everything is useless. Even if we try, we can't make things better.

The Gospel puts this into focus. Jesus tells the story of a man who worked hard to provide for himself, with no concern for God or others. It is a classic story of greed, selfishness, and self-sufficiency. The point of the story is, as Ecclesiastes laments, all of that is useless, for "Tonight you will die. And what will become of all your possessions?" In the end, possessions are not what bring happiness. Only God can provide meaning to life.

Help us find our joy in you. Your Word brings us life and sets us free.

FIRST READING: *Ecclesiastes 1:2; 2:20-23*

A reading from the book of Ecclesiastes.

The Preacher said,

"Useless, useless, everything is useless!
For example, there are people
who have worked hard
and used all their knowledge and all their skill,
but they don't enjoy the results
of what they have worked for.
Someone else enjoys them instead.
That's useless and unjust.
What good does all that hard work
do for a person?
People spend their days
doing so much hard work,
and at night they can't sleep.
That too is useless."

The Word of the Lord.

RESPONSE: *Psalm 90*

Fill us with your gift of love. Help us find our joy in you. joy in you.

VERSES:
1. God, our God, ev-er-last - ing, may our hearts al-ways turn to you.
2. God, our God, ev-er-last - ing, bless the work that we do to-day.

GOSPEL ACCLAMATION:

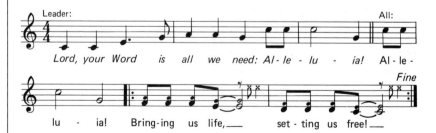

Lord, your Word is all we need: Al-le-lu - ia! Al-le-lu - ia! Bring-ing us life,____ set-ting us free!____

GOSPEL: *Luke 12:13-21*

A reading from the Gospel of Luke.

One day a man said to Jesus,

"Teacher, tell my brother to give me half
of what belonged to our father before he died."

But Jesus said,

"Why should I be the one
to settle an argument about money
between you and your brother?"

Then he said to the people,

"Be careful about being selfish and greedy.
Having a lot of money
isn't what makes you important,
and being rich won't save your life."

Then Jesus told this story,

"There was a very rich man
who had a farm that produced good crops.
He grew so much food
that soon he didn't have enough space
to store it all.
So he said to himself,

'I know what I'll do.
I'll tear down all my barns
and build bigger ones.
Then I can put everything I have in them.
And I will say to myself,

'I have everything I need for years and years.
Now I can take it easy.
I can eat and drink and do whatever I want.'

"But God said to him.

'You are so foolish! Tonight you will die!
And so what will happen to all the things
you saved for yourself?
Who will get them?'

"This is the way it is with people who are selfish
and keep things for themselves
but don't care about God."

The Gospel of the Lord.

REFLECTING ON THE READINGS
WITH CHILDREN:

Unfortunately, many of our
children will have been exposed to
the American work ethic which tells
us, "work hard, and you will
prosper." While this is, perhaps,
humanly true, it carries with it the
danger of self-sufficiency and even
selfishness. The children will also
have been exposed to materialism
and consumerism as the guarantees
of happiness.

In a language appropriate to their
age, the freeing truth of today's
Gospel must be presented. All of
society tells them otherwise. Here, in
Christian liturgy, they deserve the
truth. Children can readily see that
*while possessions are useful, and
even good, they do not, in themselves,
bring lasting happiness.* They have
already experienced the much
wanted toy that no longer amuses
them. Many will have experienced
loneliness even amidst many
belongings.

We will want to keep the focus
clear. Today's Gospel is not a sermon
against wealth, nor even an
exhortation to share. It is the stark
reality that possessions, few or many,
do not bring happiness. *Help the
children see that while having things
seems to make one more important
and powerful in the world, it is not so
with God, nor with those who truly
love God.*

101

NINETEENTH SUNDAY IN ORDINARY TIME

YEAR C

PRAYER OF THE DAY:

Everlasting God,
it is your wish
we should live with you,
even after we die.
May we never forget you,
but always behave in the way
we know pleases you
by loving you and our neighbor
as we love ourselves.
We make this prayer to you
through Christ our Lord.

FOCUS OF THE READINGS:

The focus of our readings is faith. The first reading, from the book of Hebrews, presents Abraham and Sarah as models of faith, hope and trust in God's promise. Abraham's faith was not in where he was going or what he was doing, but in the One who was leading him. Sarah was the first of a series of women to believe that God's promise of a child would be fulfilled. Because of their faith, Abraham and Sarah have become the symbol of the People of God.

The Gospel passage for today encourages us to trust in God for our daily needs. Two weeks ago we focused on the effectiveness of prayer. This Sunday the readings call us to live the faith that causes us to pray. To pray and then worry is to lack faith. Our faith is not in the things we need, but the One who provides. When we seek God first, all other things will follow.

Wherever our treasure is, there will our heart be.

FIRST READING: *Hebrews 11:1-2, 8-12*

A reading from the letter to the Hebrews.

Faith means believing in the things we hope for.
It means being sure of things
even when we cannot see them.
There were people who lived a long time ago
who had strong faith,
and God was pleased with them.

For example,
God asked Abraham to leave his home
and go to a new country far away.
God promised Abraham
that he would find a new home there
and that it would belong to him and to his family.
Because Abraham had faith in God,
he left his home and set out for this new land
which God had promised him.
When Abraham got there,
he and his family lived in tents
like foreigners in a strange place.
But Abraham always hoped and believed
that one day he would live in the city of God,
which would last forever.

And Sarah also had faith in God.
Because she believed what God promised her,
she had a child even though she was too old.

And so, because of the faith of Abraham and Sarah,
God gave them children,
and their family has grown
to be as many as the stars of heaven
and the grains of sand on the seashore.

The Word of the Lord.

RESPONSE: *Psalm 33*

RESPONSE:

Lord, be with us, with your love, be with us, all our hope is in you.

Response music continued on next page.

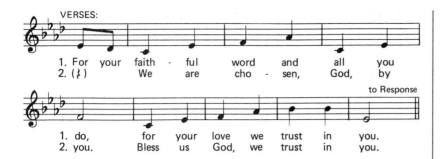

1. For your faith - ful word and all you
2. (𝄽) We are cho - sen, God, by

to Response

1. do, for your love we trust in you.
2. you. Bless us God, we trust in you.

GOSPEL ACCLAMATION:

"Wher - ev - er your treas - ure is, there will your heart be." Al - le - lu - ia!

GOSPEL: *Luke 12:22-24, 27-34*

A reading from the Gospel of Luke.

Jesus said to his disciples,

"Don't worry about the food you need
or the clothes you will wear.
Life is more than what we eat or what we wear.
Look at the birds.
They don't plant seeds or store food in barns.
But God feeds them.
And you are worth much more than birds!
Look at the wild flowers.
They don't make clothes for themselves.
But they are more beautiful
than a king all dressed up in rich clothes.
Now if God takes such good care of the flowers,
you can be sure God will take good care of you.
Have faith! God knows the things you need.
Look first for God's kingdom,
and all the other things you need
will be given to you.
So don't worry about these things.
Share what you have with the poor.
Keep your treasure in heaven
where no thieves or robbers can take it away.
Wherever your treasure is,
that's where your heart will be."

The Gospel of the Lord.

REFLECTING ON THE READINGS
WITH CHILDREN:

Again this Sunday, we want to be careful not to put God over and against the necessities of life. Jesus is not saying that we don't need food, clothing, etc. Nor is he saying that we need not work to earn these things. The comparison with the birds is based, not on need, but on "worry."

Two points may be stressed with the children.

1) We are of more value than birds. God loves us very much and wants us to have what we need to live well and to be happy. We can never stress enough with children (or adults!) how much God loves us and cares for us. Our failure, sometimes, to believe this may be an indication that we are seeking the wrong things.

2) We guard with our heart whatever is important to us. Wherever our treasure is, that's where our heart is.

TWENTIETH SUNDAY IN ORDINARY TIME

YEAR C

PRAYER OF THE DAY:

God of heaven and earth,
it is not easy to live
in the way you want us to.
Without your help
it is impossible.
We pray to you now
to help and support us,
and one day take us
to your home
where you live
forever and ever.

FOCUS OF THE READINGS:

Both of our readings tell us that those who proclaim the truth often suffer for it.

Jeremiah presented a very unpopular message—the city of Jerusalem would be destroyed because the people were unfaithful. It was not just their sinfulness, but their unwillingness to repent and change their lives. Jeremiah was constantly put in the position of choosing between being faithful to his mission and risking his life, or denying God's call and saving his own life.

The Gospel focuses on our acceptance of Jesus and his teaching. But this is not a passive acceptance, we are to witness to it without being ashamed of it. For the faithful Christian, as for Jeremiah, that will surely mean "taking up our cross." Jesus tells us that when we are willing to give up our life, we actually save it—he will take us with him to be with God.

Take up your cross and follow me. I will proclaim your power and your salvation.

FIRST READING: *Jeremiah 38:4-6, 8-10*

A reading from the prophet Jeremiah.

Some people who worked for King Zedekiah said to him,

"Jeremiah is telling our people
new things about God.
Our soldiers don't want to fight anymore
because of what he says.
The people listen to him,
and then they are confused.
He is not trying to help our people;
he is trying to hurt them!
Let us kill him."

The king said,

"Do whatever you want with him."

So they took Jeremiah out to the courtyard,
tied him with ropes,
and lowered him into a deep cistern.
There wasn't any water in the cistern, just mud,
and Jeremiah sank down into it.
Later, someone else who worked for the king went to him and said,

"King Zedekiah, it was wrong of those men
to throw the prophet Jeremiah into the cistern.
He will die of hunger in there."

So the king said,

"Take three people from here to help you.
Go and pull Jeremiah out of the cistern
before he dies."

The Word of the Lord.

RESPONSE: *Psalm 30*

GOSPEL ACCLAMATION:

1. "If you would be my dis-ci-ples, ac-cept the cross and fol-low me."
2. Al - le - lu - ia, al - le - lu - ia, "Ac-cept the cross and fol-low me."

GOSPEL: *Luke 9:23-26*

A reading from the Gospel of Luke.

Jesus said to the people,

"If you want to be my disciple,
you must not be selfish.
You must accept the cross, every day,
and live as I do.
If you try to save your own life,
you will lose it.
But, if you are willing
to give up your life for me,
you will save your life.

"What good is it if you have everything
you want in the world,
but you do not go to heaven?
For if you are ashamed of me
and what I teach you,
I will not take you with me
to be with God and the angels."

The Gospel of the Lord.

REFLECTING ON THE READINGS
WITH CHILDREN:

Draw from the children
experiences that they have had.
Many children will have already
experienced being punished for being
faithful to a friend. And it is not
uncommon for children to tell the
truth and not to be believed.
Children also have a great capacity to
put others first. All of these are
qualities that develop into the
mature attitudes demanded in
today's Gospel. *Help the children see
that "accepting the cross" and "not
being ashamed of Jesus and his
teachings" need not mean only the*
grave matter of life and death. Most
of us are not faced with those
situations. This Gospel *is lived out in
the classroom, on the ball field, in our
families, our treatment of others on a
daily basis.*

TWENTY-FIRST SUNDAY IN ORDINARY TIME

YEAR C

PRAYER OF THE DAY:

God, you love all people,
the small as well as the great,
the powerless
as well as the powerful.
Keep us faithful to you,
even in things
which seem unimportant,
so we can show
how we love you
with all of our lives.
We make this prayer to you
through Christ our Lord.

FOCUS OF THE READINGS:

The focus of both readings is universality. In the first reading, we have the prophecy that God will gather people from all over the world. Not only the Israelites, but all people will know and praise God.

The Gospel appears to contradict itself. First, Jesus says that the door to heaven is narrow, and his parable seems to indicate "getting in" will not be easy. But the passage goes on to say that people will come from everywhere and sit at the table of God's kingdom.

In fact, these are not contradictory. All people are invited to the Kingdom, without reference to race or nationality (or assumed importance). But all people must enter through Jesus, the door. There are no guarantees for "card carrying members." We are saved by believing in Jesus and being faithful to his ways.

All people will know and praise you. I am the door; come in by me.

FIRST READING: *Isaiah 66:18-19*

A reading from the prophet Isaiah.

Our God says:

"I am going to gather people
   from all over the world.
People of every country and language will come.
They will see my glory and will know me.
Then I will send some of them to other nations
   so they can tell other people who I am
   and what I have done,
   so that they, too, will see my glory
   and will know me."

The Word of the Lord.

RESPONSE: *Psalm 96*

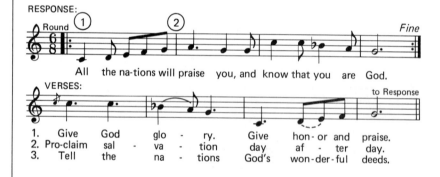

GOSPEL ACCLAMATION:

106

GOSPEL: *Luke 13:22-30*

A reading from the Gospel of Luke.

While Jesus was on his way to Jerusalem,
he stopped to teach the people
in the little towns and villages along the way.
One day someone asked him this question:

"Lord, will many people be saved or only a few?"

Jesus said,

"Work hard to do what is right.
  The door is narrow,
  but you can only come in through that door.
  Many people will try to enter heaven
  by some other way."

Then Jesus told them this parable:

"Suppose the owner of a house
  has locked the door,
  and you come later and say,

    'Open the door and let us in.'

"The owner will not open the door, but will say,

  'I don't know where you come from.'

"Then you will say,

  'But we live here. You've seen us before.
  You even taught some of our people.'

"And the owner will say,

  'No, I really don't know you!
  You only do evil things. Leave me alone!'

"Then you will be very sad and miserable
  because you will see that others
  like Abraham, Isaac, and all the prophets
  are in the kingdom of God,
  and you are left out.
  People will come from everywhere,
  and they will sit at God's table.
  The people who are the most important now
  will be the least important.
  And the people who are the least important now
  will be the most important in the Kingdom of God."

The Gospel of the Lord.

REFLECTING ON THE READINGS
WITH CHILDREN:

Our reflections with the children
should highlight two points:

1) *God does not have favorite
people. God loves all people equally
and invites everyone to the Kingdom
of Heaven.* It is important that the
children really understand this. We
live in a world that makes so many
distinctions based on race,
nationality, education, sex, money
and power. Explore this with the
children. How does our world make
some people seem better than
others? Help them see that God is
not like that.

2) Jesus demands that we truly
believe in him and live by his ways.

*Today's Gospel calls all of us to
accept all people, as Jesus did. It is
through Jesus that we are saved.*

TWENTY-SECOND SUNDAY IN ORDINARY TIME

YEAR C

PRAYER OF THE DAY:

God, we are full of joy
because you care for us,
in spite of all our faults.
Stay close to us;
fill us with your life,
for without you we are nothing.
We make this prayer to you
through Christ our Lord.

FOCUS OF THE READINGS:

Both of our readings focus on humility, not as a passive virtue, but rather one which causes us to act toward others as God does.

The first reading tells us that God is pleased with people who are humble. Notice that importance and humility are not opposites here. All are called to gentleness and humility.

The Gospel reading consists of two parables. The first one focuses on our relationship with God. The "special dinner" referred to is the banquet in the heavenly kingdom. We do not enter because of our own importance or position. We are called there, freely, by God. At that banquet, the humble are honored by God. "My friend, come and sit by me."

The second parable focuses on our relationship with others. Because God invites us freely to the "special dinner," we, too, must do the same with others. Just as we have nothing to offer God in return for this invitation, we must be kind to those who seemingly cannot offer us anything in return.

If you are humble, God will reward you.

FIRST READING: *Sirach 3:17-19*

A reading from the book of Sirach.

My children, listen to my words.
Always be gentle.
Do everything with gentleness,
and good people will love you.
Always be humble.
The more important you are,
the more humble you must be.
For God, who is very powerful,
is pleased with people who are humble.

The Word of the Lord.

RESPONSE: *Psalm 131*

REFRAIN:
Like a child rests in its mother's arms, so will I rest in you. Like a child rests in its mother's arms, so will I rest in you. *Fine*

VERSES 1-3: *to Refrain*
1. My God, ___ I am not proud. I do not look for things too great.
2. My God, ___ I trust in you. You care for me, you give me peace.
3. O Is-ra-el, ___ trust in God, ___ now and al-ways trust in God.

GOSPEL ACCLAMATION:

1. If you are hum-ble, God will re-ward you.
2. Al - le - lu - ia, al - le - lu - ia!

1.-2. If you are hum-ble, you will be blessed.

GOSPEL: *Luke 14:1, 7-14*

A reading from the Gospel of Luke.

One day Jesus was invited to dinner
at the home of a very important Pharisee.
When Jesus saw that the people who were invited
chose to sit in the special places of honor
at the table, he said to them,

"When you are invited to a special dinner,
   don't sit in a place of honor right away.
   That place might be reserved for someone else.
   Then you will have to move,
   and you will be embarrassed.
   No, sit in the least important place.
   Then the person who invited you might say,

   'My friend, come and sit by me.'

"Then you will feel honored.
   If you try to make yourself great and important,
   you will be humbled.
   But if you are truly humble,
   God will honor you and make you great."

Then Jesus said to the man who had invited him,

"When you give a special dinner or party,
   don't invite only your friends and relatives,
   and don't invite only rich people.
   Those people will invite you
   to come to dinner in their homes too.
   No, instead, when you have
   a special dinner or party,
   invite people who are poor or crippled or blind.
   Those people won't be able to pay you back
   by inviting you to dinner at their homes.
   But God will bless you
   and reward you for being so kind.

The Gospel of the Lord.

REFLECTING ON THE READINGS
WITH CHILDREN:

The second parable may be more
easily understood by the children.
Ask them what Jesus said in the
parable. Invite them to share what
this might mean in their lives.
Children already have the experience
of giving and attending parties, of
inviting and being invited, of being
included and left out. Recall for them
last Sunday's readings that assure us
that "God does not have favorite
people." It is important that the
children not take this to mean they
should not have special friends or
that their family is not more special
to them than others. Help them to
put this into focus. God does not
exclude people.

Secondly, help them understand
the meaning of the virtue of
humility. Biblically, to be humble
means to know ourselves as children
of God, to count all other people as
no less important or more important
than ourselves. And ultimately, it
means to know our need for God. We
are not on our own for salvation—
God is our creator and Savior.

TWENTY-THIRD SUNDAY IN ORDINARY TIME

YEAR C

PRAYER OF THE DAY:

God of mercy,
Jesus showed us how much
you really love us
by dying on the cross
for our sake.
Give us the generosity
to follow him
and spend our lives
helping other people.
We make this prayer to you
through Christ our Lord.

FOCUS OF THE READINGS:

There is not a unifying focus between the first reading and the Gospel. The reading from Wisdom focuses on "How can I know the will of God?" Humanly speaking, it is impossible. It is the presence of God's Spirit that teaches us discernment.

The passage for today's Gospel is part of Luke's teachings on the cost of discipleship. The focus is again the need to be ready to give up everything to follow Jesus. The parable of the builder tells us that living as a disciple is not a haphazard adventure. We must consciously make decisions about how we will act. Discipleship is a choice, and it requires daily decisions.

FIRST READING: *Wisdom 9:13, 16-18*

A reading from the book of Wisdom.

Who can really understand God completely?
Who can really understand
what God thinks or what God does?

Sometimes we don't even understand
what happens here on earth,
so how can we understand the things of heaven?

But you, our God,
have given your Holy Spirit to us.
You have given us your gift of wisdom
so that we can understand
what you want us to do.
With your Spirit,
we can know what pleases you.

The Word of the Lord.

RESPONSE: *Psalm 90*

Fill us with your gift of love. Help us find our joy in you. joy in you.

1. God, our God, ev-er-last - ing, may our hearts al - ways turn to you.
2. God, our God, ev-er-last - ing, help us know what to do to - day.

GOSPEL ACCLAMATION:

1. "If you would be my dis-ci-ples, ac-cept the cross and fol-low me."
2. Al - le - lu - ia, al - le - lu - ia, "Ac-cept the cross and fol-low me."

GOSPEL: *Luke 14:25-30, 33*

A reading from the Gospel of Luke.

One day, when a large group of people
was listening to Jesus,
he said to them,

"If you want to be my disciple,
you must love me more than anyone.
You must love me even more
than you love yourself.
If you really want to be my disciple,
you must be willing
to carry your cross and follow me."

Then Jesus gave them this example:

"Suppose you want to build something.
The first thing you would do is sit down
and think about what you need to build it
and how much it will cost.
Then you would see
if you have enough money to pay for it.
For if you don't plan before you start,
you might get only part of it built
and not be able to finish it.
And people will say how foolish you are
because you weren't able to finish
what you started.

"So, you must be willing
to give up everything you have
if you want to be my disciple."

The Gospel of the Lord.

REFLECTING ON THE READINGS
WITH CHILDREN:

You will notice that we have
excluded the lines of the Gospel that
suggest that the true disciple must
hate the members of his or her
family. Clearly this is not the
teaching of Jesus, but a technique
familiar to his audience which
carried the meaning, as we have
adapted it, "we must love him more
than anyone." It is a question of
being ready to choose him over all
things and all people.

Since that concept, in itself
difficult for children, has already been
discussed recently, it may be well to
concentrate on the parable itself.

- Help them to recall the example
  Jesus gave.
- What other examples can they
  think of?
    —Making a trip?
    —Planning a dinner?
- Help them to relate this to our
  following of Jesus. Here, too, we
  must think about what we are
  doing and make our own
  decisions based on being faithful
  to his ways. Anything that
  doesn't correspond to his ways
  must be given up, willingly.

TWENTY-FOURTH SUNDAY IN ORDINARY TIME

YEAR C

PRAYER OF THE DAY:

Forgiving God,
Jesus died
to wash away our sins.
We are sorry for all the wrong
we have done,
and we promise,
with your help,
to love you even more.
We make this prayer to you
through Christ our Lord.

FOCUS OF THE READINGS:

Both of our readings focus on the mercy of God. In the first reading, Moses pleads for his people, appealing to God's love already manifest in bringing the people out of Egypt and making a covenant with them. He acts as mediator between his people and God.

The Gospel tells us that God, imaged by the shepherd and the woman, seeks out those who are lost and rejoices at their finding.

Both readings reveal a God who loves us and wants to save us. We cannot save/find ourselves. Moses declares, "It was *you* who saved them." And Luke gives us two lovely parables in which God (the shepherd) seeks the lost sheep and rejoices when it is found. And it is God (the woman) who will not rest until the coin is found and rejoices when she finds it!

"Come and celebrate! The lost has been found!" God's loving mercy is always with us.

FIRST READING: *Exodus 32:7-11, 13-14*

A reading from the book of Exodus.

God said to Moses,

"Go and talk to your people,
for they have turned away from me.
They have made an animal out of metal,
and they are telling the people that it is a god.
Now they are worshipping that animal,
made out of metal, instead of me."

Then God said,

"These people are very stubborn.
And now I am angry,
and I am going to punish them for their sins."

Moses prayed for the people. He said to God,

"But these are good people.
It was you who saved them
by taking them out of Egypt.
You made a covenant with Abraham
and promised him that his people would be great
and would live in the land you would give them.
So don't be angry with your people now."

So God decided not to punish them.

The Word of the Lord.

RESPONSE: *Psalm 51*

In your kind-ness, O my God, have mer-cy on me, have mer-cy on me.

1. I know___ that I have sinned and done what is wrong.
2. O God___ for-give my sins and make my heart true.

GOSPEL ACCLAMATION:

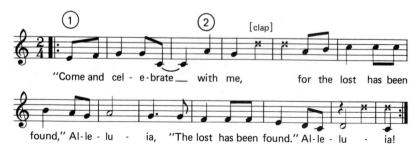

"Come and cel - e-brate___ with me, for the lost has been found," Al-le - lu - ia, "The lost has been found." Al-le - lu - ia!

112

GOSPEL: *Luke 15:1-10*

A reading from the Gospel of Luke.

When dishonest tax collectors and sinners
came to listen to Jesus,
the Pharisees and other leaders were angry. They said,

"This man, Jesus, talks to people who are sinners,
and he even eats with them!"

So Jesus told them these two parables.

"Suppose you had a hundred sheep,
and one of them got lost.
Wouldn't you leave the ninety-nine sheep
that were safe and go looking
for the one sheep that was lost?
And when you found it,
you would pick it up and carry it home.
You would be so happy
that you would call your friends and neighbors
and say,

'Come and celebrate with me
because I have found my sheep that was lost!'

"Well, God is just like that!
And everyone in heaven will rejoice
when even one person stops sinning
and comes back to God."

Then Jesus said,

"Now suppose a woman had ten very special silver coins,
and she lost one of them in the house.
Wouldn't she turn on all the lights
and sweep every room in the house
until she found the coin?
And when she found it, she would be so happy
that she would call her friends and neighbors and say,

'Come and celebrate with me
because I have found the coin that I lost!'

"Well, God is just like that!
And everyone in heaven will rejoice
when even one person stops sinning
and comes back to God."

The Gospel of the Lord.

REFLECTING ON THE READINGS
WITH CHILDREN:

After the first reading, the
question of Moses' mediation is
probably too complex to discuss
meaningfully with the children.
What is important is God's quickness
to forgive. Help the children see that
the people, in worshipping a metal
animal (golden calf) was a way of
truly denying God. They turned away
from God who had done so much for
them. We sometimes forget about
God and make other things more
important. *Yet God is always ready
to forgive.*

After the Gospel: Help the
children enter into the parable.
- Who do you think the "lost
  sheep" might be?
- Who do you think the
  shepherd is?
- Why did he rejoice?
- Who do you think the "lost
  coin" might be?
- Who do you think the woman is?
- Why did she rejoice?

Then help them see that *God sent
Jesus to look for those who were lost*,
those who had turned away from
God or did not even know God. *Jesus
still looks for us when we turn away
from God, and he rejoices when we
are found.*

113

TWENTY-FIFTH SUNDAY IN ORDINARY TIME

YEAR C

PRAYER OF THE DAY:

God,
make us faithful to you
in the small things as well as
the big things of life.
Do not let us pick and choose
when to be good,
but let us do and say
everything to please you.
We make this prayer to you
through Christ our Lord.

FOCUS OF THE READINGS:

Both of our readings focus on the sin of greed. In the first reading, Amos, the prophet of social justice, has harsh words for those who, through greed, cheat the poor. In this passage we hear God's judgment on those who exploit the poor. "I will not forget what you have done."

The Gospel too presents us with the claims of God or money. The focus here is not on money itself, but how it is acquired and how it is used. The concluding line, "You cannot serve God and money at the same time," summarizes the teaching which speaks of honesty and trust in our dealings.

Wherever your treasure is, there will your heart be. God loves the poor and needy.

FIRST READING: *Amos 8:4-7*

A reading from the prophet Amos.

Amos said to the people,

"Listen to me,
you people who don't care about the poor,
you who oppress them.
When they buy your grain,
you lie about the price,
and you cheat them out of their money.
You make the poor pay more than they should.
But God says to you,

'I see your sins,
and I will not forget what you have done!'"

The Word of the Lord.

RESPONSE: *Psalm 113*

```
RESPONSE:
1. You love the poor,      you love the need-y.___
2. Teach us to love        the poor and need-y,___

1. You give them help,     you care for them.
2. to give them help,      to care for them.
```

GOSPEL ACCLAMATION:

Leader:

Lord, your Word is all we need: Al - le - lu - ia! Al - le -

All:

Fine

lu - ia! Bring-ing us life,___ set - ting us free! ___

GOSPEL: *Luke 16:10-13*

A reading from the Gospel of Luke.

Jesus said to his disciples,

"People who can be trusted with things
   that are not important
   can also be trusted with things
   that are important.
People who are not honest about little things
   are not honest about big things either.
If you cannot be trusted
   with the things in the world,
   how can you be trusted
   with the things God gives you?

"You know that people cannot work
   for two bosses at the same time.
They will always care more
   about one than the other
   and will work harder for one than the other.

"And it's the same with you.
   You cannot serve God and money
   at the same time."

The Gospel of the Lord.

REFLECTING ON THE READINGS WITH CHILDREN:

The last line of the first reading seems unlike the God of loving kindness and mercy. Last week we focused on God's readiness to forgive, yet this week we hear, "I will not forget." Help the children see that God's anger is because the poor are being treated unjustly. God loves all people and will not tolerate the rich hurting the poor, then or now. Assure the children that the prophets preach like this to warn the people to change their ways. God is always ready to forgive when we change.

While we want to avoid moralizing with children, readings like today's demand that we look at our lives and ask ourselves honest questions. We can do this gently with the children. Jesus says that people who are not honest about little things are not honest about big things either!

- Am I honest about little things? What are some examples of "little things"?
- Can others trust me?

What does Jesus mean when he says, "You cannot serve God and money"?

Help the children realize that having money is not wrong. "Serving money"—getting it in the wrong way and using it in the wrong way, being selfish with it—that's wrong.

115

TWENTY-SIXTH SUNDAY IN ORDINARY TIME

YEAR C

PRAYER OF THE DAY:

God, full of tenderness,
you look with special pity
on people
who are poor and weak.
We, too, want to help those
who cannot help themselves.
Make us able to recognize them,
and give us a share
in your power
so that we can make their lives
easier and happier.
We make this prayer to you
through Christ our Lord.

FOCUS OF THE READINGS:

Both of our readings focus again this week on the evil of greed. And again this week, the first reading comes from the prophet Amos, who always calls us to justice, sometimes in rather harsh words. The focus here is not on having wealth, but again on the attitude one has toward it. Notice that the wealth of the people is coupled with a selfish attitude.

"You eat only the best; you live only to be amused. You have everything; you don't care about the nation."

The Gospel, too, focuses on greed and the misuse of goods. We have the same theme here as last week's first reading, the neglect of the poor by the rich. The rich man refused the basic needs of Lazarus, a poor beggar, whom he saw daily before his door. Again, the judgment seems harsh, but, as we saw last week, God will not

FIRST READING: *Amos 6:1a, 4-7*

A reading from the prophet Amos.

Amos said to the people,

"Be careful,
 you who have everything you want now!
 Some day you are going to lose it all.

"Be careful, you who have the best of everything,
 you who take life so easy,
 you who eat only the most expensive food,
 you who live only to have a good time.

"You have everything,
 but you don't care
 that your nation is being destroyed.

"But you also will be destroyed.
 Your enemies will take you first,
 and all your expensive things
 and your easy life will be lost!"

The Word of the Lord.

RESPONSE: *Psalm 113*

1. You love the poor, you love the need-y.___
2. Teach us to love the poor and need-y,___

1. You give them help, you care for them.
2. to give them help, to care for them.

GOSPEL ACCLAMATION:

"Wher-ev-er your treas-ure is, there will your heart be." Al-le-lu-ia!

GOSPEL: *Luke 16:19-31*

A reading from the Gospel of Luke.

Jesus told this story to the Pharisees:
  "Once there was a rich man
    who always wore the best and most expensive clothes.
    And he always ate the best and most expensive food.
    There was also a very poor man named Lazarus.
    He was so poor that he used to sit
    outside the rich man's house and beg for food.
    He was even happy to eat the scraps
    from the rich man's dinner.
    This poor man, Lazarus, had sores on his skin,
    and the dogs used to come and lick them.
  "When Lazarus died,
    the angels took him to be with Abraham in heaven,
    and Abraham welcomed him and took him in his arms.
    Later, the rich man died.
    But he went to a place called Hell,
    a place of great suffering.
    When he saw Abraham far off, and Lazarus with him,
    he called out,
      'Abraham, have pity on me.
      Send Lazarus to come and bring me some cool water
      because I am suffering terribly.'
  "But Abraham answered,
      'Remember that when you were on earth,
      you had everything you wanted.
      You had the best of everything,
      and poor Lazarus had nothing.
      Now he is very happy, and you are suffering.
      'But it is a long way between where you are,
      and where we are,
      and no one can cross from one side to the other.'
  "Then the rich man said,
      'Then please send Lazarus to warn my five brothers
      so that they won't come to this same place
      and suffer like me.'
  "Abraham answered,
      'Your brothers can read
      what Moses and the prophets wrote.
      They should learn from them.'
  "But the rich man said,
      'No, Abraham! They won't listen to them.
      But if someone who had died
      came back to them and warned them,
      then they would pay attention,
      and they would change their lives and stop sinning.'
  "Finally Abraham said,
      'No, if they won't listen to Moses and the prophets,
      they won't even listen to someone
      who comes back from the dead.' "

The Gospel of the Lord.

tolerate the exploitation of the poor.

Wherever your treasure is, there will your heart be. God loves the poor and needy.

REFLECTING ON THE READINGS WITH CHILDREN:

After the first reading, ask the children questions like:
- Why was the prophet Amos angry with the people?
- How did they use their money?

It will help if the children realize that there were many poor people living in Jerusalem at the time Amos was writing. He was angry because people who said they believed in God did not care about the poor and did not share with them.

After the Gospel, ask the children to recall the Gospel.
- Who are the people involved?
- Why is the rich man unhappy? What does he ask?
- How does Abraham answer him?

Help the children see that God loves the poor and want us to share with them now. How can we do that? Do we know people who are poor or who are in need? Can we help? While concrete action is the genuine response to the needs of the poor, we must be careful to discuss this within the limits of little children. They are not responsible for the miseries of the world. But the Gospel invites us to examine our attitudes about the poor and about sharing. Guide the children along those lines.

117

TWENTY-SEVENTH SUNDAY IN ORDINARY TIME

YEAR C

PRAYER OF THE DAY:

Dear God,
we believe in you
and in Jesus, who died for us,
and in the Holy Spirit,
who makes us able
to carry on your work.
Sometimes it is not easy
to believe,
and we lose courage.
Be with us always;
strengthen us by your Spirit,
that our faith may turn
the whole world to you.
We make this prayer to you
through Christ our Lord.

FOCUS OF THE READINGS:

The focus of both of our readings is faith. In the first reading, the prophet sets up the question of faith, then gives God's answer, "Be patient." We see from the context that this "patience" means faith. Those who have been evil, having a lack of faith, will fall. But those with faith will live. The message is clear—keep faith even in the midst of adverse conditions.

The parable of the mustard seed, so familiar to us, is a dramatic description of the power of faith. The contrast between the tiny seed and the power of the action (changing the location of a tree!) puts into sharp focus the faith that we are capable of having and which the Lord proposes as the norm. But faith is a gift, and so

FIRST READING: *Habakkuk 1:2-3; 2:2-4*

A reading from the prophet Habakkuk.

Habakkuk made this prayer to God:

"Dear God,
I have been crying for help for so long.
Why haven't you heard me?
There is so much violence all around me.
Won't you save me?"

And God said to Habakkuk,

"Your prayers will be answered.
The peace you want will come.
It may seem to you that it is coming too slowly.
But, be patient, wait for it.
It will come.
And then, those who have been evil will fall,
but those who have had faith will live."

The Word of the Lord.

RESPONSE: *Psalm 95*

RESPONSE:
(Leader) 1. Lis-ten to the voice of God, o-pen your hearts__ and lis-ten.
(All) 2. We will hear the voice of God, o-pen our hearts__ and lis-ten.

VERSES:
to Response
1. God, you made ev-'ry-thing. You take care of all you made.
2. God, you made us as well. You, our Shep-herd, we, your sheep.

GOSPEL ACCLAMATION:

Al - le - lu - ia, al - le - lu - ia. Al - le - lu - ia, al - le - lu - ia!

*VERSE:

Plant your Word in our hearts. Let it bear fruit in us!

*Keep singing Alleluia line. Add the verse with a solo or small group.

GOSPEL: *Luke 17:5-6*

A reading from the Gospel of Luke.

One day the disciples said to Jesus,

"Help us to believe more.
  Make our faith stronger."

Jesus said to them,

"If your faith were only the size of a tiny seed,
  like a mustard seed,
  you would be able to say to this tree,

  'Pull yourself up out of the ground,
    and plant yourself in the ocean,'

  and the tree would do it!"

The Gospel of the Lord.

we must pray for it, "Make our faith stronger."

Plant your word in our hearts. We will open our hearts and listen.

REFLECTING ON THE READINGS WITH CHILDREN:

In reflecting on this Gospel, two dangers must be avoided:
- A wonder woman or superman approach to faith.
- Minimizing the parable as a harmless figure of speech.

Help the children see that our lives and the lives around us can be different if we live by faith. Explore the parable with the children. Explain to them that Jesus often used nature to teach us. Also, Jesus often used big contrasts to "wake us up." Changing the location of trees is not what Jesus is talking about. He is talking about changing the hearts and lives of people.
- What will we accomplish by using our faith?
- How do people with faith in Jesus live?
- How does that change our world?

You might end the reflections with time for all to pray that our faith be made stronger.

TWENTY-EIGHTH SUNDAY IN ORDINARY TIME

YEAR C

PRAYER OF THE DAY:

Loving God,
you have showered upon us
so many good things
that we cannot count them.
May we never forget
all you have done for us,
and let us always thank you
for your great goodness.
We make this prayer to you
through Christ our Lord.

FOCUS OF THE READINGS:

Both of our readings have three features:

1) The dreaded disease of leprosy, for which there was no cure, and which excluded one from the community, is miraculously cured.

2) Both Naaman, as well as the leper who returned to Jesus, were foreigners, that is, outside of Judaism. Thus we see here the salvation of God reaching out beyond the confines of Israel.

3) Both of these foreigners expressed gratitude and began immediately to worship the true God. This is in striking contrast to the "other nine" who were already within the fold. We see here the spontaneous gratitude of those who receive the gift of God unexpectedly.

We have tried to combine these features in our psalm response and Gospel acclamation.

You are healed because you believe. All the nations will know you and praise you.

FIRST READING: *2 Kings 5:1-5, 10, 14-15, 17b*

A reading from the second book of Kings.

There was in Syria a man called Naaman
who was the chief in the King's army.
Naaman had suffered for many years with leprosy.
When he heard about the prophet Elisha,
he went to ask the prophet to cure him.
Elisha told him to go to the Jordan River
and dip himself in the water seven times,
and he would be cured of his leprosy.

So Naaman went and dipped himself
seven times in the Jordan River.
And when he came out of the water,
he was cured of his leprosy.

Naaman went back to Elisha, the man of God,
and said to him,

"Now I am sure
that your God is the only true God.
From now on
I am going to serve the God of Israel."

The Word of the Lord.

RESPONSE: *Psalm 96*

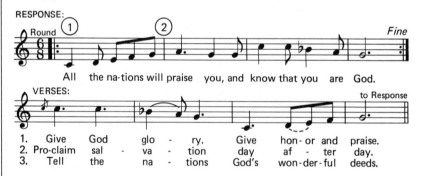

All the nations will praise you, and know that you are God.

VERSES:
1. Give God glo - ry. Give hon - or and praise.
2. Pro-claim sal - va - tion day af - ter day.
3. Tell the na - tions God's won-der-ful deeds.

GOSPEL ACCLAMATION:

"You are healed be - cause you be - lieve." Al - le -
lu - ia, al - le - lu - ia! lu - ia, al - le - lu - ia!

GOSPEL: *Luke 17:11-19*

A reading from the Gospel of Luke.

As Jesus was on his way to Jerusalem,
he walked along the border
between Galilee and Samaria.
When he came into a little town,
he saw ten people who had leprosy.
They stayed back a little way from Jesus,
but they yelled to him,

"Jesus, please have pity on us. Help us."

When Jesus saw them, he said,

"Go and show yourselves to the priests."

As they went on their way,
they were all cured of their leprosy.
One of the ten,
as soon as he saw that he was cured,
ran back to Jesus.
All the way back, he was shouting praises to God.

When he got to Jesus,
he knelt down in front of him
and thanked him for healing him.
Now, this man was a foreigner, a Samaritan.
Jesus said,

"Weren't all ten people healed?
Where are the other nine?
Why has only one person
come back to thank God?
And this man is a foreigner!"

Then Jesus said to the man who came back,

"Get up! You may go now.
You have been healed because you believe."

The Gospel of the Lord.

REFLECTING ON THE READINGS WITH CHILDREN:

Before the readings, tell the children a little about leprosy. Untreated, it consists of open sores on the skin, often resulting in disfiguration. Because it is contagious, lepers were not allowed to live inside the towns and villages. They were completely rejected by the people.

After the first reading, ask the children to recall the story.

- Who was the man with leprosy?
- What was his job?
- Why did he go to the prophet Elisha?
- What did Elisha tell him to do?
- What else do we know about the Jordan River?
- What did Naaman do after he was cured?

After the Gospel, again ask the children to recall the story.

- Where was Jesus going?
- Whom did Jesus meet on the way?
- What did they do and ask?
- What did Jesus tell them to do?

(It was the role of the priest to verify whether or not a person had leprosy. Since they would be cured on the way, the priest would find them "clean.")

- How many lepers were cured?
- How many came back to thank Jesus? Who was he?
- What did Jesus say to him?

Remind the children that both Naaman and the Samaritan gave thanks and praise to God for healing them. We want always to be grateful for the things God does for us. Usually God does things for us through other people. We want always to say, "Thank you." Being thankful is a way of worshipping God.

You might also tell the children that leprosy exists today, but that it is treated with medicine. Many people with leprosy (now called Hansen's disease) live normal lives.

121

TWENTY-NINTH SUNDAY IN ORDINARY TIME

YEAR C

PRAYER OF THE DAY:

God,
our defender and our guide,
you are always anxious
to hear our prayers.
Bring us more and more
to realize
how much we need you,
and may we
never stop praising you
for all you have done
in our world.
We make this prayer to you
through Christ our Lord.

FOCUS OF THE READINGS:

Our first reading from Timothy focuses on the need to be persistent in preaching the Word of God. The Bible is the heart of our tradition and teaches us the great truths that we must remain faithful to even in difficult times.

The Gospel reading also focuses on persistence, but this time in prayer. The passage for today is a parable. Thus, the characters should not be taken as representatives of God and the faithful. The focus is *not* that we can twist the arm of an unwilling God, but simply that persistence in prayer puts us in touch with God and opens us to the ways of God. In this sense we receive the gifts of God.

Ask, seek, knock: you will receive.
My God, I will always hope in you.

FIRST READING: *2 Timothy 3:14-17; 4:1-2*

A reading from Paul's second letter to Timothy.

Always be true to what you were taught
and what you believe.
Ever since you were a child,
you learned what is written in the Bible.
The Bible helps you understand
and believe that Jesus is our Savior.
God inspired people to write the Bible
to teach everyone to do what is right and good.

Now, in the presence of God and Jesus Christ,
I tell you: Preach God's Word!
Keep on teaching the truth even when it is hard.
Never give up.

The Word of the Lord.

RESPONSE: *Psalm 71*

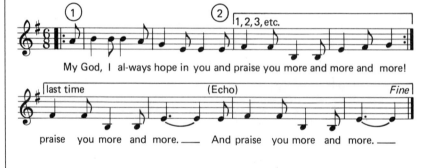

My God, I al-ways hope in you and praise you more and more and more!

praise you more and more. And praise you more and more.

GOSPEL ACCLAMATION:

1. "Ask and you will have. Seek and you will find.
2. Al - le - lu - ia! Al - le - lu - ia!

1.-2. Knock and the door will be o - pened to you."

GOSPEL: *Luke 18:1-8*

A reading from the Gospel of Luke.

Jesus wanted to teach his disciples
that they should always pray and never give up.
So he told them this story:

"Once there was a judge
who lived in a certain town.
Now this man didn't believe in God,
and he didn't care about people either.
There was a woman, who was a widow,
living in the same town.
She kept going to the judge and saying,

'I am being treated unfairly!
Do something about it. Help me!'

"For a while the judge didn't do anything.
But finally he thought,

'Even though I don't care about God or people,
I will help this woman
so she will stop bothering me.
If I don't help her, she'll never leave me alone,
and I'm tired of her coming here.' "

Then Jesus said,

"Pay attention to what this bad judge said!
Now think about this:
If people pray to God every day,
won't God, who is good, answer their prayers?
Will God refuse for a while, like this bad judge?
No, God will answer their prayers right away!
Now I ask you, when I come again,
will I find people who believe like this?"

The Gospel of the Lord.

REFLECTING ON THE READINGS
WITH CHILDREN:

As we have had occasion to reflect
on the need for prayer on previous
Sundays, we suggest you reflect with
the children on the Bible. Perhaps
you will want to reread the first
reading. Explain to the children that
Timothy was a young man when Paul
met him. Paul taught Timothy and
later prepared him to be a leader in
the Church. Now he is encouraging
Timothy to remain faithful to what
he learned and to preach the Word
of God.

- Explain that the Bible has two
  main parts, the Old Testament
  which tells the story of God's
  people before Jesus, and the
  New Testament which tells the
  life of Jesus and the Church.
- The Bible is God's Word.
  People, over many years, wrote
  down what God did and what
  God said. They wrote the story
  of how God acted in their lives.
  The Bible also has God's
  messages for us in the prophets.
- In the New Testament we read
  about the things Jesus did and
  said. When we read the Bible,
  we see God's great love for us,
  and we want to live as Jesus did.
- The Bible is really lots of books
  put together, like a library: for
  example, the Book of Isaiah, the
  Book of Samuel. There are lots
  of different kinds of books:
  stories, letters, Gospels, history
  books, prayers, etc.

You may wish to end by encouraging
the children to spend time reading
the Bible.

THIRTIETH SUNDAY IN ORDINARY TIME

YEAR C

PRAYER OF THE DAY:

God, though your Son, Jesus,
is equal to you in everything,
he became a servant
that our sins might be forgiven.
Made strong by your Spirit,
we want to imitate him,
to serve others,
especially those
who cannot help themselves,
and show the world
what sort of people
you want us all to be.
We make this prayer to you
through Christ our Lord.

FOCUS OF THE READINGS:

Both of our readings focus on humility. Humility, in the biblical sense, has little to do with the self abandonment and near rejection of the ego which has sometimes characterized the teaching of this virtue. Biblical humility is to see oneself honestly before God. We are not worthless, evil beings, we are created by God, each one precious. Humility means to see ourselves as neither better nor worse than others and to see ourselves as dependent on God our Creator, Reedemer and life-giving Spirit.

It is in this sense that our readings praise the humble. In the first reading, we hear that God does not have favorites, yet listens especially to those who are in need and to the humble. It is only those who know their need for God who truly pray.

The Gospel reading focuses on the

FIRST READING: *Sirach 35:12c-14, 16-18b*

A reading from the book of Sirach.

God treats everyone fairly.
With God, everyone is important,
not just some people.
God does not have favorites,
but he listens to those
who have been treated unjustly.
God hears the prayers of people in need,
like children who have no parents,
and wives whose husbands have died.
God listens to all people who serve others,
and God listens to those who are humble.

The Word of the Lord.

RESPONSE: *Psalm 113*

GOSPEL ACCLAMATION:

GOSPEL: *Luke 18:9-14*

A reading from the Gospel of Luke.

There were some people
who thought they were better
than other people
and that God was more pleased with them.
So Jesus told them this story:

"Two people went into the Temple to pray.
One of them was a Pharisee,
and the other one was a tax collector.
The Pharisee prayed like this:

'O God, I thank you
that I am better than other people.
I don't steal; I'm not unjust;
I don't do bad things against my wife.
And I'm not sinful
like that tax collector over there.
I fast twice each week,
and I even give ten percent of all my money
to the Temple.'

"But the tax collector stood
way in the back of the Temple.
He wouldn't even look up to heaven.
He bowed his head and prayed,

'My God, I am a sinner. Have mercy on me.' "

Jesus said,

"I tell you,
it was the tax collector who was right with God,
not the Pharisee.
For people who think they are important
and better than others will be humbled.
But people who are truly humble
and honest about themselves
will be honored and praised by God."

The Gospel of the Lord.

same. The Pharisee, in his self righteousness, was not truly praying. He was, rather, presenting his life of virtues to God. The publican, on the other hand, knew he needed God's grace to become righteous. And because he prayed, "he was right with God."

God is the strength of those who are humble.

REFLECTING ON THE READINGS WITH CHILDREN:

Ask the children to recall the Gospel story. Explain to them the meaning of the words "Pharisee" and "publican."

- Was the Pharisee really praying to God? What was he doing?

Help the children see that the Pharisee probably did live a good life. But he saw himself as "better than other people."

- What did the publican pray?
- What did he ask God for?
- What was God's response?

Three points should be explained:

1) Though the story is about a Pharisee and a publican, it is a story about all of us, today.

2) As is clearly stated in the first reading, God does not have favorites. We are created and loved by God.

3) Humility means to know we need God. God rewards the humble, because it is the humble who pray for God's help.

THIRTY-FIRST SUNDAY IN ORDINARY TIME

YEAR C

PRAYER OF THE DAY:

Loving God,
you want nothing better
than for us
to turn back to you,
away from our wrongdoing.
Help us to see the times
we do not obey
your commandments
and be ready promptly
to put right those things
our sins have damaged.
We make this prayer to you
through Christ our Lord.

FOCUS OF THE READINGS:

Both of our readings focus on the forgiveness of God. The first reading, from Wisdom, is a prayer for mercy, based on God's love for all created beings. The God who created us cannot reject us!

The Gospel presents the appealing story of Zacchaeus, the "little man" whose life was changed by an encounter with Jesus. The focus of the reading comes as the conclusion: "I came to find and save people who are lost." We see no indication in the story that Zacchaeus had any initial faith in Jesus. Perhaps it was only out of curiosity that he climbed the sycamore tree to see him. The encounter is initiated by Jesus. We have here an example of Jesus' consistent identification with sinners and the power of that identification for conversion. The identification is often expressed by Jesus eating in the home of sinners, a gesture

FIRST READING: *Wisdom 11:22-24; 12:2*

A reading from the book of Wisdom.

O God, the world is only a small part
of all that you have created.
It is like a tiny grain of sand.
And yet you love each one of us,
and you show mercy to everyone.
You help us change our hearts and lives,
and you forget about our sins.
You are the One
who made all things and all people,
and you love them all.
Your living spirit is in everyone.
Because you love us,
you correct our faults little by little,
so that we will turn to you, our God.

The Word of the Lord.

RESPONSE: *Psalm 51*

RESPONSE:

Give me a new heart, O God. Put your Spir-it in me. Keep me

with you, give me joy. Give me a new heart, O God.

GOSPEL ACCLAMATION:

1. Je - sus said: "Zac - che - us come down for I
2. Al - le - lu - ia, al - le - lu - ia! "For I

1. want to stay with you." 2. want to stay with you."

GOSPEL: *Luke 19:1-10*

A reading from the Gospel of Luke.

Jesus was going through the city of Jericho,
and many people came out to see him.
There was a man there named Zacchaeus
who was the head of all the tax collectors
and was very rich.
Zacchaeus also wanted to see Jesus
and find out who he was.
But Zacchaeus was a very short man
and couldn't see Jesus through the crowd,
so he ran ahead
and climbed into a sycamore tree
and waited for Jesus to pass.

When Jesus came to that place,
he looked up and said,

"Zacchaeus, come down! Hurry!
I want to stay at your house today!"

Zacchaeus was so excited that he hurried down
and welcomed Jesus into his home.
The people who saw this were angry and said,

"Look, this man, Jesus,
is staying in the home of a sinner!"

But Zacchaeus said to Jesus,

"Lord, I am going to give
half of everything I have to the poor.
And if I have ever cheated anyone out of money,
I am going to pay them back
four times as much."

Then Jesus said to Zacchaeus,

"Today you have been saved
because you, too,
are one of the family of Abraham.
For I have come to seek
and to save the people who are lost."

The Gospel of the Lord.

detestable to the Pharisees of his time.

*In kindness and mercy, Jesus said,
"Zacchaeus come down, for I want to
stay with you."*

REFLECTING ON THE READINGS
WITH CHILDREN:

This Gospel story will almost
always appeal to children (and adults
as well!). There is a light heartedness
to it that makes the encounter
between Zacchaeus and Jesus the
sort of occurrence we naturally want
to applaud to show our joy.

Invite the children to recall and
visualize. Help them to imagine
the scene:
- The crowds.
- Jesus and those with him.
- Zacchaeus scurrying along,
  looking for an open space, and
  finally running to climb the
  sycamore tree.

Ask the children:
- What might the crowd have
  been like?
- Why did everyone want to see
  Jesus?
- Who was Zacchaeus?
- Why did Jesus and Zacchaeus
  meet? (It is important that the
  children see that Jesus spoke
  first to a sinner. Jesus sought
  him out.)
- What did Jesus say to
  Zacchaeus? (Emphasize that he
  ate in Zacchaeus' house.)
- How did Zacchaeus respond?

Two points should be emphasized:

1) Jesus came to look for sinners
so he could save them.

2) When we truly meet Jesus, we
change our lives.

THIRTY-SECOND SUNDAY IN ORDINARY TIME

YEAR C

PRAYER OF THE DAY:

God,
you call everyone
to live with you forever.
Make strong our belief in Jesus,
the first one
to rise from the dead,
so that we may continue doing
what he wishes
and follow him
to your home in heaven.
We make this prayer to you
through Christ our Lord.

FOCUS OF THE READINGS:

Both of our readings focus on the resurrection of the dead. The first reading recounts the martyrdom of seven brothers and their mother. Each, in turn, suffered cruel tortures (we have chosen to omit the details in the adaptation for the children) for refusing to disobey God's law. In this passage we have one of the few references to a belief in eternal life found in the Old Testament. Within Judaism, there were those (the Pharisees) who believed in the Resurrection and those (Sadducees) who did not, but rarely is this mentioned in the Old Testament. But here, the seven brothers, along with their mother, proclaim that God will raise them up and give them life.

The Gospel also focuses on the resurrection of the dead. Jewish law required a man to marry the childless wife of his dead brother. This was to assure the procreation of the family. The Sadducees pose a

FIRST READING: *2 Maccabees 7:1, 14*

A reading from the second book of Maccabees.

At one time there were seven brothers
who were put into jail
because they followed the Jewish laws.
And their mother was also put into jail.
While they were in prison,
the King tried to make them eat pork,
which is against the Jewish law.
They were whipped and had to suffer
because they would not disobey God's law.
All seven were killed
because they remained honest and faithful.
One of them said, just before they killed him,

   "We are sure that God will raise us to life again.
      But because you are evil,
      you will not be raised to life."

The Word of the Lord.

RESPONSE: *Psalm 27*

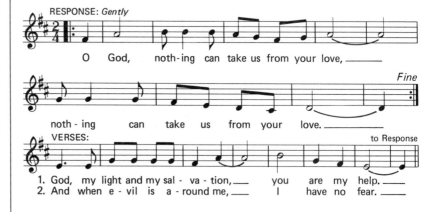

RESPONSE: *Gently*

O God, noth-ing can take us from your love, _____

noth-ing can take us from your love. _____ *Fine*

VERSES: to Response

1. God, my light and my sal-va-tion, ___ you are my help. ___
2. And when e-vil is a-round me, ___ I have no fear. ___

GOSPEL ACCLAMATION:

Your Word is a-live and it lives in our hearts. Al-le-lu-ia to God for the Word in our hearts.

GOSPEL: *Luke 20:27-28a, 34-38*

A reading from the Gospel of Luke.

There were some people, called Sadducees,
who came to Jesus
and asked him a tricky question.
(They asked him what marriage
would be like in heaven.)
Jesus said to them,

> "Eternal life is not like life here.
> In heaven, people don't get married
> like they do here on earth.
> People who are worthy to live forever
> will be like angels.
> They will be true children of God
> and will never die anymore."

(Jesus knew that they asked this question
because they didn't believe
that people will rise after death and live forever.)
So Jesus said,

> "You don't believe people can live after death.
> But even Moses proved they do.
> When he wrote about the burning bush,
> he called God 'the God of Abraham,
> the God of Isaac, and the God of Jacob.'
> Now God is the God of living people,
> not of dead people.
> Everyone is alive for God."

The Gospel of the Lord.

question which pushes this law to its limit. If seven brothers, each in turn, marry the wife of their eldest brother, whose wife will she be in the resurrection? Their intention is to discredit, as nonsense, the notion of the resurrection. But Jesus seizes the opportunity to teach that eternal life is altogether different from this life. In doing so, he affirms the resurrection of the dead.

Nothing can take us from your love. You bring us life and set us free.

REFLECTING ON THE READINGS WITH CHILDREN:

We often come to a reflection on eternal life when faced with life threatening situations or the death of someone close to us. For many children, the context for this sort of faith experience has not presented itself. Secondly, at their age, death seems impossible. Therefore, the question of faith in the resurrection is of little value at this point. Children repeat, as belief, what significant adults present as truth.

Perhaps it would be well to leave them with two thoughts.

1) Sometimes people are made to suffer, and even die, for being faithful to what they believe. You might explain the word "martyr" and its place in our tradition. But, when faced with hard times, we know that nothing can take us from God's love. God will be faithful.

2) Heaven (eternal life) is completely different from life here and now. We don't know what it will be like, but we know *we will be free* from all harm *and will live with God forever.*

THIRTY-THIRD SUNDAY IN ORDINARY TIME

YEAR C

PRAYER OF THE DAY:

God,
you support us
in good times and in bad.
Protect us
when we are laughed at
for following Jesus.
Help us say and do
the right things,
so that through us
other people may come
to believe in your Son
and make this world
a place of love and of peace.
We make this prayer to you
through Christ our Lord.

FOCUS OF THE READINGS:

Our readings focus on fidelity. The first reading, from the prophet Malachi, draws a clear distinction between good and evil, reward and punishment. For the prophet the end is clear—those who remain true, who worship God, will be saved.

The Gospel passage deals with the end time. As we come to the end of the liturgical year, the liturgy takes us back to the question of the First Sunday of Advent, "When will the end of the world come?" Here, Jesus warns that before the end comes, Christians will be tested and tempted by false prophets and antichristian forces. But, as our response to the first reading affirms, nothing can take us from God's love. Jesus echoes

FIRST READING: *Malachi 3:19-20a*

A reading from the prophet Malachi.

Our God says,

"The time is coming when people who do evil
and who think they are better than others
will be punished.
They will suffer for the evil they have done.
But it will be different for those of you
who worship me.
You will have justice and healing."

The Word of the Lord.

RESPONSE: *Psalm 27*

GOSPEL ACCLAMATION:

GOSPEL: *Luke 21:7-19*

A reading from the Gospel of Luke.

Some of the disciples asked Jesus
when the end of the world would come.
Jesus said to them,

"Before the end comes,
lots of things will happen.
People will come and claim to be me.
They will say,

'I am the Christ.
The time for the end of the world is here.'

"But don't believe them and don't follow them.
And when you hear about wars and riots,
don't be afraid.
Lots of awful things will happen on earth.

"People will hate you
because you believe in me and follow me.
They will put you in jail
and accuse you of doing wrong.
Then you can show them
how strong your faith is
by telling them about me.
Don't worry about what to say.
I will give you all the wisdom
and the words you need,
so you will say the right things,
and no one will be able to say you are wrong.
Nothing and no one can hurt you.
You will be saved because you believe in me
and have stayed faithful to me."

The Gospel of the Lord.

that here, "Don't worry, I will give
you the wisdom and words you
need." He assures his disciples,

*You will be saved, for you believe
in me. You will be saved because you
stayed with me.*

REFLECTING ON THE READINGS
WITH CHILDREN:

Invite the children to reflect on
the human virtue of fidelity. You
might ask them what qualities they
look for in a true friend. You might
set up some role-playing examples in
which a friend must choose whether
or not to be faithful. Ask the children
to discuss the pros and cons. The
point here is not to put the children
to the test, but to help them see that
fidelity requires choice. The ultimate
question is "how would you want a
true friend to respond?" Jesus wants
us to remain faithful as his true
friends. And he promises to help us
when we are faced with difficulty in
remaining faithful.

The children themselves will be
able to supply examples of when they
must choose to be faithful. They will
frequently couch this in language of
"good and bad," "being honest or
lying," etc. While the reading refers
to apostasy or martyrdom, the life
experiences of little children are real
for their age. Help them develop a
sense of fidelity which will serve
them well in serious matters later.

CHRIST THE KING
YEAR C

PRAYER OF THE DAY:
God of heaven and earth,
you have made Jesus
ruler of all you have created.
Today, we give ourselves
to him once again.
He is our leader,
our shepherd, our guide.
With the power of your Spirit
to make us strong,
we will follow Jesus
to his home with you,
where he lives and reigns
forever and ever.

FOCUS OF THE READINGS:

Both of our readings focus on
Kingship. The first reading presents
one of the many accounts of David's
ascension as King of Israel. The focus
of this account is to show David as
"Shepherd King," clearly acclaimed
by his own people.

The Gospel comes from Luke's
passion narrative. It was chosen,
undoubtably, because of its emphasis
on the Kingship of Jesus.

The dramatic juxtaposition of
Jesus' death and Kingship pulls our
faith to its limits. Like David, Jesus
is recognized as King by his own
people. But his people are not to be
found in a political or geographical
reality. Throughout Luke's Gospel,
from the Infancy Narratives forward,
his people are the sinners, the
outcasts. As the others mock, it is the
criminal, the social outcast, the
abandoned, who knows his need for
God, who recognizes Jesus as King.
"When you come into your kingdom,

FIRST READING: *2 Samuel 5:1-3*

A reading from the second book of Samuel.

The people of Israel came to David and said,

"When Saul was our king,
    you were the one who helped us.
And God said to you,

    'You will be the shepherd of my people,
    and you will be their leader.' "

So that day
David made a covenant with the people,
and they anointed him as King of Israel.

The Word of the Lord.

RESPONSE/GOSPEL ACCLAMATION:
Psalm 47

RESPONSE:
To you, great King of all the earth: sing al - le - lu - ia, sing! To
you, our Lord, our God and King: sing al - le - lu - ia, sing!

GOSPEL: *Luke 23:35-47*

A reading from the Gospel of Luke.

Jesus was hanging on the cross.

The people who were there watching
made fun of him, saying,

"He saved other people.
If he is truly the Christ, God's chosen one,
let him save himself."

The soldiers also made fun of him and said,

"If you are the king of the Jews, save yourself."

At the top of his cross, there was a sign which said,

"This is the King of the Jews."

One of the criminals yelled at him,

"Aren't you the Christ?
Then save yourself and save us too!"

But the other criminal scolded him,
and then said to Jesus,

"Jesus, when you come into your kingdom,
remember me."

Jesus said to him,

"I promise you,
today you will be with me in Paradise."

It was now about noon,
and the sun stopped shining,
and it was dark until about
three o'clock in the afternoon.
Then Jesus cried out loud,

"Father, take my life. I give you my spirit."

And he died.
One of the Roman soldiers who saw all of this
began to praise God,
and he said,

"Surely, this was a great and good man."

The Gospel of the Lord.

remember me." And for those of us
who know ourselves . . .

He is our Lord, our God and King.

REFLECTING ON THE READINGS
WITH CHILDREN:

After the first reading, ask the
children to recall what other name
the people used for David besides
King. What does the term Shepherd
imply? Why do you think the people
called David both Shepherd and King?

After the Gospel, ask the children
what kind of king Jesus is. Do you
ever use the word Shepherd when we
speak of Jesus? Who is the one
person in this Gospel who asked
Jesus for help? What did he ask?
What did Jesus say?

Help the children see that Jesus
wants to be our King, a shepherd
King, who cares for us and will take
care of us if we let him reign in
our hearts.

Holy Days,
Feasts of the Lord,
and
Solemnities

PRESENTATION OF THE LORD

YEAR C

PRAYER OF THE DAY:

O God,
you have shown
such love for us.
You sent
your only Son, Jesus,
to save us.
You have given us great joy.
You have given us Light,
through Jesus Christ,
your Son.

FOCUS OF THE READINGS:

The focus of our readings is God's presence in the temple, the one to be adored. In the first reading, the prophet Malachi tells us that God will send a messenger to prepare for the one to come. The Lord of the covenant is coming to the temple and will call all people to change their lives. Christian tradition has seen in this prophecy the persons of John the Baptist and Jesus.

The Gospel recounts the day that Mary and Joseph present Jesus in the temple. There, in the temple, he is recognized by both Simeon and Anna as the fulfillment of God's promise. He is the Savior of the Israelites and the Gentiles as well. But the Gospel also forewarns that this Savior will suffer and will be a sign of contradiction among his own people.

Jesus is the Light and Savior of the world.

FIRST READING: *Malachi 3:1-4*

A reading from the prophet Malachi.

Our God says:

"See, I am sending my messenger
 to prepare the way for me.
The One you are waiting for is coming.
The Lord of the covenant
is coming to the temple
 and will call everyone to change their lives
 and do what is right.
Then the people will make offerings
 that are pleasing to me,
 just as they did long ago."

The Word of the Lord.

RESPONSE: *Psalm 24*

O - pen the gates! O - pen the gates! Let the King of glo-ry in!

GOSPEL ACCLAMATION:

"I have seen the Sav - ior, the light of the world. I have seen the Sav - ior," Al - le - lu - ia!

GOSPEL: *Luke 2:22, 24-25, 27-36, 38-40*

A reading from the Gospel of Luke.

Mary and Joseph brought Jesus
to the temple in Jerusalem
to present him to God
and to make an offering of two turtle doves.
That same day,
a man named Simeon came to the temple.
He was a good and holy man
and was waiting for the Messiah to come.
When Simeon saw the child, Jesus,
he took him in his arms and praised God
and said,

"Now, God, you have kept your promise.
  I have seen the Savior.
  He is the light of the Gentiles,
  and the glory of your people Israel."

[Jesus' mother and father were amazed
at what Simeon said about him.
Then Simeon blessed them and said to Mary,
Jesus' mother,

"This child will be a sign
  for all the people of Israel.
  Some people will accept him and be saved.
  Others will reject him.
  And in your heart
  you will suffer because of this."]

There was also a holy woman,
a prophetess named Anna,
who was in the temple.
When she saw the child,
she, too, began to praise God.
And she talked about him to everyone
who was waiting for the Messiah to come.

Mary and Joseph went back to Nazareth.
And the child, Jesus, grew in size and strength.
He was filled with the wisdom and grace of God.

The Gospel of the Lord.

[ ] *Reader may omit text that appears in brackets.*

REFLECTING ON THE READINGS
WITH CHILDREN:

Explain to the children that it was
customary to take the first child
(son) to the temple to be consecrated
to God. Since this rite was specific to
the first male child only, we will not
want to compare it to Christian
baptism. This was a Jewish ceremony
which included a rite of purification
and the offering of a sacrifice. In this
case, the offering was two turtledoves,
the offering of the poor.

Two points might be emphasized
in today's Gospel.

1) Simeon, the holy man,
recognized Jesus as the Light and
Savior of the world. *He is our Light
and our Savior.* Help the children
understand what this means in our
everyday lives.

• How is Jesus our Light?
• How is Jesus our Savior?

Remind the children that we
often use a candle as a symbol
of Christ:

• Easter candle,
• a baptism candle,
• an altar candle,
• a sanctuary lamp.

2) Anna, the prophetess, "talked
about him to everyone who was
waiting for the Messiah." Many
people today are waiting for a sign of
hope, for help, for light, for salvation.
Can we talk to them about Jesus?
*Can we, like Anna, tell others the
Good News of Jesus?*

BIRTH OF JOHN THE BAPTIST

YEAR C

PRAYER OF THE DAY:

O God,
you are with us every day.
Each one of us
has been given special gifts.
John the Baptist
was chosen
to preach to the people.
Help each of us
to see our gifts
and to use them
to spread your Good News
through Jesus Christ,
your Son.

FOCUS OF THE READINGS:

Our readings focus on the call of the disciples.

The first reading is one of four passages in Isaiah referred to as "Songs of the Servant." The church has normally seen these passages fulfilled in Christ. Today, this second servant song is applied to John the Baptist. The reasons are obvious. The prophet was called and named before birth. God fills him with strength and honor, and his mission is to preach.

The Gospel picks up these themes with the birth of John the Baptist. Even before the child is born, his name, John, has been determined. He lived in the desert where God filled him with strength and holiness to preach to the people, announcing the coming of the Messiah, the light.

FIRST READING: *Isaiah 49:1, 3, 5-6*

A reading from the prophet Isaiah.

This is what the prophet Isaiah said:

"Listen to me, people everywhere!
God chose me even before I was born.
When I was still in my mother's body,
God gave me my name.
God's hand is always upon me
to give me strength.
And I am honored in God's eyes.

God said to me,

'You are my servant.
You are the one
who will lead my people back to me.
And I will make you a light to all people
so that they may be saved.' "

The Word of the Lord.

RESPONSE: *Psalm 71*

GOSPEL ACCLAMATION:

GOSPEL: *Luke 1:57-66, 80*

A reading from the Gospel of Luke.

When it was time
for Elizabeth to have her child,
she gave birth to a son,
and her neighbors and relatives
rejoiced with her.
When the baby was eight days old,
they came to circumcise him.
The people wanted to call him Zechariah
because that was his father's name.
But Elizabeth, his mother, said,

"No, his name will be John."

The people said,

"But no one in your family is called John."

So they asked his father, Zechariah,
what he wanted to name the baby.
Zechariah asked them
for something to write on, and he wrote,

"His name is John."

And immediately after this,
Zechariah could talk again,
and he began to praise God.
Everyone who heard about this
wondered what it all meant.
They were talking about it
all over the hill country of Judea
where Elizabeth and Zechariah lived.
The people asked themselves,

"What is this child going to be
when he grows up?"

John grew and became strong and holy.
And he lived in the desert
until it was time for him
to preach to the people.

The Gospel of the Lord.

REFLECTING ON THE READINGS
WITH CHILDREN:

Before the Gospel, tell the children
we are going to hear the story about
the birth of John the Baptist.

- Does anyone know the name of
  his parents?
- What do you know (remember)
  about Elizabeth? about
  Zechariah?

If the children do not know the
background of these two, tell them,
so that the Gospel for today will
make sense.

- Zechariah was a priest who lost
  his speech because he didn't
  believe the message of the angel.
- Zechariah and Elizabeth were
  old and had no children.

After the Gospel, recall the story.
If the children have difficulty
verbalizing it, ask questions that will
help them.

- Why do we celebrate the feast of
  John the Baptist?
- What do you know about John
  the Baptist?
- Where did he live?
- What did he preach about?
- What did he do? Where?
- Who is the special person John
  baptized?

God did a very special thing for
Zechariah and Elizabeth. But the
birth of John the Baptist is special
for us too.

- What do you think makes this
  feast so special?
- What do you want to remember
  from today's celebrations?

139

SS PETER AND PAUL, APOSTLES

YEAR C

PRAYER OF THE DAY:

You are our rock,
O God.
We know you are there
when we need you.
Help us to learn
from the strength
of Peter and Paul.
Let us never forget
your love.
We ask this
through your Son,
Jesus Christ.

FOCUS OF THE READINGS:

The readings focus on the special mission of two of the greatest leaders of the church. The first reading is somewhat of a farewell discourse. Paul seems certain that, having gone the limit, he will be killed for the faith. As he approaches his martyrdom, Paul is confident and even joyful. The Gospel gives us the beginning of Peter's ministry. Having professed faith in the person of Christ, he is assured of the permanence of the church and his role in it.

FIRST READING: *2 Timothy 4:6-8, 17-18*

A reading from Paul's second letter to Timothy.

I am sure that I am going to be killed,
because I preach about Jesus.
I have done my best in the race,
and I have stayed faithful.
So I know that the Lord will give me a crown
on that special day when he comes back.
He will reward everyone who loves him
and stays faithful.
The Lord has always been with me
and made me strong
so that I could proclaim the Word of God
to people everywhere.
The Lord has always helped me,
and he will save me from every evil
and keep me safe for heaven.
May everyone give praise and glory to the Lord,
forever and ever. Amen.

The Word of the Lord.

RESPONSE: *Psalm 71*

RESPONSE:
I will pro-claim your pow - er. I will pro-claim your won-der-ful deeds! I will pro-claim sal - va - tion, and your faith - ful love! ___

GOSPEL ACCLAMATION:

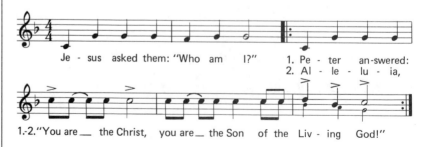

Je - sus asked them: "Who am I?" 1. Pe - ter an-swered: 2. Al - le - lu - ia,
1.-2. "You are ___ the Christ, you are ___ the Son of the Liv - ing God!"

GOSPEL: *Matthew 16:13-19*

A reading from the Gospel of Matthew.

When Jesus and his disciples
were in the area of Caesarea Philippi,
he asked his disciples,

"Who do people think I am?"

They said,

"Some people think you are John the Baptist,
and others think you are the prophet Elijah.
But there are others
who say you are Jeremiah
or some other prophet."

Jesus asked them,

"And who do you say I am?"

Simon Peter answered,

"You are the Christ.
You are the Son of the living God."

Jesus said,

"Simon, you are blessed.
You did not learn that
from any human being.
No, God told you that.
From now on you will be called Peter,
which means rock.
I will build my Church on this rock,
and it will be strong.
Nothing will be able to destroy it.
I will give you the keys
to the kingdom of heaven,
so that what you decide on earth
will be the same in heaven."

The Gospel of the Lord.

REFLECTING ON THE READINGS
WITH CHILDREN:

Since the Gospel reading appears
elsewhere in the Sunday readings
(Twenty-First Sunday in Ordinary
Time/Year A), it would seem
appropriate today to concentrate on
the two men themselves. Peter and
Paul stand out among the saints, and
even the apostles, as two giants of
the early church. Their common
feast has been celebrated in the
church since the year 258.

There are several books for
children which contain the lives of
Peter and Paul which may be useful
for presenting the highlights of their
lives. We will want to avoid,
however, pictures and stories which
do not correspond to the Biblical
presentation. For example, many
books for both children and adults
show pictures of Paul falling from a
horse on the road to Damascus.
There is no indication in any of the
several accounts of Paul's conversion
which suggests that. The accounts
of their lives should focus on reality
and the great contribution of these
two men.

THE TRANSFIGURATION OF THE LORD

YEAR C

PRAYER OF THE DAY:

O God in heaven,
you have given us
the greatest gift of all.
You sent Jesus
to live with us
and to show us how to love.
We will listen, God.
We will do our best for you
and your Son, Jesus,
our Lord.

FOCUS OF THE READINGS:

In each cycle, the Gospel account of the Transfiguration is the same as the Gospel reading for the Second Sunday of Lent. We suggest you use the reflections for that Sunday. We reprint them here for your convenience.

FIRST READING: *2 Peter 1:16-19*

A reading from the second letter of Peter.

Brothers and sisters,

When we told you about the power of the Lord,
Jesus Christ, and how he would come again,
we were not just telling you interesting stories
that someone made up.
No, we saw the majesty of Jesus.
We were with Jesus on the holy mountain
when God showed how special Jesus is,
and we heard the voice of God saying,

  "This is my beloved Son.
   I am very pleased with him."

We are sure now
that what the prophets said a long time ago
is true.
You should listen very carefully
to what they said
because it is like a lamp shining in a dark place
until the daylight comes.

The Word of the Lord.

RESPONSE/ GOSPEL ACCLAMATION: *2 Peter 1:17*

A voice from heav-en said,___ "This is my be-lov-ed Son."___
___ Al - le - lu - ia. Al - le - lu - ia. ___ Al - le - lu - ia. Al - le - lu -
ia.___ Al - le - lu - ia. Al - le - lu - ia. Al - le - lu - ia.

GOSPEL: *Luke 9:28-36a*

A reading from the Gospel of Luke.

One day, Jesus took Peter, James, and John,
and went up on a mountain to pray.
While Jesus was praying,
his face changed,
and his clothes became shining white.
Then Moses and Elijah were there with Jesus,
and they, too, were shining in glory.
They were talking with Jesus
about how he was going to die in Jerusalem.

Peter, James and John had fallen asleep.
When they woke up,
they saw Jesus shining in glory,
and they saw the two men with them.
As Moses and Elijah were leaving,
Peter said to Jesus,

"Master, it's good for us to be here!
Let us make three tents:
one for you, one for Moses,
and one for Elijah."

Peter was so confused by what was happening
that he didn't know what he was saying.
As he was speaking,
the shadow of a cloud came over them.
When it was all around them,
they became frightened.
Then a voice came from the cloud saying,

"This is my Son, my chosen one.
Listen to him."

After the voice had spoken,
they saw only Jesus standing there.

The Gospel of the Lord.

REFLECTING ON THE READINGS
WITH CHILDREN:

While heeding the call of God can be understood by children, the notion of being killed for the faith may not serve as a suitable model of response.

Ask the children to recall what they heard. If they have difficulty recalling, you may wish to help them with questions such as:

- Who did Jesus take with him to the mountain?
- What happened while they were there?
- Who did Peter, James and John see with Jesus?
- What did Peter say? What did Peter, James and John hear God say?

Ask the children if they have ever seen previews of coming attractions on television or in a theatre. Help them understand that previews tell us about the coming attraction and help us look forward to it.

At the Transfiguration, Jesus was giving a preview of what he will be like after the Resurrection. He was also showing us that we will be like him. We will live with him in glory. As Jesus was showing this to Peter, James and John, God told them what we must do to live with Jesus forever.

Do you remember what God said to Peter, James and John? God tells us, too, "This is my beloved Son; listen to him."

How do we listen to Jesus today:

- in the Bible?
- in our parents and others who teach us?
- in the good thoughts we have that encourage us to do the right thing, and so forth?

THE ASSUMPTION OF MARY

YEAR C

PRAYER OF THE DAY:

O God in heaven,
you sent your only Son, Jesus,
to live among us.
You made Mary his mother.
How happy she must have been
to share in Jesus' life.
Let us learn from Mary, O God,
and from Jesus Christ,
your Son, our Lord,
forever and ever.

FOCUS OF THE READINGS:

Both of our readings, as they are chosen and placed together for this feast, tell us something about the place of Mary in the church. The reading from *Revelation*, rich in symbolism, presents Mary in various aspects of her role in the church. She is the Mother of the Son, born to be the Messiah. She is the image of the church with the 12 stars (12 tribes of Israel, 12 apostles) around her head. And the crown seems to indicate her entrance into heaven where she received the reward of those who remain faithful (*2 Tim.* 4:8).

The Gospel reading, usually called "The Visitation," indicates the real meaning of today's feast. Mary is the Mother of the Lord, and all generations will call her blessed because she believed. The feast of the Assumption places Mary among the Blessed, and indeed the model of the Blessed.

REFLECTING ON THE READINGS WITH CHILDREN:

Rather than reflecting on the readings specifically, it may be well to reflect on the meaning of the feast.

FIRST READING: *Revelation 12:1-2, 5-6, 10b*

A reading from the book of Revelation.

I, John, had a vision.
I saw a woman with the sun shining on her,
and the moon was under her feet.
She was wearing a crown on her head,
and it was made of twelve stars.
The woman was expecting a child,
and she was crying in pain.
She had a baby boy,
and he immediately
was taken up to God's throne
because this child
was to become the ruler of the world.
And the woman went to the desert,
where God had prepared a place for her.

Then I heard a voice in heaven say,

"Christ has come with all the power
and authority of God's kingdom.
Now salvation is here."

The Word of the Lord.

RESPONSE: *Psalm 24*

GOSPEL ACCLAMATION:

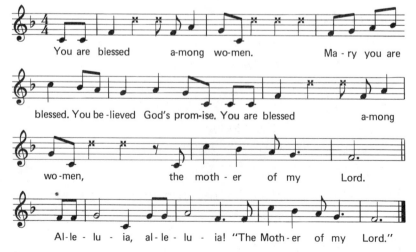

*After Gospel, repeat Acclamation from here.

144

GOSPEL: *Luke 1:39-56*

A reading from the Gospel of Luke.

When the angel Gabriel told Mary
that her cousin, Elizabeth,
was also going to have a baby,
Mary went as quickly as she could to the town
where Zechariah and Elizabeth lived,
up in the hill country of Judah.
As soon as Elizabeth heard Mary's voice,
the baby inside her began to move.
Elizabeth was filled with the Holy Spirit,
and she said to Mary,

"Of all the women on earth,
you are most blessed.
And the baby in your womb is also blessed.
I am so honored because you,
the mother of my Lord,
have come to visit me!
You are blessed, Mary,
because you believed in the promise
that God made to you."

And Mary said,

"I sing with praise the greatness of the Lord,
and my heart finds joy in my Savior.
The Lord has chosen me, a humble servant;
now all people will say I am blessed.
The Lord, who is mighty,
has done great things for me.
Holy is God's name.
God has destroyed the power
of people who are proud
and honored those who are poor and humble.
God has given good food to hungry people
and sent the rich away with nothing.
God has come to help the people of Israel
because of the promise
made to Abraham and Sarah
and their family forever."

Mary stayed with Elizabeth about three months
and then returned to her home in Nazareth.

The Gospel of the Lord.

The feast celebrates Mary's entrance into heaven. It tells us that human beings are destined to live, like Mary, in heaven, in the presence of God. But why was Mary taken to heaven? Why has the church celebrated this feast centuries before it was proclaimed as dogma in 1950? This would be a good time to help the children see the "blessedness" of Mary as she is presented in Scripture.

Ask the children what they remember about Mary. The obvious is that she gave birth to Jesus. Help the children recall the main features of Luke's story of the Annunciation.

- What does this tell us about Mary? *She was a woman of faith.*

Mary at Bethlehem

- What does this tell us about Mary? *She was a wife and mother.*

Mary at the Temple

- What does this tell us about Mary? *She was a woman who followed her religion.*

Mary at Cana

- What does this tell us about Mary? *She was a woman who cared for the needs of others.*

Mary at the foot of the Cross

- What does this tell us about Mary? *She remained faithful to the end.*

Mary at Pentecost

- What does this tell us about Mary? *She was a woman of prayer.*

Help the children see that these qualities are what makes Mary special and why we know she is in heaven. Mary is a human being, a woman of great faith to be imitated by all believers. And we too, when we live that way, will be in heaven.

Note: This may be an occasion to give the children a small picture or holy card of Mary.

145

TRIUMPH OF THE CROSS

YEAR C

PRAYER OF THE DAY:

Praise you, O God,
for loving us enough
to send your only Son
among us.
Your love is never ending.
Your love lives on
with Jesus Christ,
your Son,
forever and ever.

FOCUS OF THE READINGS:

Our readings focus on the entire life of Christ. It would be a mistake to see the cross, the death, and resurrection as the total message of today. Both of our readings put the Triumph of the Cross as the climax of a total life given for us, beginning with the Incarnation.

The first stanza of the first reading tells us that Jesus was always God. At a point in history, he became a human being and lived in every way like us. Because, as a human being, he obeyed God in everything, even though it meant he would be killed, God raised him to a new life after he died. Death on a cross has become the sign of God's power over death.

The Gospel gives us the reason for Jesus' coming to earth. "God loved the world so much." Jesus is the visible expression of God's unconditional love for us. Everyone who believes that Jesus came, lived and died for us, and was raised to new life, will live forever.

FIRST READING: *Philippians 2:5-11*

A reading from Paul's letter to the Philippians.

Brothers and sisters,

You must think and live like Christ.
Even though he was always God,
Jesus did not try to hold onto that.
Instead, he became a human being just like us.

He lived a humble life
and obeyed God in everything,
even though it meant he would die on a cross.
Because he obeyed God in everything,
God raised him up and gave him the name
which is above every other name,
so that at the name of Jesus,
everyone should kneel and worship him.
Everyone in heaven,
on earth and everywhere
should give glory to God
by proclaiming, "Jesus Christ is Lord!"

The Word of the Lord.

RESPONSE: *Psalm 34*

Glo-ri-fy God, glo-ri-fy God, glo-ri-fy God with me. Let us praise God's ho-ly name. Glo-ri-fy God glo-ri-fy God's ho-ly name!

GOSPEL ACCLAMATION:

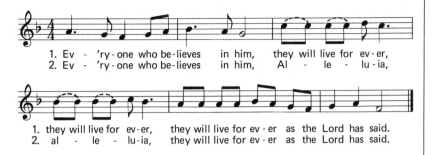

1. Ev - 'ry-one who be-lieves in him, they will live for ev-er,
2. Ev - 'ry-one who be-lieves in him, Al - le - lu - ia,

1. they will live for ev-er, they will live for ev-er as the Lord has said.
2. al - le - lu - ia, they will live for ev-er as the Lord has said.

GOSPEL: *John 3:14-18a*

A reading from the Gospel of John.

Jesus said to Nicodemus,

"God's Chosen One must be lifted up
so that everyone who believes in him
will live forever.

"Yes, God loved the world so much
that God sent the only Son into the world,
so that everyone who believes in him
will live forever.

"God did not send the Son
to judge the world,
but to save it.
And everyone who believes in him
will live forever."

The Gospel of the Lord.

REFLECTING ON THE READINGS WITH CHILDREN:

Neither of our readings has a "story line" which will be easy for children to follow, understand and retain.

You might ask the children to recall what they heard in the first reading. It might be helpful to read the text slowly, stopping after each stanza. Ask the children what they think is the most important line in each stanza. Perhaps you could help them arrive at the following and write these on a large poster.

- He became a human being just like us.
- He obeyed God in everything.
- God raised him up.
- Jesus Christ is Lord.

We, like Jesus, want to obey God in everything. And we, like Jesus, will be raised up after we die.

- Why do you think God sent Jesus?

Let's listen to the Gospel and hear what St. John tells us.

After the Gospel, ask the children what John tells us about why Jesus came into the world. God loved the world (us) so much.

Ask the children what sentence was repeated three times. Add this to the large poster.

- Everyone who believes in him will live forever.

Note: As there are no leaflets for the feasts, you may wish to have the important lines of the first reading already prepared on a paper which the children can take home, decorate and put in their room. (You might change the pronoun He to Jesus.)

ALL SAINTS

YEAR C

PRAYER OF THE DAY:

We love you, God.
As members
of your family,
we want to show you
our love by living
as Jesus did,
in your name,
forever and ever.

FOCUS OF THE READINGS:

The feast of All Saints focuses attention on two of our fundamental beliefs as Christians: we are baptized into a community, and we will live forever. We celebrate today our union with all those believers, children of God, who have been "rewarded in heaven," and now see God.

The first reading focuses on our life as Christians here and now. *We are children of God now!* As such, we must try to be good and pure as we wait for the day when Jesus will come again and we will see him as he is and be like him. And so, the reading also pulls us into the future. We live a life of "already/not yet." We are *already* children of God, but we are *not yet* perfect like Jesus.

The Gospel, too, focuses on the already/not yet, but with an emphasis on the future. We are assured of reward in heaven, the blessing to come, when we live the life of Jesus. It is this assurance of seeing God and eternal life of blessing that motivates us to live the beatitudes here and now. Combined, these readings present the Christian view of both present and future.

The saints are those children of God who have lived the beatitudes.

FIRST READING: *1 John 3:1-3*

A reading from the first letter of John.

Brothers and sisters,

See how much God loves us!
We are called the children of God.
And that is who we really are, God's children.
We know that when Jesus comes again,
we will be like him
because we will see him as he really is.
Everyone who believes this
tries to be good and pure,
just as Jesus is good and pure.

The Word of the Lord.

RESPONSE: *Psalm 15*

RESPONSE:

Those who seek your face, Lord, with a pure heart shall stand in your Ho - ly Place!

GOSPEL ACCLAMATION:

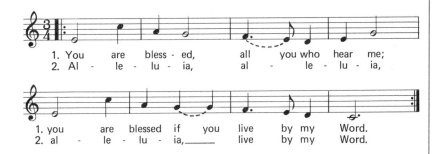

1. You are bless - ed, all you who hear me;
2. Al - le - lu - ia, al - le - lu - ia,

1. you are blessed if you live by my Word.
2. al - le - lu - ia,_____ live by my Word.

GOSPEL: *Matthew 5:1-12*

A reading from the Gospel of Matthew.

Jesus and his disciples went up on a mountain,
and they sat down so Jesus could teach them.
Jesus said to his disciples,

"Blessed are people who know they need God,
   for the kingdom of heaven belongs to them.
Blessed are people who are sad now,
   for later God will comfort them.
Blessed are people who are humble,
   for God will give them everything.
Blessed are people who work for justice,
   for God will give them all they need.
Blessed are people who give mercy to others,
   for God will have mercy on them.
Blessed are people
   who have hearts that are pure,
   for they will see God.
Blessed are people who make peace,
   for they will be called children of God.
Blessed are people who suffer
   for doing what is right,
   for the kingdom of heaven belongs to them.

["And you are blessed when people hurt you
   and say bad things about you
because you believe in me.
   Be happy and glad,
   for God will reward you in heaven."]

The Gospel of the Lord.

[ ] *Reader may omit text that appears in brackets.*

REFLECTING ON THE READINGS
WITH CHILDREN:

We want to emphasize with the
children that we live the beatitudes
because we are children of God. The
beatitudes are, for Christians, a way
of life. We do not need to earn our
relationship with God by living the
beatitudes, we are already children
of God.

You might compare this to family
relationships. Members of a loving
family do not need to earn the love of
one another by being good and kind.
They are good and kind because they
already love one another.

We belong to the family of God.
We are truly God's children and so
we live as children of God. We know
that we are not perfect, but one day
we will see Jesus, our brother, as he
really is and we will be like him. The
beatitudes tell us how we should live
until that day.

The saints are people who did
that. They live forever with God.
Today would be an ideal time to
share the lives of some saints who
are special to your parish or city.

ALL SOULS

YEAR C

PRAYER OF THE DAY:

Your love is strong,
O God.
Nothing can stop you
from loving us.
Help us be strong too,
O God,
strong enough to live
as Jesus lived,
in your name.
Amen.

Note: In keeping with the Directory for Masses
With Children *(Paragraph 43), the authors
have elected to use readings from selections
offered for* Masses for the Dead *instead of the
All Souls readings because they seem better
suited "to the capacity of children."*

FOCUS OF THE READINGS:

Our readings focus on death and
eternal life. The first reading
assures us that nothing, not even
death, can separate us from the love
of God. God intended us to live
forever and revealed that explicitly
in Jesus Christ. We have God's
promise and nothing can take that
from us.

The Gospel gives us the image of
the seed which must die in order to
bear fruit. The grain of wheat, when
buried, becomes hidden. Only this
burial will allow it to grow into what
God intended it to become. Jesus
himself was the example of this for
us. Only by dying could he rise to
new life. Death, then, becomes the
process through which we become the
person God intended us to become, to
be lifted up by Christ, and to live with
him forever. We come to this new
life not only through physical death,
but by being willing in our daily lives
to give up our lives for others.

FIRST READING: *Romans 8:31-34, 38-39*

A reading from Paul's letter to the Romans.

If God is on our side,
who will be against us?
Surely not God,
who was willing to give up even Jesus
for our sake.
God has saved us through Jesus.
No one can take that away from us.

If God is on our side,
who will reject us?
Surely not Christ Jesus,
who died and was raised to life
and is now with God to help us.
I am sure that nothing
will ever take us away
from the love of God.
Not death, not anything in life,
nothing now or in the future—
nothing will ever take us away from God's love,
which is in Christ Jesus, our Lord!

The Word of the Lord.

RESPONSE: *Psalm 27*

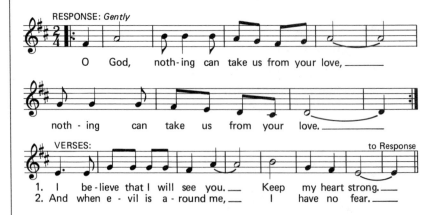

GOSPEL ACCLAMATION:

1. "Those who give up their lives for me, they will live for ev-er,
2. "Those who give up their lives for me," Al - le - lu - ia,

1. they will live for ev-er, they will live for ev-er," as the Lord has said.
2. al - le - lu ia, "They will live for ev-er," as the Lord has said.

GOSPEL: *John 12:24-25, 32-33*

A reading from the Gospel of John.

Jesus said to Philip and Andrew,

"You know that if you do not bury
a grain of wheat,
it stays just one grain of wheat.
But if you do bury it in the ground,
it grows and becomes many grains.

"In the same way,
people who try to hold onto their lives
will lose them.
But those who are willing
to give up their lives
will live forever.
And when I am lifted up,
I will bring all people to me."

When he said this,
Jesus was telling them
how he was going to die.

The Gospel of the Lord.

REFLECTING ON THE READINGS
WITH CHILDREN:

Let the sung response be the
reflection on the first reading.
Through the gentleness and
memorable quality of the refrain, the
children will conclude that nothing
can take us from God's love.

After the Gospel, show the
children a seed. Ask them what a
seed will become if it stays on the
table or in an envelope. Most
children will know that a seed must
be planted in order to grow. It must
be buried in the earth. Discuss this
process with them. After it is buried,
we no longer see it. It seems like
nothing is happening to it. Then one
day, we see a sprout. It's growing.
That means it's really alive. Now it
doesn't look like a grain, but wheat.

Jesus tells us that our death is
like that. When people die, it looks
like the end. But, like the grain of
wheat, they are alive and one day will
be raised to a new kind of life. We
don't know what we will look like or
be like, but we will be alive. Jesus
showed us that this is true because
he died and was raised to a new life
and he is now alive and with us.

DEDICATION OF ST. JOHN LATERAN

YEAR C

PRAYER OF THE DAY:

Loving God,
you have given each of us
a place to call our own—
a home in your own house.
Thank you, God,
for the love
you share with us,
forever and ever.

FOCUS OF THE READINGS:

Today's feast focuses on the church. The particular church, St. John Lateran in Rome, is the cathedral church of the Bishop of Rome and is also therefore the symbol of the universal church. Several choices for readings are permissible for this feast, all of which point to the true nature of the church.

In the first reading, Paul tells us that we are the temple of God. Since the word "you" is in the plural in Greek, it is clear that Paul speaks of the Christian community as the church.

The Gospel is good news for sinners! The church, the presence of Christ, is for sinners! Christ is the church, and he says to Zacchaeus, "I want to stay at your house." The church is the gathering of sinners— those who are lost— around the Lord.

REFLECTING ON THE READINGS WITH CHILDREN:

The concept of church as Body of Christ or Presence of Christ will be too abstract for most children. Children will naturally associate church with the building. However we can at least plant the seeds.

After the first reading, ask the children to recall the image Paul used. A building is a place where people live or work.

- What special "building" are we?

FIRST READING: *1 Corinthians 3:9b-11, 16-17*

A reading from Paul's first letter to the Corinthians.

You are like a building that belongs to God.
God asked me to begin forming you,
and I used all my talent
to build a good foundation for you.
And that foundation is Jesus Christ.
So, really, you are God's temple,
and God's Spirit lives in you.
God will punish anyone
who tries to destroy that temple.
For God's temple is holy,
and you are God's temple!

The Word of the Lord.

RESPONSE: *Psalm 122*

RESPONSE: In the House of our God, in the House of our God, we give praise to the Lord in the House of our God.

VERSES:
1. I was glad when they said to me: "Let us go to the House of God!" And now in God's House we are standing.
2. It is here that we find peace for our families and friends, here that we find justice.

to Response

GOSPEL ACCLAMATION:

1. Jesus said: "Zaccheus come down for I want to stay with you."
2. Alleluia, alleluia! "For I want to stay with you."

GOSPEL: *Luke 19:1-10*

A reading from the Gospel of Luke.

Jesus was going through the city of Jericho,
and lots of people came out to see him.
There was a man there, named Zacchaeus,
who was the head of all the tax collectors
and was very rich.
Zacchaeus also wanted to see Jesus
and find out who he was.
But Zacchaeus was a very short man
and couldn't see Jesus through the crowd.
So he ran ahead
and climbed up into a sycamore tree
and waited for Jesus to pass by.

When Jesus came to that place,
he looked up and said,

"Zacchaeus, come down! Hurry!
I want to stay at your house today!"

Zacchaeus was so excited that he hurried down
and welcomed Jesus into his home.
The people who saw this were angry and said,

"Look, this man Jesus
is staying in the home of a sinner!"

But Zacchaeus said to Jesus,

"Lord, I am going to give
half of everything I have to the poor.
And if I have ever cheated anyone
out of money,
I am going to pay them back
four times as much."

Then Jesus said to Zacchaeus,

"Today you have been saved
because you, too,
are one of the family of Abraham.
For I have come to seek
and to save the people who are lost."

The Gospel of the Lord.

Try to help the children see that we use the word "church" in two ways. It is the building, but also the group of Christians who go there. You might suggest this as a comparison. If we have a Christian gathering—for example a Mass in the park—that is also the church. If a group of Christians gather to prepare food for the poor, that is also the church. Whenever we do things in the name of Christ, that's the church. When we say we belong to the church, we don't mean the building; we mean the Christian community.

The children will relate much more easily to the story of Zacchaeus. If you feel it appropriate, reflect only on the Gospel. The encounter between Jesus and Zacchaeus is joyful and easy to enter into. Perhaps there is a little Zacchaeus in all of us!

We suggest you follow the same reflections given for the Thirty-first Sunday in Ordinary Time, Year C. They are reprinted here for your convenience.

This Gospel story will almost always appeal to children. There is a light heartedness to it that makes of the encounter between Zacchaeus and Jesus an event we naturally want to applaud to show our joy.

Invite the children to recall and visualize. Help them to imagine the scene.

- The crowds,
- Jesus and those with him,
- Zacchaeus scurrying along, looking for an open space, and finally running to climb the sycamore tree.
- What might the crowd have been like?
- Why did everyone want to see Jesus?
- Who was Zacchaeus?
- Why did he want to see Jesus?
- How did Jesus and Zacchaeus meet? (It is important that the children see that Jesus spoke first to a sinner. Jesus sought him out.)
- What did Jesus say to Zacchaeus? (Emphasize that he *ate* in Zacchaeus' house.)
- How did Zacchaeus respond?

Two points should be emphasized:

1. Jesus came to look for sinners so he could save them.

2. When we truly meet Jesus, we change our lives.

PART TWO

1. Introduction to the Sunday Readings

"What we have heard, and what we have seen with our own eyes; what we have watched and touched with our own hands, we proclaim to you so that you may be in union with us, as we are in union with God and with the Son, Jesus Christ. And we are writing this to you so that our joy may be complete" (1 John 1:1, 3, 4).

The first disciples, filled with the joy of the Resurrection, were consumed with the desire to proclaim the Good News! This Good News of God's faithful and unconditional love continues to be proclaimed in the church today, especially in the liturgy. In a special way, this saving Word is embodied in the sacred scriptures. The Second Vatican Council reminds us that God is truly present to us in the scriptures, and that this Word reveals God's saving love and also nourishes us on our journey of faith. For this reason, the church teaches that all the Christian faithful should have easy access to the sacred scriptures and that translations and versions should be prepared which could more easily be read and understood by the people of God. (Paragraphs 22 and 25, *Constitution on Divine Revelation.)*

The church is also concerned with the availability and understanding of the scriptures for children, who, as members of God's family, have their rightful place in the church.

"Jesus said, 'Let the little children come to me; do not stop them; for it is to such as these that the kingdom of God belongs.' Then he put his arms around them, laid his hands on them, and gave them his blessing" (Mark 10:14, 16).

Jesus made a special point of welcoming children. In his great love for them, he put his arms around them and gave them his blessing. The scripture readings in SUNDAY have been adapted so that children may more easily understand the Word of God, and through that

Word, be touched and blessed by this same Jesus who is ever present in his Word.

These children have the right to hear God's Word, and God wants them to hear it. We are all aware, however, of the difficulty they have in understanding the Word since the scriptures were written in a language for adults which is beyond the capacity of little children.

Happily, the Congregation for Divine Worship recognized this difficulty and provided a means for solving it. The *Directory for Masses With Children*, issued on November 1, 1973 opens the door for realizing the dream of parents, catechists and priests to make the Word of God accessible and understood by children. This challenging document calls us to use *"words and signs"* in our liturgies which are *"sufficiently adapted to the capacity of children"* (Par. 2). The challenge to provide such adaptation, especially of the scripture readings, is aided by the prudent and useful guidelines provided within the document itself where ministers of the Word with children are encouraged to make selections and adaptations of texts guided primarily by the *"spiritual advantage which the readings can offer children"* (Par. 44).

All those who minister to children in a formal capacity, as well as parents who long to share their faith with their own children, are aware of the necessity for such adaptation. It is to assist in this important ministry that we have prepared scripture readings for each Sunday. Our selection and adaptation of these readings has been guided by four principles.

1. Retain the Sunday Readings of the Liturgical Year.

The Bible, a collection of seventy-three books, was written over a period of some 1800 years, in various places by a myriad of authors. Through these books, we come to see that each human being neither receives nor transmits God's revelation in exactly the same way. The various authors wrote on different topics using a variety of literary forms such as poetry, prose, narration, epic story, letter, etc. By recognizing the variety of the readings, we are open to more of God's revelation to us.

The church has spread these readings over the course of a three-year cycle during which we hear selections from both the Old and New Testaments, including nearly every book in the Bible. Through them we are in touch with the faith community throughout the ages and we hear God's call for a response in our own time.

In the Liturgy of the Word, children, too, receive God's wonderful revelation through the readings and are invited to respond in their daily lives. In almost all circumstances, therefore, the choice of readings already assigned for each Sunday has been preserved. In this way, the children may experience the mystery of God's love for them as it is unfolded during the liturgical year.

There are, however, some readings which are particularly problematic for children. In these instances, an alternative reading has been selected in accordance with the *Directory for Masses With Children.*

"If all the readings assigned to the day seem to be unsuited to the capacity of children, it is permissible to choose readings or a reading from the Lectionary for Mass or directly from the Bible, taking into account the liturgical seasons" (Par. 43).

Young children often have difficulty being attentive to three readings within one liturgical celebration. With this in mind, we have presented two readings for each Sunday.

Because of the harmony which usually exists between the first reading, from the Old Testament, and the reading from the Gospel, we have generally adapted these two. On occasion, however, when deemed more suitable for children, the second reading replaces the Old Testament reading. It remains for the minister of the Word to determine the suitability of reading only the Gospel or using the two readings presented.

"If three or even two readings on Sundays and weekdays can be understood by children only with difficulty, it is permissible to read two or one of them, but the reading of the gospel should never be omitted" (Par. 42).

2. Remain Faithful to the Meaning of the Text.

Since Christ himself is present in his Word and in the assembly of the faithful, the scriptures, as the inspired Word of God, always speak to us on some level. While not all of the meaning of each text is clear to adults, and certainly not to children, it is true for both adults and children that frequent reading of the scriptures reveals more and more of the meaning of that which was received initially as a seed to be nurtured. It is often through unfamiliar parables and images that God's message is revealed, and it is our prayerful meditation of these parables and images that cultivates in us a profound sense of the mystery of God's presence and unconditional love for us.

Children, who are especially open to wonder and mystery, are often easily led to a deeper level of faith and a desire to respond to God through the proclamation of the Word. Any adaptation of the readings must, therefore, remain faithful to the rich images and literary forms used by the sacred writers to reveal God's love and saving power. In order that this fidelity be safeguarded, the *Directory* insists that adaptations *"should be done cautiously and in such a way that the meaning of the texts or the sense and, as it were, style of the scriptures are not mutilated"* (Par. 43). And further: *"Paraphrases of scripture should, therefore, be avoided"* (Par. 45).

In all cases, the authentic meaning of the text has clearly been preserved, even when this meaning will not be immediately evident to all children.

3. Use Language That is Intelligible to Children.

It is evident that children sometimes fail to understand the Word simply because it is couched in words beyond their learning. If children are to understand the scriptures and be nourished by them, every effort must be made to make adaptations using a language appropriate to their capacity of comprehension. There is no question here of watering down the Word of God or of rendering it in current colloquialisms. It is, rather, a question of being familiar with the vocabulary level and language structure of the age range for which the adaptation is being made. Often the meaning of an entire passage will be made clear to children by reducing multisyllabic words to a simpler vocabulary or by rearranging the order of the words in a sentence. In instances where sentences are unusually long or contain a number of clauses, we have separated these into shorter, more direct sentences.

Some exceptions to the principle of simpler vocabulary have been made. Frequently the names of cities, the use of words or phrases in Hebrew or Aramaic have been retained. For example, in *Mark* 5:21-43 (Thirteenth Sunday of Ordinary Time, Year B*)*, we have kept the phrase *"Talitha kum"* which means "Little girl, get up, I tell you." And in *Mark* 7:31-37 (Twenty-third Sunday of Ordinary Time, Year B*)*, we retain the word *"Ephphatha"* which means "be opened." These words and phrases are as foreign to adults as they are to children, yet they have become part of our scriptural heritage and do not pose a problem for us. In fact, these bits and pieces of the original language seem to make a particular passage come alive for us. By retaining these, we hope to enlarge the biblical vocabulary of the children and at the same time expose them to some of the flavor of the time in which the scriptures were written.

Apart from these few exceptions, there has been a consistent effort to present the readings in a simple, direct language which should be easily understood by children between the ages of seven and twelve. Recognizing that children's comprehension levels may vary greatly, even within a two year span, we have concentrated on the vocabulary level of the seven- and eight-year-old. In this way, the readings will be easily understood by older children and by some younger children. Many catechists and ministers of the Word will have children much younger, perhaps three to six years old. Until such time when readings are prepared specifically for these children, we encourage ministers of the Word to freely adapt these readings still further. Again, we call upon the guideline given in the *Directory for Masses With Children* which tells us that the primary goal is *"the spiritual advantage the readings can offer the children."*

4. Use a Language Which is Inclusive of All God's People.

Since the renewal of the liturgy, which made possible the use of the vernacular, the Christian community has become more aware of the language used in liturgical celebrations, especially the Eucharist. While this language has been almost exclusively masculine, many now recognize that whatever the origins of this practice, both historical and grammatical, the use of exclusive language does not represent the true meaning of the sacred scriptures or the true nature of the church and should, therefore, be avoided in revisions of liturgical texts and translations of the Bible.

Because children relate more easily with concrete terms than with abstract concepts, the need for inclusive language is particularly important. The use of exclusively masculine or feminine language at liturgical celebrations may develop for them a limited image of God, God's people and ministry in the church. The readings in liturgical celebrations proclaim God's saving Word for all people and it is important that children hear and understand this. We have, therefore, adapted the readings using a language which is inclusive of both men and women when this is clearly the intention of the sacred writer.

In presenting these Sunday readings adapted for children, we wish to encourage all ministers of the Word, the professionals, the volunteers, and especially the newcomers, to continue in their important ministry in the church. As a further aid, we have included this background information on the Sunday readings and liturgical seasons. This weekly Leader Guide includes suggestions for reflecting on the Word with the children, background materials for the minister of the Word, dramatizations, music, responses, Gospel acclamations, seasonal reflections and a prayer for each Sunday.

With SUNDAY, we wish to affirm and support those who desire to share the Word of God with children, of whom Jesus said, *"The Kingdom of God belongs to such as these"* (Mark 10:14).

2. Introduction to the Liturgical Seasons

Most people enjoy celebrations. Birthdays, weddings, graduations, football victories, centennials, ship launchings are just a few of the occasions people celebrate, sometimes quietly and intimately, sometimes loudly and with great gusto.

The church, for all its seriousness of purpose, is no laggard when it comes to celebrating. Indeed, the liturgy, the heartbeat of the church, is celebration. We do not say or read the liturgy, we celebrate it. Every time we come together for the liturgy we celebrate an event, a happening in the long history of God's dealings with men and women down the ages. Liturgy is the unfolding of the story of our salvation through, with, and in Jesus Christ.

This celebration takes place within two inter-linked cycles: one which we call the seasons and the other, the saints. The cycle of seasonal liturgies (Advent, Christmas, Lent, Easter and Ordinary Time) commemorates the principal events of our redemption, while the sanctoral cycle, as it is called, commemorates particular men and women who have lived out that redemption in a special way.

Liturgical celebrations are important because the church assembles not just to look back to long-past events, but to participate fully in those same saving events. Through the liturgy, the full effects of the work of our salvation are made present: we become part of them, they become part of us. The unfolding in the liturgical seasons of the life and times of Jesus Christ is at the same time an invitation to us to actively participate in that life. Each liturgy presents us not with a faded memory or a lesson from the past, but with the grace-filled effects of that event, made present in the proclamation of God's Word and the celebration of the sacrament by a people called by God. To celebrate the liturgy is as effective for our redemption as if we had been personally present on the historical occasion commemorated. So, celebrating Christmas is more than a pleasant memory; it is involvement with the incarnation of our Savior, Jesus Christ.

Sunday is central to the church's annual cycle of celebrations. It is a journey on which we follow in the path of Christ, fully and really. By so doing we are caught up in his great journey, the victory over sin and death, which we call the paschal mystery.

A final word. The events of our salvation in Christ were, on his part, acts of worship of the God who sent him. Our participation in the unfolding history of our redemption—celebrated in the church's year and in the power of the Spirit—is, therefore, a participation in the greatest possible act of worship. What could be more important than the church's liturgy?

3. Season of Advent

Advent is a time of expectation, a time of preparing for the coming of the Lord. Expectation and preparation are part of the Christian way of life. We are on a journey of faith, pressing forward with greater or lesser zeal, toward the kingdom. In one breath we can say, "The Lord has come," and in the next, "He will come again." To celebrate the future hope of Christians is to celebrate that element which makes faith complete.

The Advent liturgy keeps this expectation alive. The Gospel readings in all three cycles of the lectionary begin the season on the First Sunday of Advent with Jesus' warning about the unexpectedness of the end of all things and our need to be prepared for it, at whatever time it should come. The Second and Third Sundays of Advent throw a spotlight on the person and teaching of John the Baptist. This emphasis might appear at first sight to place John in the role of prophet of the imminent birth of the Savior at Bethlehem, until we remember that, according to the Gospels, John exercised his ministry long after Jesus' birth, directly before his public ministry.

It is only on the Fourth Sunday of Advent that the Gospel readings unequivocally turn their attention to the events leading up to Jesus' birth to Mary. It would help our understanding of the full meaning of Advent if we were to remain more faithful to the pattern laid down by the season's Gospels. Commercial pressures and pre-Christmas Nativity plays, not to mention Christmas parties in early December, diminish the meaning of the preparation of Advent.

Consequently, long before the season begins, children will have been looking forward to the actual celebration of Christmas and the gifts which will accompany it. This is a pity. Such early anticipation of the climax diminishes the force and meaning of the time of preparation.

We should perhaps recognize more clearly other liturgical signs of the season and point them out to the children. First, there is the omission of the *Glory to God*, a hymn of joy, at all eucharistic celebrations of the season, though it is doubtful that a young child will notice this anyway. More noticeable is the use of liturgical colors for vestments and, in some churches, the absence of flowers. Once upon a time, Advent was invested with many more signs of penance, and perhaps the attempt to make it into a mini-Lent was going too far, but at least we should not treat Christmas as if it were already here.

What the liturgy of Advent does, and what we should help the children to begin to understand, is fill us with expectation and an attitude of hope. The readings tell us that we should be on the watch, always ready, not only for the celebration of the birthday of Jesus, but also for his second coming, which puts the first one into perspective. Christianity is a faith for the future.

4. Introduction to the Prophet Isaiah

During cycle A, all of the Old Testament readings for the liturgy come from the book of *Isaiah*, and in cycle B three come from *Isaiah*; cycle C presents passages from four different prophets. Throughout the Advent season, even the Gospel readings are heavily laced with quotations from the book of *Isaiah*. Because this book plays such an important part in our Advent readings, we will give a brief, general introduction to it as a backdrop for the more specific, liturgical introductions for the individual Sundays.

It is generally agreed by biblical scholars today that the sixty-six chapters of the book of *Isaiah* are not the work of a single prophet, but rather the work of two, or possibly three writers. While many theories about this have been presented by various scholars, it is commonly thought that the book can be divided into two major sections: chapters 1-39 being the work of the eighth century prophet, Isaiah, and chapters 40-66 the work of a prophet who lived after the Babylonian exile, perhaps in the fourth century B.C. The major reason for dividing the book into these two sections is that the content, style of writing, and audience are clearly different after chapter 39. Accordingly, chapters 1-39 are called *First Isaiah*, and chapters 40-66 are called *Second Isaiah*. (You may also find them called "Proto-Isaiah" and "Deutero-Isaiah.") The readings for cycle A come from *First Isaiah* and in cycle B from *Second Isaiah*.

First Isaiah (Chapters 1-39)

Isaiah identifies himself in the opening verse of the book, and throughout the early chapters, gives us some of the details of his life. He speaks of his call and his fear of responding to that call. In chapter six he tells of his conversion from this fear to a willingness to be the spokesperson of God. From his writing we know also that Isaiah was married to a prophetess and that they had at least two children. He was an educated man who had easy access to the kings of his time, and to other members of the royalty. He tells us that he prophesied during the reigns of "Uzziah, Jotham, Ahaz, and Hezekiah, kings of Judah" (1:1). This places Isaiah in Jerusalem during the eighth century B.C.

Isaiah's task was to guide his nation through a critical period. The people were rooted in the tradition of King David and longed for a return to that golden period in their history. During the eighth century, God's promise of a "lasting dynasty in the House of David" seemed doomed. The prosperity and glory of Judah as a leading nation were fading, and the Assyrians were a constant threat to their security and independence.

From Isaiah's prophecies, it seems that God's people responded to these events by yielding to the temptation of compromising with foreign nations and, as it were, bargaining for their security rather than trusting in God. Coupled with this was the arrogant attitude that if God were truly on their side, they could do as they pleased and God would come through in the end. For Isaiah, both of these attitudes were sins of pride against the very holiness of God.

At this same time, the nation was changing from an agricultural society to a more stratified society with a class structure. Isaiah witnessed the increasing gap between the rich and the poor and the injustices that resulted from it. Those who were prosperous soon forgot the communal nature of God's chosen people!

These sins of pride and blatant injustices reflected the neglect of the moral standards expected in the covenant and resulted in a breakdown of national strength and security. Isaiah preached that God, who is holy and faithful, would surely save Israel, but would also surely punish them for their sins. Hence, Isaiah consistently proclaimed that the fall of Israel and Judah would be the punishment of their infidelity, and at the same time, he gives a constant call to return to the covenant, to live justly and to trust in the God who would forgive and redeem them.

Second Isaiah (Chapters 40-66)

Whereas the prophet of *First Isaiah* clearly identifies himself, the prophet of *Second Isaiah* remains anonymous. From his writing, however, we can say that he lived during the time of the Babylonian exile. Throughout his prophecy, the destruction of the city of Jerusalem and the temple, the suffering of the people in exile are presumed. His is a message of comfort and hope (40:1). He assures the people that God will restore Israel through Cyrus, the King of Persia.

Second Isaiah's writing is highly liturgical, using psalms and hymns as a primary literary form. His attention is focused on the restoration of Jerusalem and the temple, the place of worship. God's people will be brought back from the desert (40:3) and will be made secure in Jerusalem.

Second Isaiah speaks of God in a language that seems to take on a more personal dimension. He speaks of God's intimate relationship with the people of Israel and describes God's fidelity and salvation in personal, relational images of mother, father and shepherd. The time of redemption also seems to take a more personal shape. Primarily, redemption or salvation meant freedom from oppression and a time when Israel would again be a secure, powerful nation. It was a time when God would restore strength and power to Israel. This time was called messianic time which means "the time of anointing." From this we have our word, "Messiah" which means "the anointed one."

During the time of *Second Isaiah*, this messianic hope became focused on a person who would be God's anointed one. This Messiah is described as the servant of God who will proclaim truth and will atone for the sins of the people. Though he will suffer greatly, God will vindicate him. Quite obviously, Christianity has seen in these passages the foreshadowing of Jesus. These passages which describe the servant are called the "songs of the suffering servant." The notion of a person being the redeemer, the savior, and who embodies the suffering of the people distinguishes *Second Isaiah* from all former prophecy, including *First Isaiah*.

Above all, *Second Isaiah*, while exposing again the sins of Israel, proclaims the message that salvation is sure. God is our Redeemer.

5. *Introduction to Jeremiah, Baruch, Zephania & Micah*

The prophets of the Old Testament provide us with the backdrop for the New Testament and prepare us for the coming of Christ. As we read the prophets in the context of liturgy, we must always remember the nature of their ministry. They worked in and through the political and social order of their day, challenging and exhorting the people, especially the leaders, to return to the covenant and remain faithful to the ways of God.

During cycles A and B, we hear from the prophet Isaiah. In cycle C, we hear the message of four different prophets from the 7th and 8th century BC.

Jeremiah

Jeremiah appears as perhaps the most human of the prophets. Often reluctant to fulfill his role, his writing reveals the pain and agony he experienced in being faithful. Yet, as a public figure, Jeremiah maintained uncompromising fidelity, though he was often commanded to present God's message through rather strange signs. For example, he was commanded not to marry or have children as a sign to the people that they were not living in harmony with God and that a complete restoration was in order. Jeremiah lived a life of hope and despair; he was loved and hated, ridiculed and respected. Through it all, his message was consistent: return to the covenant. Live in justice and God will save you.

Baruch

Baruch is best known as the secretary to Jeremiah. What we know of him is gleaned from the book of *Jeremiah* rather than from the book which bears his name. Much of the book of *Jeremiah* was either dictated to Baruch or written by him, and he sometimes delivered the messages to the people in Jeremiah's name. The last ten chapters contain a lengthy biography of Jeremiah, written by his faithful servant, Baruch.

Zephania

Zephania was a man of great conviction who spoke out fearlessly against the infidelities of his people. Though he issues strong warnings, he speaks of the "Anawim," the faithful remnant who will enjoy salvation. Of his personal life, we know almost nothing, except that he was decended from Hezekiah, who may be the King Hezekiah so often mentioned in the Old Testament.

Micah

Micah came from the small village of Morsheth in Southwest Judah. Coming from a peasant background, he was familiar with the injustices suffered by the poor at the hands of the rich. In unpolished and often blunt language, he spoke out against every kind of injustice; those of the leaders, the priests and prophets, as well as the common people. Because of his constant demand for justice as the true worship of God, Micah is known as the prophet of social justice.

6. The Season of Christmas

That the Son of God should have taken upon himself our human nature is the most astounding and incomprehensible truth we can imagine. Indeed, it is beyond all imagining: for we know the truth only because it has been revealed to us by the power of the Holy Spirit. The joy and excitement which permeates this season is not misplaced.

The exchange of gifts which marks this entire season is thoroughly appropriate as an active symbol of God's gift to us, sinners as we are. But should we be carried away by emotion and excitement, the liturgy firmly stresses the seriousness and, if you will, the practicality of the gift. *". . . The child born today is the Savior of the world"* (prayer after communion), *". . . all the ends of the earth shall see the salvation of our God"* (first reading). *"Today in the town of David, a Savior has been born to you"* (Gospel). The child born in the stable has come not just to be among us, but to save us from our sins.

Soon after Christmas Day, we celebrate the feast of the Holy Family. Less than helpful artistic representations of what the life of Jesus, Mary and Joseph was thought to be like, and moralizing meditations of Christian family life, have tended to obscure the truth of this feast. As the Gospel for cycle B tells us: *"Meanwhile, the child grew to maturity, and he was filled with wisdom; and God's favor was with him."* Jesus was truly a human being, like us in all things but sin. He lived, learned, loved and laughed like any other child of his time. He was one of us. Yet, even in the midst of the joys of Christmas, a more sombre note is struck. All three Gospels of the lectionary cycle for the Holy Family speak of tension, threat, perplexity, like distant thunder announcing an impending storm. The flight from Herod's persecution, Simon's prophecy of the piercing sword, and the loss of the child in Jerusalem warn us of a mission to be accomplished.

The epiphany sheds a sharper light on that aspect of the season. *"Today you revealed in Christ your eternal plan of salvation and showed him as the light of all peoples"* (Preface of the Epiphany). He is not a passive Emmanuel, a God-among-us with no function. On the contrary, he is the Savior of all, sent by God to proclaim the Good News and lead all peoples to the peace and joy of the Kingdom. That this is God's will is made abundantly clear at the very end of the Christmas season when, at the baptism of the Lord, we hear a voice from heaven, *"This is my Son, the Beloved; my favor rests on him."*

Savior, Son, beloved though he is, Jesus seeks our free cooperation. For his mission to succeed, we must respond with a constant "yes!" The first and most complete "yes" was uttered by Mary. The solemnity of Mary is celebrated on January 1st and is a reminder of the humility and love with which we must match—that of Jesus himself. *"Let it be done to me according to your word!"* is echoed by *"your will be done"* as Jesus prayed in Gethsemane.

7. Introduction to the Infancy Narratives

All of our Gospel readings for the Christmas season, as well as the last Sunday of Advent, come from the Infancy Narratives of Matthew and Luke. These wonderful stories tell us, in vivid images, of the unique Son of God who was born of a young virgin, and the virgin's name was Mary. They present Jesus as the One of whom the prophets spoke, the One who fulfills the expectations and desires of the people of Israel. He is Messiah and Savior, Light to the Gentiles and Lord of all.

The Infancy Narratives are a witness to all that the early Christians believed about Christ. But, in reading, praying and proclaiming the Infancy Narratives, we need to guard against two extremes. The first is to assume that these events were meant to be presented literally and are, therefore, historically accurate in every detail. On the other hand, we want to avoid rejecting the narratives as not historical and, therefore, regard them as pure legend. The purpose of the Infancy Narratives, in the view of most scripture scholars, may best be summarized in the words of the Jerome Biblical Commentary: *"The details of the narratives are symbolic and Biblical. They communicate the mystery of redemption, not a diary of early events."*

We have, perhaps, become accustomed to the Christmas story with all the details of the shepherds, the star, magi, angels, manger, etc. seen together. Yet, when we look at the two narratives separately, we find two stories that are entirely different in their presentation, both in the telling of events and in mood. For example, Matthew speaks of the star guiding the magi to Bethlehem where they adore the newborn King. Luke, on the other hand, tells us of the shepherds who, at the word of the angels, came to Bethlehem to find the child, lying in a manger.

Matthew, a Jew writing for Jewish converts, presents Jesus as one who experiences the struggles of his people, even from his birth. Throughout the narrative, we read of fear, suspicion, danger and concern for the survival of the infant. In Matthew's narrative, Jesus shares in the struggles of his Jewish ancestors and, at the same time, fulfills their hopes for salvation.

Matthew uses the language and images familiar to his Jewish audience. His narrative is written within a patriarchal context. The annunciation is made to Joseph. Joseph is to name the child. Joseph leads the family to safety, and when they return from Egypt, he settles in Nazareth.

Luke, too, used the language and images which would speak to his people. But he and his Christian community were not primarily Jewish, but Gentile in origin, with a variety of backgrounds. So his narrative is one which appeals to a more universal audience. His narrative is written around a whole host of characters, Jewish and non-Jewish, rich and poor, men and women. His audience was not part of the struggle common to Matthew's community; so his narrative is filled not with struggle but with songs of joy, sung by Zachariah, Mary, the angels, and Simeon.

Nor is Luke's community a patriarchal society. In his Gospel, the annunciation is made to Mary. Mary is to name the child. Mary takes the good news to the hill country of Judea. Mary is addressed by Simeon and Anna in the temple, and Mary treasures all these things in her heart.

Whatever the differences in detail, both Matthew and Luke present the central mystery: Jesus was conceived by the power of the Holy Spirit and was born of the Virgin Mary. We are invited through their vivid and varied images to read the story of the birth of this child and, in faith, to see "more than meets the eye."

8. Season of Lent

Lent is the season with the strongest liturgy. Ashes, palms, purple vestments, omission of alleluia—all intertwined with finely tuned texts—contribute to a liturgy which makes a deep impression on all who take part in it.

Lent is a time of preparation. First and foremost, the church is concerned with the preparation of the catechumens who are to be initiated into the Christian community at the Easter Vigil services. On the First Sunday of Lent they appear before the community which gives its assent to them becoming elect, and so may embark on the final period of prayer and purification.

Lent is a time of reflection and celebration in which, especially on the third, fourth and fifth Sundays, the community prays with the men and women who are soon to become their brothers and sisters in the Lord. As the Gospel stories of Jesus' encounter with the Samaritan woman at the well (third Sunday), of the healing of the man born blind (fourth Sunday) and the raising of Lazarus (fifth Sunday) unfold, all those assembled for worship are plunged once again into a renewed understanding of what it is that happens to us when we are initiated into the community which is Christ.

Lent is also a time of renewal. If the baptismal waters beckon the initiates onward, the ashes are a spur to those who have long since been members of the Christian community but have lost something of their first innocence. As the baptized accompany the soon-to-be-baptized on their journey of faith, they enter a period of prayer and fasting which must be a constant feature of the Christian way of life.

This is brought home to us graphically on the first Sunday in all three cycles when we hear the account of Jesus' time of prayer, fasting, and temptation in the desert. As he sets out on his journey to Jerusalem and his Passover, we are reminded that our own journey will not reach its destination if it is not accompanied by the rejection of sin and a renewed adherence to the will of God.

That there is a destination of glory is emphasized in the account of the Transfiguration of Jesus, presented in the Gospel of the second Sunday in all three cycles. Thereafter, cycle B continues the theme of dying and rising, particularly exemplified in Jesus' words that: *"unless a grain of wheat falls on the ground and dies, it remains a single grain; but if it dies, it yields a rich harvest"* (fifth Sunday).

Cycle C is more concerned with repentance and forgiveness. The moving and mysterious story of the adulterous woman (fifth Sunday) underlines the truth that if we turn from sin, the Lord will more than match our conversion with his loving forgiveness. On the preceding Sunday, we listen to the parable of the Prodigal Son, which perhaps best sums up our relationship with God. While we witness the catechumenal journey, we are reminded that we, too, share fully in a loving relationship with God. We have fallen away. But still, like the father of the Prodigal Son, God anxiously awaits our return so that we can be restored to our true home.

Passion Sunday, with its blessing and procession of Palms and the reading of the accounts of the Passion by Matthew, Mark and Luke, launches us into the final period of Lent. Paradox, as always, is there: a triumphal entry into Jerusalem, only to end in Jesus' ignominious death. But, of course, we know that death is not really the end.

9. Introduction to the Gospel of John

Who is John?

The disciple who wrote the fourth Gospel tells in the last verses: *"This is the disciple who is bearing witness to these things, and who has written these things. And we know that his testimony is true."* This eyewitness to the life of Jesus is the "beloved disciple," the apostle John. He is one of the first to be called by Jesus. While fishing with his brother, James, and his father, Zebedee, he *"left everything and followed him."* John, unlike the other three evangelists, was with Jesus on some rather privileged occasions: the wedding feast at Cana, the healing of Peter's mother-in-law, the healing of Jairus' daughter, the Transfiguration, and he was seated next to Jesus at the Last Supper. His Gospel reveals the closeness of their relationship.

When and why did John write and for whom?

John's Gospel, composed near the end of the first century (90-100), was written for Christians who had never known the earthly Jesus. For John, Christians living in the second century and beyond have the same intimacy with the Lord as did those who were privileged to walk with him on earth. He sees Jesus as living among us in a sacramental way.

As a Palestinian Jew, John explains for his audience many of the things that would not be understood either by non-Jews or by those who lived after the events had taken place. For example, he explains why it would be unusual for Jesus to be speaking with the Samaritan woman (*John* 4) and why the parents of the blind man refused to speak (*John* 9).

What are the special characteristics of John's Gospel?

There are many unique characteristics of the fourth Gospel that make it quite different from the other three: his emphasis on the sacramental life of the church, his highly symbolic language and his emphasis on discipleship rather than a hierarchical church based on the apostles.

John presents the divinity of Christ through the signs that Jesus gives. Rather than concentrating on the miracles themselves, John sees in them the signs of who Jesus is. So, for example, at the wedding feast of Cana, John concludes by saying, *"this was the first of his signs, and his disciples believed in him."*

There are seven such signs in John's Gospel. There are seven *"I am"* sayings:*"I am the bread, the light, the door, the shepherd, the Resurrection, the way, the vine."* When we recall that *"I am"* is the name of God revealed to Moses, we see in these *"I am"* sayings the revelation of Christ's divinity. This revelation reaches its climax in the confession of Thomas, *"My Lord and my God."* John's sacramental presentation is climaxed in the response of Jesus, *"Blessed are those who do not see (me) and have believed."*

It is for us, those who have not seen Jesus with our eyes, that John has written about the *"signs Jesus did in the presence of the disciples,"* that we *"might believe that Jesus is the Christ, the Son of God, and that believing, we may have life in his name."*

10. Easter Season

For fifty days, up to the celebration of the Spirit at Pentecost, the church rejoices in a special way in the risen Lord and in the life which he gave to his people. Yet the Resurrection is incomprehensible without the dying which goes before it. So Easter season begins with what we call the Easter Triduum. This starts with the celebration of the evening mass of the Lord's Supper, continues through the Good Friday Passion celebration, and so to the excitement of the Easter Vigil—three celebrations making the summit of the church's year.

Yet, not three celebrations, but one. The Triduum celebrates in word, song, silence and ritual the paschal mystery of Jesus Christ, his passing over from death to life, from this world to the reign of God. The entire life of Jesus may be seen as a journey, and it is in the last three days of Holy Week that we see and experience the journey reaching its conclusion. At the evening mass on Holy Thursday, we commemorate the passover meal which Jesus had longed to eat with his disciples (*Luke* 22:15). On Friday, we contemplate the moment when Jesus gave himself as the sacrificial victim of the new passover. Then, at the vigil service, Jesus' passover journey is completed, and we celebrate the Resurrection.

Others have also been on a journey, a passover. For some time past, the catechumens have been journeying in faith, and the Easter Vigil is that moment when, through the initiation sacraments of baptism, confirmation and Eucharist, their journey is united with Christ's. They participate in his dying and rising and become fully one with the Christian community. Thereafter, Easter season is the welcoming of the new members into the community and a continuing celebration of the Resurrection event.

With the feast of the Ascension of the Lord, we focus more sharply on the fact that Jesus' mission must become ours. We are to be his witnesses to the world. Even as Jesus is taken up into heaven "to sit at the right hand of God," where he reigns in glory, he promises that he will send his Spirit to be with us in carrying out this mission.

The Easter season is completed at Pentecost as we celebrate the coming of the Holy Spirit upon the church, which, transformed and empowered, proclaims God's Word to the nations.

11. Introduction to the Acts of the Apostles

In all three cycles, the first reading throughout the Easter season comes from the *Acts of the Apostles*. It might be helpful, therefore, to have a short introduction to this exciting book.

Who wrote the Acts of the Apostles?

The introductions to the third Gospel and the *Acts of the Apostles* indicate that they were written by the same author. From earliest times, it has been accepted that both were written by Luke as a single, two-volume work and were later separated in the canon of the New Testament.

Luke was a companion of St. Paul on at least one of his missionary journeys. In his letters, Paul refers to Luke as the beloved physician and twice mentions that Luke is with him as a co-worker. Luke describes himself as a careful writer who researches well before committing his story to writing.

What is the purpose of the Acts of the Apostles?

Luke tells us that in his first book, the Gospel, he *"dealt with all that Jesus did and taught before he was taken up."* His purpose in *Acts* is to show the development of the church after Pentecost. *"When the Holy Spirit comes upon you, you are to be my witnesses in Jerusalem, throughout Judea and Samaria and to the ends of the earth"* (Acts 1:8). The rest of the book unfolds this mission, beginning with the speech of Peter on Pentecost in Jerusalem and concluding with the arrival of Paul in Rome, the city which symbolized *"the end of the earth."*

Through the speeches and activities of the disciples, but principally those of Peter and Paul, Luke stresses two main ideas. First, Jerusalem is the mother church, the place of its birth and the seat of its teaching. Second, through the power of the Holy Spirit, the church reaches out from Jerusalem to embrace the entire Gentile world. Luke recounts in vivid detail the missionary journeys of Paul which take him all over the known world. Throughout these journeys, Paul looks to the twelve apostles in Jerusalem for approval of his teaching. After telling us that Paul was taken to Rome and put under house arrest, Luke abruptly ends his book. His mission has been accomplished. Peter had proclaimed the Good News in Jerusalem and Paul had carried it to the ends of the earth.

Why is this book so appropriate for the Easter season?

Through the activities of the early disciples, we learn of the struggles and persecutions as well as the joys and successes of the early church. Under the guidance of the Holy Spirit, the first Christians lived in community, witnessed to the risen Lord, taught his message, preached his Word, healed in his name, baptized converts and endured persecutions. From Jerusalem, the disciples proclaimed, in word and deed, the Good News of the Easter message: He is risen!

12. Sundays of the Year

Advent, Christmas season, Lent, and Easter season are the times of calling. In those seasons we celebrate the Incarnation and all the other events which made up Jesus' life on earth. It is a time of calling because it broadly commemorates the calling together of the community. "Come, follow me" is the key phrase.

A call is no use without a response. The Spirit has been sent upon the church so that we may make that response. The Sundays which follow Pentecost (the "green" Sundays) are, in a certain sense, the time of the Spirit in which the church sets forth to proclaim the living Word of God. There is no imposed thematic structure for the 33 Sundays. They follow a pattern whereby the Gospel of Matthew is proclaimed in cycle A, Mark in cycle B, and Luke in cycle C. The first reading from the Old Testament is selected to match some particular truth contained in the Gospel of the day.

The season is concluded by the celebration of Christ the King. It is as if we are saying, *"The humble infant who grew to adulthood, preached the good news of reconciliation, brought it about in his death on the cross and rising from the dead, who sent his Spirit upon the church to complete his work, he is the King of all creation. Glory to him forevermore. Alleluia! Amen!"*

13. Formation of the Gospels

Over the course of the three-year cycle, we hear from each of the four evangelists and so receive the Good News of Jesus Christ from four united, yet quite distinct, sources. During cycle A, the Gospel of Matthew is read; during cycle B, we have the Gospel of Mark; cycle C presents the Gospel of Luke. The Gospel of John is read for most of the Sundays of the Easter season in all three cycles.

Each of these evangelists has a unique portrait of Jesus to present. As we prepare to enter into their Gospels during the liturgy, we might ask ourselves what factors might account for four different portraits of the same person, Jesus the Christ?

In searching for our answer, it is important to realize that the Gospel, the Good News, was handed on orally for over thirty years before it was written down in any organized way. Thus, the four written Gospels, as we have them today, represent not the beginning but the final step in their formation. In a document issued by the Pontifical Biblical Commission in 1964, the three stages in the formation of the Gospels are clearly outlined.

The *first stage* of the Gospels is, of course, the actual ministry of Jesus. The Good News, from which we get our word "gospel," was first proclaimed by the life, death and resurrection of Jesus himself. In his preaching, his miracles, his encounters with others, he proclaimed the Good News of salvation. It is, therefore, the words and deeds of Jesus during his earthly ministry that are the source for all Christian tradition, both oral and written and, hence, the first stage in the formation of the Gospels.

Traditionally, we say that this first stage lasted about three years, that is, from the baptism of Jesus until his crucifixion.

The *second stage* in the formation of the Gospels is the ministry of Jesus as it was understood and preached orally by the disciples between the Resurrection of Jesus and the actual writing of the Gospels. This stage is very important in the formation of the Gospels, because it is here that the various portraits of Jesus begin to emerge. The early disciples had only one goal in preaching the Good News: to bring all people to the saving power of Jesus Christ, the Lord.

Obviously, Jesus did and said more than we find in the written Gospels. And so, even as we do today, the early preachers recounted those stories, deeds and words of Jesus which they found most appropriate for their local community in a particular time and in a particular place. Also, as is true today, no two preachers had the same style. Hence, the Gospel came to take a slightly different shape in the various communities where the disciples went to preach. Some stories, deeds and words took on prominence in one area, others in another area. This second stage, which we might call "the oral Gospel," became the substance for the Gospels as we have them today.

The *third stage* in the process of the formation of the Gospels spans a great number of years, perhaps from 65 to 110 AD. After years of handing on the Gospel through oral preaching, disciples of those earlier eyewitnesses, the apostles, began the process of putting it into writing. Mark was the first to undertake this task sometime between 65 and 70 AD. The Gospels of Matthew and Luke were written between 80 and 90 AD, using much of Mark's Gospel as well as material from other sources, including the oral tradition in their local areas. The Gospel of John, written between 90 and 110 AD, seems to be dependent on entirely separate sources. His Gospel departs radically from the style and content of the first three. The individual style and content of each of the four will be discussed in separate introductions to each of the Gospels.

All four, however, gathered their primary material from the oral tradition known to them. Each evangelist sought to bring the Good News to his contemporary community and so selected the material needed for his purpose and arranged it in the order and style best suited to his audience.

Some stories or incidents in the life of Jesus appear in only one of the four Gospels. For example, the "Pearl of Great Price" appears only in *Matthew*, the parable of the Good Samaritan is found only in *Luke*, the story of the woman at the well is told only by John. Sometimes the same story will be found in two or more of the Gospels but in a different order of events, with different details, and perhaps even a different meaning. In other words, the evangelists used the deeds and sayings of Jesus differently according to their audiences and their own understandings of the meaning of Jesus. The result of this is that we now have four accounts of the Gospel, each with its unique presentation of the life, death and resurrection of Christ.

In reading the four Gospels separately, allowing for the intention of each evangelist, we experience the richness of the early church as it sought to live and proclaim the meaning of the risen Lord. This is precisely why the church presents them separately in the three-year cycle.

14. Introduction to the Gospel of Matthew

"*As Jesus was walking, he saw a man named Matthew sitting by the customs house, and he said to him, 'Follow me.' And he got up and followed him*" (*Matthew*, 9:9).

Who is Matthew?

In the list of apostles, he is identified as "Matthew, the tax collector" (*Matthew* 10:3). Is Matthew, the tax collector and apostle, the author of the Gospel which bears his name?

Given the situation of the Gospel, which dates it near the end of the first century, around 80-90 AD, this seems unlikely. However, we may say that the author of this Gospel is a disciple of the apostle and that he relies on the oral tradition that comes from Matthew's eyewitness account.

It was not at all unusual at that time to attach the name of an important person to one's work, either to give it prominence or to honor the person so named. It would seem that the author of this Gospel has done so here. As is traditional, however, we continue to refer to the author as Matthew. Of all four evangelists, Matthew is the most clearly Jewish.

Why and when did Matthew write?

The Gospel of Matthew was written near the end of the first century. His community had experienced a separation from the synagogue, the center of their relationship with God. The Jewish authorities had agreed that anyone who acknowledged Jesus as the Christ should be expelled (*John* 9:22). Accustomed to the rituals and ways of the synagogue, these Jewish Christians needed the assurance that Jesus himself was the Messiah and was now the center of their relationship with God. The primary purpose of Matthew's Gospel, therefore, is to show Jesus as the Messiah.

What are the specific characteristics of Matthew's Gospel?

Writing for a community of Jewish converts, he uses images, stories, references and literary techniques that are well-known to Jewish people. Matthew uses more Old Testament passages than the other three Gospels combined. He frequently frames the teachings of Jesus in a dialogue with the Jewish teaching authorities, to whom he is superior.

Matthew appeals to the background of his audience. He does this by comparing Jesus to the figures of Jewish history who represented all that was ideal, all that looked forward to salvation. Jesus is the new Moses, the liberator par excellence. As Moses led the people from slavery in Egypt, so Jesus liberates us from the slavery of sin. As Moses gave the Ten

Commandments on Mt. Sinai, so Jesus gives the fulfillment of this law in his sermon on the Mount. Jesus is the new David. Just as David, the ideal king, was promised an everlasting kingdom, so Jesus is the Son of David, the king who inaugurates the kingdom of heaven here among us. This identification between Jesus and the Old Testament figures is seen clearly in Matthew's presentation of Jesus' family tree (*Matthew* 1:1-17). Whereas Luke traces the geneology to *"Adam, son of God"* (*Luke* 3:23-38), Matthew begins with *"Jesus Christ, son of David, son of Abraham."*

At the same time, this Jewish community was faced with an influx of Gentile converts. How does a people, who thought of themselves as the sole inheritors of God's salvation, come to accept the possibility of universal salvation? Matthew's Jesus reveals the fulfillment of God's promise to the Jews and the unfolding of a more universal plan of the same God. He insists that Jesus could be recognized as Messiah but was rejected by the Jews. This rejection has turned the mission of Jesus to the Gentiles. Matthew, at the end of the first century, wants his contemporary Jewish Christian community to avoid the blindness of earlier Jews. He calls them to faith in Jesus—the new Moses, the Son of David—who brings the old law to fulfillment in the reign of heaven, a reign which includes the Gentiles as well as the chosen people.

The portrait of Jesus that emerges from Matthew's Gospel is Messiah, in the person of Emmanuel—God with us.

15. Introduction to the Gospel of Mark

Who is Mark?

While we know very little about the actual person of Mark, some hints within his Gospel allow us to make at least some attempt at a description. His careful attention to details and his vivid accounts may indicate that he was an eyewitness to the life of Jesus. Traditionally, it has been thought that Mark was a disciple and secretary to Peter. Some have suggested that he is the young man described in 14:51-52. Here, Mark tells us that during the arrest of Jesus, a young man, wearing only a linen cloth, followed him at a distance. Fearful that he, too, might be arrested, the young man ran off naked, leaving the linen cloth in their grasping hands. Still others have suggested that he is the John Mark who traveled with Paul during his first missionary journey (*Acts* 13:14). Having deserted Paul, the two were later reconciled (*2 Timothy* 3:11-12).

Why and when did Mark write and for whom?

It is generally agreed by scholars that Mark's Gospel was the first to be written. Perhaps the most consistent opinion is that Mark, a Jew, wrote for Gentile Christians in Rome, sometime in the late 60s or early 70s. It seems clear from his emphasis on the suffering of Jesus that Mark is writing for people who themselves are undergoing persecution and who need to be encouraged by the example of the suffering Christ. During this time of persecution, they may have been tempted to doubt the viability of Christianity or to abandon it altogether out of fear of suffering or even death.

What are the special characteristics of Mark's Gospel?

As the first of the evangelists, Mark has truly invented a unique literary form, which has come to be known as "gospel." Certainly, before the writing of the first Gospel, there existed the oral preaching of the disciples and the letters of St. Paul. But here, for the first time, the deeds and sayings of Jesus were collected in a single narrative in an attempt to present the meaning of Christ in the lives of believers at the time of the writing. Mark, taking into account the needs of his audience, selected the events and sayings from the life of Jesus and arranged them in such a way that this audience would understand their meaning in their own lives. Later, Matthew and Luke organized their Gospels around the material found in *Mark*.

Mark's Gospel is clearly divided into two parts. In the first half of the Gospel, Jesus reveals great power and authority, both in action (miracles) and in teaching. Great emphasis is placed on the "authority" of Jesus—a constant source of misunderstanding. Often it is the demons who recognize him rather than those who should be his disciples. This leads to his frequent command to keep silent about his miracles. This messianic secret, so characteristic in *Mark*, is the evangelist's way of insisting that the authority and power of Jesus are not to be identified only in his miracles, but also in his death and resurrection. Until he is recognized for who he truly is, he does not want his name or his actions revealed.

The second part begins with the focal point of the Gospel. This comes in 8:29 when Jesus asks the disciples, *"Who do you say that I am?"* The answer to his question (*"the Son of man who must suffer many things, and be rejected by the elders and the chief priests and the scribes, and be killed, and after three days rise again"*) leads us into the second part of the Gospel. From this point on, Mark will insist that fidelity to this Christ is the hallmark of discipleship. The disciple is one who, like Jesus, suffers what is necessary for the mission. Only if one truly understands the cross will one understand resurrection. Mark's is a message of victory through suffering.

The portrait of Jesus that emerges in Mark's Gospel is Jesus—Son of God, Son of Man—who suffered the human condition and invites us to follow him. We are called to resurrection. But the journey there is by way of the cross.

16. Introduction to the Gospel of Luke

Who is Luke?

The New Testament tells us more about Luke than any other evangelist. He was the companion to St. Paul on his missionary journeys and remained his "dear friend," "co-worker," and "beloved physician." He himself tells us that he was a careful writer (*Luke* 1:1-4) who wrote both the life of Jesus and the early life of the church (*Luke* 1:1). Luke was a convert from paganism who was familiar with both Jewish and Gentile customs.

When and why did Luke write and for whom?

The Gospel of Luke, written perhaps between 75 and 90 AD, emphasizes the universal salvation of all people, Jew and Gentile alike. Luke's primary purpose in writing seems to be to renew the faith and fidelity of Christian converts living outside of Palestine who had lost some of their earlier zeal. They had allowed community factions to occupy their attention and Luke reminds them that true discipleship means responding to the Gospel in concrete, daily situations within the community. Their very community life is to be a witness.

What are the specific characteristics of Luke's Gospel?

Luke presents the story of Jesus within the framework of a long journey. As Jesus presses on toward Jerusalem to his death, resurrection and ascension, he teaches, exhorts, and manifests his power as Lord. To those who follow him on this journey, he reveals his mission, a mission which, for Luke, has four specific characteristics: the prominence of the Holy Spirit, the importance of prayer, an attitude of joy and a special concern for marginal people such as foreigners, women and social outcasts.

He recounts stories of such people which are found only in his Gospel: the Good Samaritan, the sinful woman, the ten lepers, the widow at Nain, the good thief, the pharisee and the publican, and the prodigal son. And Luke includes more women in his Gospel than the other three combined. To all people, and especially to those without status, Luke gives the assurance of the tender mercy of God.

More than either Matthew or Mark, Luke presents the Holy Spirit as the creative power of God: in the Incarnation, in the mission of Jesus, and in the lives of the disciples. Jesus announces his mission on earth with a quotation from the prophet Isaiah, *"The Spirit of God is upon me"* (*Luke* 4:18). It is this same Spirit that works in and through the disciples as a sign of God's saving power on earth.

God's saving power is cause for joy and Luke's Gospel abounds with this attitude. His Infancy Narrative contains four songs of joy sung by Zachariah, the angels, Mary and Simeon. And Luke tells us that there will be great joy in heaven over each sinner who repents.

The mission of Jesus and, therefore, of his disciples, is accomplished through prayer. Unlike the accounts of Matthew and Mark, Luke tells us specifically that Jesus was at prayer when he was baptized, at the Transfiguration, before choosing the twelve apostles, and before teaching the Lord's prayer. Frequently, Luke introduces a teaching or a healing story with the phrase, "while he was at prayer."

The portrait of Jesus that emerges from Luke's Gospel is the Lord of all, whose Spirit enlivens the disciples, and who calls us to live out his mission in daily, real-life situations within the Christian community.

"And the Word was made flesh and dwells among us . . ."
John 1:14

PLANNING AND EVALUATION

Centering song or music_____

Welcome: *(Inspired by focus of readings)*

Readings:

First _____ Reader _____

Responsorial Psalm _____ Singer _____

Gospel Acclamation_____ Reader _____

Gospel_____ Reader _____

Reflections on Readings: *(Personal notes)*

Special Activities: *(Dramatization, reading in parts, environment, etc.)*

Symbolic Actions: *(Including special rites, gestures, banner, etc.)*

Prayers: *(Creed, prayer of the faithful)*

Evaluation of the Celebration of the Word:

   What went well:

   What needs improvement:

Please duplicate this form for your leaders. Use it every week.

Supporting the vital role of parents . . .

BRINGING GOD'S WORD INTO THE HOME

The celebration of the word with children offers parishes a natural way of involving parents in the Christian initiation and formation of their children at home. The vision of the *Directory for Masses With Children* and the *Order for the Christian Initiation of Adults* as it applies to children brings a new focus on parents and significant adults in the lives of children. This involvement of parents means more than simply organizing religious education programs to which parents bring their children. It means adults (parents) are responsible for personally sharing their faith with those children who are part of their lives.

We can support adults in this Christian duty by the kind of material we give them to use at home. Something as simple as a weekly children's leaflet with the Sunday scriptures adapted in language children understand can make the difference in whether or not this sharing of Christian faith actually happens.

Don't misunderstand. The medium, as the expression goes, is still the message. This is not to say that children's leaflets are the message. *God's Word made flesh in us is the message.* The way we live and how we respond to God's word is a primary source of influence on children. That is why we need to reflect with children on what God is saying to us when we gather each week to celebrate God's presence in the word.

Children's leaflets help make this happen. Sending leaflets home with God's word illustrated for children to see and reflect upon through the week is a vital part of the SUNDAY celebration series. So often, parishes invest only in materials for leaders to use when children gather—and fail to provide parents with the help they need to nurture the faith of their children at home. Parents and children need this simple support. The SUNDAY leaflets for parents and children have been carefully thought out and designed to keep in focus on God's word—not on what someone else tells parents and children to hear *about* God's word.

Should children's leaflets have lots of activities?

The function of children's leaflets is to put into the hands of parents and children God's word in language and illustrations children understand. No more and no less. Attempts are often made by publishers to give children things to do—crossword puzzles and fill-in-the-blanks kind of learning activities. Often these activities

175

distract children from focusing on God's word and responding in prayer or quiet reflection.

Leaflets filled with learning activities and gospel applications often reveal a lack of faith in the power of God's word to initiate in children their own original and creative response. Children's leaflets, such as those in the SUNDAY series, can successfully focus the child on God's word by providing illustrations—conceived to embrace the message of the scriptures—that the child can color or paint as a reflective activity. Or, the child might be invited to create a prayer in response to the readings. We facilitate. God's word creates.

Should children's leaflets be graded?

There is a notion carried over from the sacramental preparation (or classroom) model that raises this question about grading children's leaflets, liturgies and the scripture readings. The Christian initiation model sees older children as companions on the journey; their interaction with younger children is formative of the entire community. In other words, Christian initiation has less to do with age than it does with disposition of the heart. Also, in the home, parents do not relate to their children as a graded system but as a family sharing common experiences.

Furthermore, the lectionary is not a textbook of God's word. Though we learn from the readings, the lectionary is not a book for education but for celebration—designed to facilitate children's participation in the liturgical experience of God's presence in the word. While some parishes may feel a need to gather the very young children (3 to 5 years old) for a greatly simplified celebration, older children can gather in a mixed age group and be enriched by their varied responses to God's word. Children's leaflets that include picture-story illustrations, such as those in the SUNDAY series, help even very young children grasp enough understanding of the scriptures to feel they are part of the celebration. Leaflets such as MY SUNDAY SHEPHERD provide a special service to parents with children 3 to 5 years old. They include an illustration and a prayer guide parents can follow through the week, enabling them to pray in a way that their children can pray with them.

Do families really use the leaflets at home?

This question often masks another concern, parish finances, for good reason—parish budgets are usually tight. We want to be sure money is well spent. We get uneasy when we can't see someone using something for which we have paid good money. A leaflet blowing across the empty parking lot makes one wonder, not only about what's happening at home, but also about what support we give parents from the pulpit and the quality of our liturgies.

Experience has shown that the children's leaflets are not only used, but families have complained when they didn't get theirs. Experience has also shown that when the use of leaflets is encouraged from the pulpit, parents respond positively. Admonitions may reduce parking lot litter but will accomplish little toward an intelligent use of the leaflets at home.

We need to keep focused on what we're about—enriching the community's response to God's word. If our liturgies provide adults and children with a rich experience of God's presence in the celebration of the word, families will value God's word and carry that sense of presence into the home. Although we may not see to verify and measure it, the adapted readings carried home in the children's leaflets will help families sustain the spirit of God's presence in the word at home. This happens in simple ways: at mealtime conversations, at bedtime prayer, when the children are coloring or painting the scripture illustrations.

Even in the best of parish worlds, we cannot be certain that families will not occasionally leave leaflets behind. We can be certain, however, that if we do *not* provide parents with leaflets, then *none* of the families will take them home. That may give us control, but it does not give families the support for which they hunger.

their children than through sharing the celebration of the word throughout the liturgical year. Such sharing draws children into the heart of the Christian community and invites us all to grow up in Christ.

Gerard A. Pottebaum

When is the best time to distribute the children's leaflets?

The best time is after mass. It seems obvious, but some communities give leaflets to the children during their celebration of the word. Children's leaflets that contain the readings adapted for children are not to be used as some parishes use missalettes. (Nor should children's leaflets that contain activities and paraphrases of the readings be used at the celebration.) A basic liturgical principle is involved here: God's word is to be proclaimed and heard in a dramatic ritual style. (Those who cannot hear may want to read from a book.) Also, the celebration of the word is not the time for learning activities. It is the time to celebrate God's presence in song and prayer and shared reflections.

Other parishes distribute children's leaflets at the end of their celebration when they return to the adult assembly. Such use invites distractions during the celebration of the eucharist. Again, this practice should be avoided.

The most suitable time to distribute leaflets is after mass. Then the leaders of the celebration of the word have a chance to make contact with the families. The children are excited about receiving the leaflets and begin to look at them during the ride (walk) home. Their interest provides an opportunity for family members to share their responses to God's word.

There is no more natural way in which to involve parents in the Christian initiation of

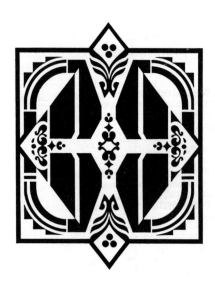

Resources

Note: This listing of publications includes both basic documents and materials that will help you implement the celebration of the word with children. While these materials come from a variety of publishers, they are available through a single source (prices subject to change):

Treehaus Communications, Inc.
P.O. Box 249
Loveland, Ohio 45140
(800) 638-4287
Fax: (513) 683-2882

A Child Shall Lead Them:
A Guide to Celebrating the Word With Children

Anyone who celebrates the Word with children should follow *A Child Shall Lead Them.* It places celebrating with children within the context of the spiritual life of children. Moreover, it captures the vision and sensitively applies the guidelines of *The Directory for Masses With Children.* Highly recommended for inservice training, the Guide follows the celebration step-by-step, giving detailed reflections and ideas on each step as the ritual unfolds. An indispensable resource for anyone who celebrates the Word with children.

Editor/Contributing Author: Gerard A. Pottebaum
Contributing Authors: Sister Paule Freeburg, D.C. & Joyce M. Kelleher.
144 pp. Treehaus/1992 ISBN 0-929496-65-5
$9.95

To Walk With A Child:
Homiletics for Children/A Guide

As the practice of celebrating the Word with children spreads, the need for training homilists becomes more crucial. This is not a book of a hundred-and-one sermon ideas. Rather, it helps homilists and children to see life from inside the Word, drawing upon their rich imagination, as well as this sense of awe and celebration in the presence of God. By Gerard A. Pottebaum.

170 pp. Treehaus/1993 ISBN 0-929496-95-7
$9.95

CIC UPDATE
The Christian Initiation of Children Newsletter

The CIC UPDATE Newsletter is published four times a year. Its purpose is to keep readers informed of developments in the Christian initiation of children, particularly as envisioned by the RCIA and the *Directory for Masses With Children.* You can receive CIC UPDATE through individual or bulk subscriptions. For complete information contact Treehaus Communications, Inc. (800) 638-4287.

The Rite of Christian Initiation of Adults
Study Edition

The complete text of the rite together with additional rites approved for use in the dioceses of the United States of America. The order for the Christian initiation of children is an integral part of the RCIA and the context within which the Christian initiation of children is to function.

396 pp. LTP/1988 ISBN 0-930467-94-9 $8.00

The Directory for Masses With Children

This document provides the official guidelines for eucharistic celebrations with children as well as for celebrations of the word with children at gatherings attended largely by adults. The *Directory* is essential reading for those who want to enrich children's worship. It is concerned with all the ways of initiating children into full and active participation in the liturgical life of the church. Its perspective is broad and its guidelines practical.

24 pp. USCC/1973 ISBN 1-55586-291-8 $1.95

The Liturgy Documents: A Parish Resource

The most important and useful documents of the liturgical reform are collected here: *Constitution on Sacred Liturgy*; the *General Introduction to the Lectionary for Masses*; *General Norm for the Liturgical Year and the Calendar*; the *Directory for Masses With Children*; *Environment and Art in Catholic Worship*; *Fulfilled in Your Hearing* (about the Sunday homily); *This Holy and Living Sacrifice* (rationale and norms for distributing communion under both species), and excerpts from the *Ceremonial of Bishops* (many principles applicable to parish celebrations). With review and brief commentary.

400 pp. LTP/1991 ISBN 0-929650-46-8 $9.95

The Church Speaks About Sacraments With Children

This brief volume contains excerpts from basic church documents related to the Christian initiation of children. Mark Searle provides an illuminating commentary that will help pastoral leaders formulate guidelines for the initiation of children.

66 pp. LTP/1990 $4.50

Issues in the Christian Initiation of Children: Catechesis & Liturgy

Edited by Kathy Brown and Frank C. Sokol, this volume draws on the experience of various contributors in dealing with central questions posed by the *Rite of Christian Initiation of Adults* as it affects the initiation of children.

219 pp. LTP/1989 ISBN 0-930467-97-3 $7.95

Sharing our Biblical Story
Revised Edition

Joseph P. Russell has written an idea book for religious educators and parents that shows how to base Christian education on the Bible stories that occur in the context of worship. This book focuses on biblical stories from each of the three cycles (with variations in readings as they appear in the lectionaries of different denominations), provides background material and offers suggestions for emphasis.

346 pp. Morehouse-Barlow/1988
ISBN 0-8192-1425-6 $19.95

Children's Liberation: A Biblical Perspective

Relatively little has been written about children in the Bible, especially about the primacy given to them in the gospel of Jesus. This enlightening volume provides rich insights into understanding that unless we are as children, we will not enter the reign of God. By scripture scholar, Joseph A. Grassi.

128 pp. Liturgical Press/1991 $5.95

The Spiritual Life of Children

Robert Coles, professor of psychiatry and medical humanities at Harvard University, has spent 30 years listening to children around the world and is one of the most respected contributors of our time to our understanding of the culture of children. In this book, Dr. Coles shows us children face to face with the idea of God, in whose presence they seem to be fearless. Children discourse on the nature of God's wishes, on the devil, heaven and hell, faith and skepticism. Recommended for parents as well as parish leaders.

378 pp. Houghton Mifflin/1991
ISBN 0-395-55999-5 $10.95

The Children's God

David Heller, a clinical psychologist, interviewed forty children of four different religious back-grounds (Jewish, Catholic, Baptist, and Hindu) about God. Though he finds some differing views attributable to age, gender, and religious background, he discovers to a surprising degree a common vision of God that cuts across ethnic and religious differences.
151 pp. Univ. of Chicago Press/1986
ISBN 0-226-32636-5 $8.95

*The Religious Potential of the Child
Second English Edition*

This book describes an experience with children from ages three to six, an experience of adults and children dwelling together in the mystery of God. Author Sofia Cavalletti offers a glimpse into the religious life of the atrium, a specially prepared place for children to live out their silent request: "Help me come closer to God by myself." Preface by Mark Searle.

248 pp. LTP/1992 ISBN 0-929650-67-0 $12.95

Children, Liturgy, and Music

Edited by Virgil C. Funk, this book of 15 articles combines theological expertise with pastoral experience to help your parish implement the *Directory for Masses With Children.*

136 pp. The Pastoral Press/1990
ISBN 0-912405-73-2 $9.95

The Christian Initiation of Children: Hope for the Future

Robert D. Duggan and Maureen A. Kelly provide a challenging vision and practical suggestions for restructuring parish religious education practices to complement the implementation of the *Rite of Christian Initiation of Adults.* An excellent description of the convergence of liturgy and catechetics and its ramifications for shaping the future church.

138 pp. Paulist Press/1991 ISBN 0-8091-3258-3 $6.95

*The SUNDAY Handbook for Ministers
of the Word*

A practical resource for every minister of the word—provides methodology a well as an overview of biblical texts and liturgical seasons. Developed under the direction of Christiane Brusselmans.

32 pp. w/pocket cover Treehaus/1989
ISBN 0-929496-06-X $7.95

SUNDAY Lectionary for Children

The Sunday lectionary adapted for children,

endorsed for liturgical use by the Canadian Conference of Catholic Bishops, features: inclusive language, large type, lines of text end to complement natural speaking breaks, adapted in keeping with the *Directory for Masses With Children,* handsomely bound for use in celebrations of the word. Year A, B, and C in separate volumes. Developed under the direction of Christiane Brusselmans with Sr. Paule Freeburg, D.C., Rev. Edward Matthews, Christopher Walker.

172 pp. Treehaus/1991-92 ISBN 0-929496-38-8 (Year A); ISBN 0- 929496-57-4 (Year B); ISBN 0-929496-91-4 (Year C) $29.95 each when purchased in a set ($49.95 individually)

SUNDAY Leader's Weekly Guide

Each volume covers 52 Sundays and special feasts. Each celebration features: 1) Focus of the Readings; 2) Ideas for Reflecting on the Readings with Children; 3) the Sunday readings adapted for children; 4) Music for Responses and Gospel Acclamations; 5) Prayer of the Day. Also features Background to the Sunday Readings and Liturgical Seasons as well as Planning & Evaluation Form.

Developed under the direction of Christiane Brusselmans with Sr. Paule Freeburg, D.C., Rev. Edward Matthews, Christopher Walker.

178 pp. Treehaus/1990-93 ISBN 0-929496-93-0 (Year A); ISBN 0- 929496-58-2 (Year B); ISBN 929496-92-2 (Year C) $29.95 each when purchased in set of 3. ($49.95 individually.) Contact Treehaus for bulk discounts.

SUNDAY Family Leaflets

These four-page and six-page weekly leaflets are for use at home or school after the Sunday celebration. They feature: the Sunday readings adapted for children ages 5 to 12 years; picture-story illustrations of the readings; prayers; and description of biblical people and places. Essential for family involvement and continued reflection on the word at home. Weekly / Treehaus / Call (800) 638-4287 for bulk rates & discounts.

MY SUNDAY SHEPHERD
Family Leaflets

These full-color seasonal leaflets are for families with children 3 to 5 years old. Designed to help the young child take those first steps—hand-in-hand with parents—in celebrating the gospel story on Sunday and responding in praise throughout the week. *My Sunday Shepherd* initiates the young child gradually into the liturgical life of the church through a prayerful family life. Each leaflet features a story-picture of the Sunday gospel on one side and, on the other side, a prayer guide that helps parents pray in a way that enables their children to pray with them and to respond to God's word throughout the week. Set of 8 leaflets and 1 Parent Guide for each of the following seasons: Advent/Christmas; Lent/Easter Sunday; Eastertide/Pentecost.

Weekly during these seasons / Treehaus / Call (800) 638-4287 for subscription information and bulk discounts.

SUNDAY Scripture Response Posters

A complete series of 53 beautiful posters (17 x 22 inches), designed to be decorated or colored by leaders, helpers, or parents, for use during the celebration of the word. Each poster features the enlarged text of Responses and Gospel Acclamations and a large picture-story illustration of the Sunday scriptures. Especially helpful for younger children. Available for all three cycles, Year A, B, and C.

Weekly / Treehaus / Call (800) 638-4287 for prices and discounts.

How to Celebrate the Word With Children . . . and Why
Video

Features a demonstration celebration with commentary by Father Edward Matthews, one of the primary authors of the *Directory for Masses With Children*.

30 minutes with guide / Treehaus /1990 $49.95

SUNDAY: A Basic Celebration Resource
Video

A video "dictionary" for the SUNDAY Celebration of the Word material, hosted by Christiane Brusselmans and Gerard A. Pottebaum. Each element of the SUNDAY Celebration of the Word material is defined, along with its uses. An important tool for any parish developing liturgies that respect the spiritual life of children.

21 Minutes / Treehaus /1990 $19.95

Lectionary for Masses and Other Celebrations With Children

In 1991 the United States bishops approved a *Lectionary for Masses With Children*, a translation by the American Bible Society (Contemporary English Version-CEV). After confirmation by the Holy See, this lectionary will be published and authorized for use in Fall 1993.

There will be a single volume for each year of the three-year cycle (plus major feast days) and a separate volume for weekdays. Several publishers will be publishing their own editions. While not available as we go to press, these volumes may be ordered through Treehaus Communications, Inc. Prices are still to be determined. Call (800) 638-4287 for information.

Index of
Scripture
Readings

Index of Scripture Readings